GENDER
Socialization
and the
Making of
GENDER
in the
Indian Context

GENDER
Socialization
and the
Making of
GENDER
in the
Indian Context

Sujit Kumar
Chattopadhyay

Los Angeles I London I New Delhi
Singapore I Washington DC I Melbourne

First published in 2018 by

 SAGE Publications India Pvt Ltd
B1/I-1 Mohan Cooperative Industrial Area
Mathura Road, New Delhi 110 044, India
www.sagepub.in

SAGE Publications Inc
2455 Teller Road
Thousand Oaks, California 91320, USA

SAGE Publications Ltd
1 Oliver's Yard, 55 City Road
London EC1Y 1SP, United Kingdom

SAGE Publications Asia-Pacific Pte Ltd
3 Church Street
#10-04 Samsung Hub
Singapore 049483

Published by Vivek Mehra for SAGE Publications India Pvt Ltd, typeset in 10/12 pt Century Schoolbook by Fidus Design Pvt. Ltd., Chandigarh and printed at Sai Print-o-Pack, New Delhi.

Library of Congress Cataloging-in-Publication Data
Name: Chattopadhyay, Sujit Kumar, author.
Title: Gender socialization and the making of gender in the Indian context / Sujit Kumar Chattopadhyay.
Description: Thousand Oaks, California : SAGE, 2017. | Includes bibliographical references and index.
Identifiers: LCCN 2017032995 (print) | LCCN 2017043626 (ebook) | ISBN 9789386602589 (Web PDF) | ISBN 9789386602572 (Epub) | ISBN 9789386602565 (hardback : alk. paper)
Subjects: LCSH: Sex role—India. | Sex differences (Psychology)—Social aspects—India. | Women—Identity. | Men—Identity.
Classification: LCC HQ1075.5.I4 (ebook) | LCC HQ1075.5.I4 C47 2017 (print) | DDC 305.30954—dc23
LC record available at https://lccn.loc.gov/2017032995

ISBN: 978-93-866-0256-5 (HB)

SAGE Team: Amrita Dutta, Sandhya Gola, Shaonli Deb and Ritu Chopra

To

*all my respected teachers from KG to PG, with
deepest gratitude, admiration and devotion;*

*my wife Bani Chattopadhyay and daughter Anwesha
Chattopadhyay for their love, encouragement and support;*

*my father Late Dr Chittaranjan Chattopadhyay,
mother Late Saraju Chattopadhyay and elder sister
Prabhati Bhattacharya for their blessings, teachings
and values that made me what I am today*

and

*my father-in-law Late Amulya Ratan Banerjee and
mother-in-law Late Manorama Banerjee for their
affection, divine favour and invisible guidance.*

Thank you for choosing a SAGE product!
If you have any comment, observation or feedback,
I would like to personally hear from you.

Please write to me at **contactceo@sagepub.in**

Vivek Mehra, Managing Director and CEO, SAGE India.

Bulk Sales

SAGE India offers special discounts
for purchase of books in bulk.
We also make available special imprints
and excerpts from our books on demand.

For orders and enquiries, write to us at

Marketing Department
SAGE Publications India Pvt Ltd
B1/I-1, Mohan Cooperative Industrial Area
Mathura Road, Post Bag 7
New Delhi 110044, India

E-mail us at **marketing@sagepub.in**

Get to know more about SAGE

Be invited to SAGE events, get on our mailing list.
Write today to **marketing@sagepub.in**

This book is also available as an e-book.

Contents

Preface and Acknowledgements

I was born and brought up in a village of the state of West Bengal, under the territory of India, during the period when India was fighting for becoming a self-reliant country just after winning the Independence. As a newly free country, India had to fight against all odds—social, political, economic and cultural. The political and the economic fields were entrenched by deep-rooted legacies of the Western, especially the British, influences. The political legacies were completely gender-biased and the laws were basically anti-women. The other organs of the government, that is, the executive and the judiciary were just reflecting the patriarchal gender perception in the name of the State. The social and the cultural fields were also full of superstitions, dogmas and unethical practices. Women were basically viewed with an objectified, fragmented and dehumanized approach. I grew up in the midst of such an atmosphere, with all the misconceptions, confusions and contradictions emerging out of the broader social setting on which I had practically little control.

Whereas the social setting was full of conservative ideas, the family background in which I grew up was more or less liberal. Gopal Chandra Chattopadhyay, my grandfather, born in 1874, was a renowned doctor of the time. He spent much of his youth in different parts of India and abroad during the years of his professional career. He stayed for quite a long time in Singapore. He received an award from George VI for his contribution in surgery. Philanthropic as he was, concentrated more on intellectual exercise than on the accumulation of wealth. Chitta Ranjan Chattopadhyay, my father, was also a renowned doctor of the time in the rural area where he lived at his choice. He tested his fate in different states such as Uttar Pradesh, Bihar, Orissa, Assam and West Bengal and subsequently was settled in Uchalan, a village under the district of Burdwan. My father was well versed in four languages—English, Bengali, Hindi and Sanskrit. He was also a graduate of the University of Calcutta and received the title 'Sahityapadhyay' from the University of Calcutta for writing a dissertation on the poet Kalidasa. Like my grandfather, my father also lived a liberal life concentrating mostly on intellectual exercises. Aditya Ranjan Chatttopadhyay, my uncle and immediately next brother of Chitta Ranjan, was the headmaster of Uchalan High School. He was also a doctor but practised irregularly. Gyan Saran Chattopadhyay, one of my uncles was a student of Meghnad Saha and was the recipient of 'Premchand Roychand' scholarship. He also chaired office of the Dean of Science and Engineering in Jadavpur University from where he retired from the Department of Computer Engineering. Gyan Saran travelled throughout the world and was a visiting professor of nearly all the prestigious universities of the world. He represented India in different international seminars of science and engineering. Satya Saran Chattopadhyay, my youngest uncle, retired as professor of commerce from the University of Burdwan. He authored two much-needed books on business management, published by World Press, Calcutta.

Owing to be brought up in such an enlightened atmosphere, I faced no difficulty in receiving the influences of liberal thinking in my boyhood. As quite open my eyes were, I had the perception of all things in my family—good or bad. The worst thing I experienced in my family was its gender-biased attitude as a result of which, in my opinion, the fate of the daughters of the family was not so good. Starting with my mother I can say that she was the victim of the notion of gender inequality and misogyny. She lost her mother in her infancy. But her father, my grandfather, did not give all the care that a motherless child should get. In spite of my mother's profound aspiration of being educated, her father did not allow her schooling. Whereas her elder brother, my uncle, got every facility for education, as a result of which he obtained a PhD degree in his subject, English literature, and became a professor of Jogmaya Devi Girls' College, Kolkata. What a miserable depiction of the difference between son and daughter! My grandfather held double MA and was a lawyer. He also composed several novels and authored some research books on the tradition and culture of the district of Bankura where he lived in a municipal town of Sonamukhi. My grandfather did all the arrangements for the education of his son. He himself was highly educated in calculation of his time.

But in case of my mother, my grandfather displayed misogyny in respect of his approach to the education of the female child. My mother, in spite of being deprived of all the facilities due to her, became literate through her own efforts and accomplished reading of almost all the novels of Bankimchandra, Rabindranath, Saratchandra, Tarashankar, Bibhutibhusan, Ashapurna Devi and such others. She also read *Ramakrishna Kathamrita* and books of Achintya Kumar Sengupta written on Ramakrishna. She was quite familiar with the biography of nearly all the sages and hermits of India. In her childhood, she came in close contact with one hermit who was the direct disciple of Swami Bijoy Krishna Goswami, and in her youth she became a disciple of Swami Nigamananda. She also read thoroughly the biographies of the two. She was the most liberal woman I have ever seen. But owing to the suppression imposed by the patriarchal values of her father first and subsequently of her father-in-law's house, especially of her husband, she did not come to reflect the features of modernity that she carried in her implicitly. When I had been forming gender identity of my own and started evaluating the world around me, I found her to be fully socialized in respect of gender norms and practices, gender stereotypes and, especially, gender role. But somehow and somewhere there was a contradiction in my mother's mind, so far as I felt, about what she had been performing and what she actually wanted to be in respect of gender. Perhaps this is the starting point of my confusion about all that is going on in the name of gender. Since my boyhood I perceived that behind the system of becoming masculine and feminine, there is obviously a role of some social and cultural processes which I identified in my matured age as gender socialization.

It is due to the system of gender socialization, being basically an unequal socialization for men and women, that my elder sisters could not fulfill their dreams like my mother. My eldest sister Saraswati was not given school education beyond Class IV. Another elder sister, Prabhati, the one immediately next to Saraswati, was really talented. In course of passing her time with my grandfather Gopal Chandra, she often expressed her desire of getting trained to mount the horses of my grandfather who had to keep them for visiting patients at distant places. Up to Class IX Prabhati achieved a brilliant result.

She had a flair for writing poems and stories with a fine control over language. But she was forced to get married with an illiterate person, and she had to sacrifice all her dreams unfulfilled. In her mid-age, Prabhati completed graduation with honours in political science from a college under the University of Calcutta. This proves her deep love and affinity to education. This also proves that in the name of gender in general and in the name of femininity in particular how much discrimination, oppression and subservience Prabhati had to undergo in a family where nearly all the senior members were enviably educated. Prabhati was perhaps the personified example of the renowned statement of Beauvoir, 'one is not born, but rather becomes, a woman'. The most puzzling issue for me at my tender age was that all our brothers did not have to face such obstruction for education. We, being the sons, were treated differently in the matter. So again I was confused with all that is going on in the name of gender. Internally, I raised a protest against the system of gender socialization which inspires man and woman to be developed in different ways. This book is perhaps an indirect consequence of my negative experiences of gender socialization in my boyhood.

Coming to my married life, I again found the negative implication of gender socialization in my wife, Bani, who also had to sacrifice her dreams unfulfilled just because of her gender. In lieu of providing enlightened educational exposure, her paternal family thought it prudent to initiate her in the traits of inferiority, subservience and domesticity. She developed a strong feminine sense which was perceived by her not as spontaneous and natural but as constructed, dictated and imposed. She now admits straightway that if she was given the scope to be socialized in a more liberal and open manner, she perhaps could do a lot of what is exclusively fixed for the male gender. Bani is a gifted singer with a highly melodious voice. She is also a good critic of my works. In terms of my personal experiences about her, I believe that if there was no external intervention, like the process of gender socialization, she might have been more successful with independent attitudes in her life. However, I must mention that it is due to the conservative attitude of my father-in-law that I have got a very good wife at least. Against the background of my experiences about gender, I decided to provide a gender-free atmosphere for my daughter, Anwesha, at least in my family.

I never allowed and imposed any artificial method of gender socialization on her. I never taught her to smile, walk and dress this way or that. I am waiting for a perfect human being to emerge from her—not a man or woman.

In this way, I have experienced many examples of the formation of gender through gender socialization and training of gender stereotypes and gender roles. In my father's family, I found the construction of gender day by day. I witnessed the role of family, peer group, school and media in the formation of gender. Having been hailed from a rural area, I closely visited the influences of the cultural forms such as folk songs, folk tales and rhymes. I also understood that these forms of culture are being used for inculcating the gender messages, gender stereotypes and gender roles of the women. Thus, in short, my past experiences have been my present master. Through a number of books that I have written on gender, I exposed and discussed many an issue. But through this book I have presented the ideological forms of the legitimization of gender inequality and gender discrimination and this ideological form operates through the process of gender socialization. So, this book argues that in order to hit the very complex domain of gender inequality and gender discrimination it is necessary to hit the methods of their legitimization, that is, gender socialization.

In course of writing this book (a long manuscript), I could not devote any time to my family. So thanks are due to my wife Bani and daughter Anwesha who were patient enough to grant me this relaxation. Bani knocked me almost regularly for limiting the length of the manuscript. Anwesha also inspired me in various ways. I do not want to leave the scope of acknowledging their debts in this regard as I think that in some way or another this book is also a record of the bond of their love and affection.

Sujit Kumar Chattopadhyay
Circus Maidan, Bankura

Introduction

Since the UN declaration of 1975 as Women's Year and the period between 1975 and 1985 as Women's Decade, women's problems and issues are getting intellectual attention throughout the world. Gender issues in general and gender inequality and discrimination in particular have been receiving considerable attention from the policy-makers and planners. Thoughtful intellectual analysis of gender issues—its nature, formation on the one hand and social problems, especially of the women emerging out of it, on the other—have become the subject of popular discussion everywhere. The debate regarding the biological nature of gender versus the social and cultural nature of gender has brought the entire issue of gender to the centre of sociological investigation. The advent of feminism as a separate school of thought has linked the issue of gender with the practical life of the women and based on the experiences of the women, feminism has presented the whole intellectual arrangement of discussion. Different approaches such as sociological, functional, psychological, biological and feminist approaches have come to view the concept of gender from theoretical angles. As such the problems of gender inequality, discrimination and violence have also been viewed in terms of gender. But in spite of so many approaches, the primary reason of gender inequality and related problems is not sufficiently clear. This book is an effort of searching the answers to the questions as to why in spite of intellectual enlightenment, women still are to pay the cost of being women and as to what social and cultural factors are responsible for the continuity of the discriminating practices of gender inequality. It has been argued in this book that it is through the gender socialization that gendered norms and practices and discriminating gender messages are being sent to men and women since their childhood as a result of which inequality of sexes arises and continues.

Since, unlike sex, gender is a social and cultural construct, the process of gender socialization has a great role to play in the shaping of personality. As sex is assigned at birth, gender is assigned at the social and cultural level, and it is never a matter of choice. So far as the history of gender is concerned, it has always been the result of individual urge of co-opting the social and cultural norms and practices and of fulfilling the social expectations thereof on the part of the individual. To a number of sociologists, socialization is the spontaneous process of learning by which individuals, men or women, conform to the basic social norms. As Gillin and Gillin state

> By the term 'socialization' we mean the process by which individual develops into a functioning member of the group according to its standard, conforming to its modes, observing its traditions and adjusting himself to the social situations.[1]

Socialization when conceived in view of gender perception is called gender socialization. Under socialization programme, society in general is the goal of all discussions but under gender socialization all discussions revolve round the concept of gender in particular. Gender socialization is the continuous process by which men and women are socialized into different sex roles, and accordingly it is ultimately an inequality of socialization of gender. As Giddens has pointed out:

> Through contact with various agencies of socialization, both primary and secondary, children gradually internalize the social norms and expectations which are seen to correspond with their sex.[2]
>
> Thus through the internalization of sex role, sex behavior and sexist viewpoint of society, in general, stakeholders are encouraged to develop gender identity—masculinity and femininity—which creates gender differences and ultimately gender inequality in society. So the socialization process which teaches men and women gender identity and differences and which inspires individual to adopt the social role corresponding to their gender through various agencies like family, school and media and through various religious and cultural activities is called gender socialization.[3]

---

[1] John Lewis Gillin and John Philip Gillin, *Cultural Sociology* (New York, NY: The Macmillan Company, 1948), 11–17.

[2] Anthony Giddens, *Sociology, 4th ed.* (Cambridge, UK: Polity Press, 2001), 108.

[3] Sujit Kumar Chattopadhyay, *Fighting Gender Inequality: A Tribute to Nirbhaya* (Kolkata: K. P. Bagchi & Company, 2015), 12.

There are a number of methods by which an individual adopts the norms and practices of gender socialization, and they are imitation, assimilation and social learning. Through imitation, the boys and girls come to adopt the gender-specific behaviour and traits, and thus they come to conform to the social expectations and rules. The matters of imitation happen in family, school, peer group and the media. That apart the cultural capital of the society also encourages the boys and girls to imitate the gender-specific norms and practices. Assimilation is a more indirect, introvert and voluntary method of co-opting the gender-specific norms and practices. The children, with the formation of the gender identity in course of their physical and mental movement towards maturity, perceive as to what kind of gender-specific behaviour is expected from them and in violation of which how much they have to pay as punishment for deviation to the gender norms, and accordingly they come to assimilate the gender norms and practices through various sources. The social learning is also another method of internalizing the gender norms and practices. Social learning is possible through various channels such as the family, school, peer group, the media and the cultural texts of the society. Through social learning, the concept of gender comes to be implemented as a result of which a boy is inspired to be masculine and a girl is encouraged to be feminine. When a baby is born, he/she remains open to any kind of expression irrespective of gender. But in course of the process of receiving the society's directions for co-opting the gender-specific norms and practices through various agents such as family, peer group, school and media, the baby becomes a gendered person. So there is a close link between the perceptions of gender on the part of the individual and the social expectations and arrangements by which gendered norms and practices come to be enforced in society. This book is a documentation of these social arrangements by which a baby comes to perceive himself/herself ultimately as boy or girl, and subsequently man or woman.

The intellectual discussion of gender socialization cannot be opened without discussion on gender study and social psychology, which is dealt with in Chapter 1. Chapter 2 of the book deals with the different issues linked to gender: what it is; its nature, formation and effects. Sociologically, it is evident that the issue of gender is not biological like sex. It is a social and cultural construct. But the intellectual debate is still open on the issue as to how much sex is a determining factor in the perception of gender. The intellectual threads of the issue of gender must include the differential treatments given by the society to a male child and a female child during the period of formation of gender. Last, the effects of gendered thinking, gender laws, norms and practices are a great concern for the free development of a boy or a girl. Especially women are to face the effects of gender formation/construction very badly. The gender ideology of the society, the techniques of gender socialization and the gender norms and practices are modelled upon the values of patriarchy. So, in the long run, all the ideas of gender go against women, and they are to pay the price of being women at every stage of their life.

Chapter 3 deals with the discussion on gender socialization: its nature and role in the making of gender. Gender socialization is a more focused form than socialization itself. Socialization encourages the spontaneous participation of the individual in the social processes whereas the gender socialization is often directed to the enforcement of the social norms and practices compulsorily and also coercively. It is the gender socialization that slowly and gradually brings men and women in the realm of gender ideology modelled upon the patriarchal values and inspires them to conform to the gender norms and practices set by that ideology. That men and women feel and think differently and that they come to perform different sex roles and that they come to reinforce different sets of gender stereotypes are mostly the result of gender socialization. Gender socialization is chiefly based on the notion of differential treatment of men and women. Thus, the objective of the gender socialization is to enforce the differential socialization for men and women and, accordingly, it is a type of socialization of inequality between men and women. Judged from this angle, it may be said that gender socialization is primarily aimed at undermining the position of women and enforcing the notion of inferiority, subservience and domesticity as the basic stereotypical traits of women. So in order to understand the logical connotation of the problem of gender inequality, the concept of gender socialization is to be dealt with much attention and intellectual openness.

Chapter 4 deals with the sociocultural dynamics of family and its role in gender socialization. A child is born in a family and subsequently in course of his life that baby as a grown up person dies in the family itself. The family supports the human being financially, physically, mentally and also culturally up to a minimum age of 25 years or more. We, human beings, get our primary identity in respect of name, birth and descent in terms of family. We learn the sexual attachment and detachment in the family; we experience the basic understanding in respect of gender stereotypes especially masculinity or femininity through the image of our parents; we get the source of imitation, assimilation and learning also in the family. Thus, there is enough scope for the family to exert a tremendous influence over the child from many angles, and accordingly the family has emerged as a very strong agent of gender socialization. Its system of nomenclature, its inextricably closed relation with the institution of marriage, its residential system, its possession of property and its system of offering a line of descent has made the family a viable institution of all societies and across all cultures. Thus, with the help of all these convenient aspects, the family has been successful in moulding the basic form of gender perception of its members. So, it is natural that the family has come out successful in causing gender socialization of the male and female members within it. In sociology, the family is generally projected as an agent of conventional socialization. But here, in this book, family has been represented as the primary agent of gender socialization and for the purpose of unfolding the sociocultural dynamics of the family, a system of analysis of its structure and functions is presented. It is evident from the analysis that all the structural and functional uniqueness of the family move towards one single agenda: gender socialization and the shaping and reshaping of gender. Students of sociology, gender studies and culture studies will get enough of new angles of discussion in this chapter.

Chapter 5 deals with the role of peer group in gender socialization. Peer group is also a primary group influencing the behaviour and attitudes of men and women and thereby claims much attention on the discussion of its role in this regard. But in the books of general sociology, the chapter on the agents of socialization does not give much importance on peer group. Most of the discussions spare some lines or at best a small paragraph to peer group. But this book, first time as a matter of sociological enquiry and investigation, has presented peer group with all its

uniqueness and complications. This chapter is the documentation of all the positive and negative aspects of peer group as to
how it teaches conformity, how it inspires peers to deviation
and how successfully it sends the gender messages to the
peers and thereby causes gender socialization.

Chapter 6 deals with the role of school in gender socialization. A number of recent sociological studies have revealed that
there are ample of materials—cultural and cognitive factors—in
the school premise and school systems of education that often
serve as a factor of constraint in intellectual development of
the students, especially the girl students. The experiences
afforded to girls and boys within schools are known to affect
gender differentiation both directly, by providing differential
skill practice and reinforcement,[4] and indirectly, by providing
input that leads children to actively socialize themselves along
gender-differentiated pathways. In view of the role of school in
creating and reinforcing gender differences between boys and
girls, it can be said that school serves as a gender barrier, that
is, barrier for the development of especially the girl students.
Such gender-biased role of the education may be termed as gate-
keeping function of the educational system which means that
it does not allow the access of all but some to education based
on gender. The gender-biased role of elementary education
has turned the school as a major agent of gender socialization.
Schools participate in the process of gender socialization chiefly
through three aspects: formation of *gender stereotypes, differential treatment and differential socialization and gender role.*
Curriculum materials, that is, textbooks often contain gender
stereotypic attitudes and behaviour. 'Children internalize gender stereotypes and prejudices, which in turn guide their own
preferences and behaviours.'[5] Stereotypes may be described as
some fixed beliefs, ideas and notions about gender created by
patriarchy and assimilated by the society. 'In fact stereotypes
are representative of a society's collective knowledge of customs,

[4] C. Leaper and R. S. Bigler, "Gender," in *Social Development: Relationships in
   Infancy, Childhood, and Adolescence,* eds M. K. Underwood and L. H. Rosen
   (New York, NY: Guildford Press, 2011).
[5] J. E. O. Blakemore, S. A. Berenbaum, and L. S. Liben, *Gender Development*
   (New York, NY: Taylor & Francis, 2009).

myths, ideas, religions, and sciences'.[6] Teachers, classmates and
the textbooks directly influence gender differentiation by providing boys and girls with differential treatment and different
learning opportunities and feedback. Girls and boys today are
receiving separate and unequal educations due to the hidden
agenda of curriculum aimed at differential gender socialization
that takes place in our schools, and accordingly the system
results in differential patterns of the formation of gender identities of students. The school is very much concerned with the
gender role distribution in society through which the agenda of
gender socialization is implemented. Women in every society
are socialized and indoctrinated toward a set of roles and since
these roles are different for men and women, they are termed
as gender roles. Thus, the school contributes to the process of
gender socialization in a variety of ways. Of late, owing to the
drastic changes in the rate of female education and female
gender role, the role of school as well as the process of gender
socialization has undergone a marginal transformation with the
keynote remaining the same.

Chapter 7 deals with the role of the media in gender socialization. Although it is admitted by sociology in particular and
social sciences in general that media is the most potent weapon
of influencing the attitudes and behaviours of the people, a
few of sociology books have offered a scientific and empirical
study of the role of media in socialization. This book, combining
theoretical discussions with empirical case studies, delineates
the possibilities and potentialities of media as an agent of
gender socialization with equal emphasis on the complexities
and contradictions in it. In a lengthy discussion, the volume
has included both the print and the electronic media and has
outlined the processes by which media comes to reinforce the
gender norms and practices. An emphasis on cyber media as the
newest form of media influences and aggression has obviously
given the book a separate status. Media is keen on reinforcing
the gender biases spontaneously and through social method
of the teaching–learning. Thus in a number of ways, the role of
media has been considered important in the process of gender

---

[6] C. N. Macrae, C. Stangor, and M. Hewstone, *Stereotypes and Stereotyping*
(New York, NY: The Guilford Press, 1996).

socialization. This role has been especially come in the centre of discussion in view of the advent of globalization which has changed the structure, content and the implication of media in recent days and thereby has made the topic much more compelling as well as interesting.

Chapter 8 deals with the role of religion in gender socialization. 'It is a matter of theoretical and practical experience that in all societies and all types of culture sex differentiation and discrimination have been present in a variety of forms. It is also a fact that in most of the cases 'female sex is the direct victim of such differentiation and discrimination.'[7] Like all other forms, religion also adds fuel to the running of the system of gender inequality and gender discrimination. Religion is no exception in this regard and in consideration of its many a retrogressive features, it can be said that it serves as the faithful agent of patriarchy, and accordingly it plays an important role in sending the gender messages to the members of the society. Religion and its norms and practices play a very significant role in gender socialization among rural girls who try to find out their future sex roles drawing materials from these norms. Religious vows express the feeling of women and accordingly act for the training of the girl child for taking up a future role as mother, wife, etc. Through vows gender messages are easily transmitted among the women of all ages and thus religious vows act as a medium of gender socialization and the resultant gender inequality. The ritual vow songs teach the girl child to ask the boons of being a good daughter, good wife, good daughter-in-law, good mother and so forth. The ideal of womanhood incorporated in the ritual vows is one of chastity, purity, gentility, tenderness, domesticity and surrender to the male sections. 'Pati Param Guru' or the ideal of 'Potivrata' is romanticized through the rituals of the vows. Thus, these religious vows play a very powerful ideological role in gender socialization of the girl child in favour of patriarchy.

Chapter 9 deals with the role of religion in gender socialization through its different myths and concepts. In all religions, especially in Hinduism we get a number of references of concepts like previous birth, rebirth, hell and paradise, concept of atonement

---

[7] Sujit Kumar Chattopadhyay, *Gender Inequality, Popular Culture and Resistance in Bankura District* (New Delhi: Primus, 2016), 19.

and belief in supernatural and these concepts actually serve as the agent of patriarchy since they teach the women to take a particular sex role encouraging women to be submissive, chaste, tolerant and self-effacing. Logical analyses of these concepts of religion have revealed a very close connection between the religion and gender ideology, gender messages and gender socialization. It is also through the religion and the concepts preached by it that the social and psychological setting of the feminine gender is created. How the gender discrimination and gender inequality developed as a system of oppression against the women and how the textual script has been used with a view to objectifying, fragmenting and dehumanizing the women are best explained with the help of these concepts and approaches. This chapter is especially unique in the sense that it examines the theories and concepts of religion from a well-argued viewpoint that will come as enough help for decoding the gender messages inherent in the religion.

It is argued in this book that gender socialization thus implemented through various agents and religious norms and practices is primarily responsible for making differential gender of men and women. Gender messages sent through gender socialization actually come to enforce the patriarchal values in the society. Since gender socialization is basically aimed at creating and enforcing inequality of sexes and since it is prone to give this inequality a social form and justification, it is very much necessary to delineate the role of those social organizations and institutions by which gender socialization comes to operate. Side by side understanding the role of religion is also important in order to unfold the social, cultural and ideological bases of gender socialization. One of the powerful reasons why gender inequalities have existed for centuries is its inner dynamism, including its ideological legitimization in religion. It is therefore argued here that any external intervention to change this very complex domain of social relationship based on discrimination must base itself on the prior knowledge of the complexities of how gender inequalities survive and are legitimized in society. So understanding the nature of religion is very much important for also understanding the nature of gender socialization. Religion is not only a metaphysical matter to the people but also a means of expressing their thoughts, beliefs, understanding about all kinds of things over the centuries. Different forms of religion and the norms and practices preached by them have represented so many retrogressive features that have been considered by the sociologists as detrimental to development especially of the women. Religion and all its techniques have taken a male-biased approach to support the patriarchy which, like all societies, prefers sons over daughters and devalues the women ideologically and culturally, and insist them to represent the virtue of self-effacement and self-sacrifice exclusively in the interest of the male gender. In this way, through defending the patriarchal intention of degrading the position of women religion has produced gender inequality through its various norms and practices, and this inequality is perhaps the most pervasive form of social inequality in society. So the interesting relationship between gender inequality and various social institutions and religion calls for a thorough empirical and analytical probing which has not been done so far academically and it is the central object of this study. A serious social scientific study of interrelationship between agents of gender socialization and the process of gender socialization is absent in the existing studies of sociology. No serious attempt has been made so far in studying as to how various institutions such as family, school, peer group, media and religion can be used as an ideological tool for the making of gender and also for degrading the status of the women. This study is an attempt to fill the gap.

The observations, analyses and conclusions reached in this study are based on in-depth studies, surveys and field works done by many organizations. Additionally, this study also consults the existing documentation of the discourses on socialization. We have also taken the help of other books on feminism and feminist issues with a view to enriching and understanding the gender aspect of the socialization process which is commonly viewed as gender socialization. Differences are the result of two separate socialization processes of the two sexes. Through the use of a variety of techniques of socialization such as imitation, role-modelling and normative attitude, children's behaviour is channelized to take a particular shape and form. The differential treatment is meted out by a variety of social agents such as family, peer group, school and media and also by religion. The end product is a package of personality traits attributed to women and men, what psychologists label as femininity and masculinity. Understanding 'gender' is the key to the study of gender socialization through the above-mentioned agents over the years. These agents have been teaching gender roles for men and women in compliance with the social norms and expectations corresponding to their sexes. Sociologists today share the view that gender inequalities result because men and women are socialized into different roles. So the process of gender socialization is primarily responsible for providing a functional, logistic and ideological support to the gender inequalities and discriminating gender norms and practices in all countries and across all cultures. The roles women play in society and the images we have of them have developed not simply from the exigencies of biology and social situations but are rather deeply rooted in social arrangements and culture and religion. Due to the lasting appeal of the agents like family, peer group, school, media and religion, it has been considered by the patriarchy as important medium of injecting its teaching. The influence of these agents is enormous in forming sex role behaviours. Each culture has a set of institutional structures and practice to teach sex roles. Individuals learn to be male or female by learning effective means of communication and social behaviours that are required for their respective gender.

In the field of gender socialization, religion is mainly used for sex role stereotyping and construction of gender. Girls are taught to be religious since their childhood. So messages of gender are inculcated early in their life and since then girls are socialized and acculturated toward a set of roles fixed by vow-rhymes such as *Sibabrata, Punyipukur, Itu, Tush-tushuli, Mangalchandi* and so on,[8] and sex role and gender socialization thus have been implemented intentionally. So the religion and its norms and practices and the concepts preached by it have constantly inspired the women to achieve feminine signs (*mayeli lakshan*), both physical and mental, which will ensure gender roles by the female. Corresponding to the gender roles it is desirable for the Indian women to be docile, domestic, generous, innocent, polite, religious and submissive. On the other hand, males are inspired

---

[8] The meaning and brief introduction of these forms of vows are given in the glossary.

by different institutions of the society to achieve the masculine features (*purushali lakshan*) such as aggression, dominance, authoritarian attitude, economic independence, etc. In this way, 'sex role stereotyping and construction of gender' serves as a powerful patriarchal ideological foundation of gender inequality which subsequently expresses itself through some attitudes and customs. Therefore, without challenging the process of gender socialization, the movement against gender inequality is bound to face a setback.

PART I

Themes

1

Gender Study and Social Psychology: A Theoretical Approach

Even though gender study is a relatively new phenomenon in higher education, social science and related research area, it is today well established as an interdisciplinary field of study which draws on knowledge from psychology, political science, economics, anthropology, sociology, management, development study and all the social sciences. After the assessment of the plan, policies and experiences of the United Nation's First Development Decade in the 1960s, it was argued by the social scientists in general and the feminist scholars in particular that emphasizing economic growth and the 'trickle-down' approach as key to reducing poverty is not enough for the development especially for the women. It was also argued that development should not only be restricted to economy and financial privilege but it should be all-round development spreading its impact on social, political, educational, cultural and all other relevant areas that shape and reshape the basic personality type not only of the men but also of the women in order to flourish as perfect social being. Subsequently such arguments resulted in the move to consider gender equality as a key element of development. The concern with gender relations in development has strengthened the affirmation that equality in the status of men and women is fundamental to every society and unless this is achieved, no effort to all-round development will come true and this concern has prompted to introduce newer perspectives on gender line of development such as gender budgeting, gender financing, gender planning and so on. The result of gender versus development debate is the realization

that development requires more than the creation of opportunities for people to earn sustainable livelihoods—it also requires the creation of a conducive environment for men and women to seize those opportunities. Development implies not only more and better schools but also equal access to education for boys and girls. Development requires good governments that give men and women equal voices in decision-making and policy implementation.[1]

Although starting from the perspective that gender matters in development, gender issues became a robust field of research, analysis and discussion within a very short span of time, and concepts and ideas such as feminism, gender inequality and women empowerment came to dominate the field of sociology, anthropology, social psychology as alternative models of theories. The result is the institutionalization of gender scholarship and research on women-centric discussion in social sciences and social psychology. In course of this trend, introduction and formation of course materials for the women's study in academic circles also began.

The dialogue between 'social psychology' and 'gender study' has been a part of the same theoretical framework that operates on the discussion of gender socialization. It often remains a puzzle for most people as to how gender socialization turns into differential socialization, especially for the women, and why at all the society in general and the women in particular endorse the vocational treatment of the process of gender socialization which ultimately marginalizes the women and confines them at home. With a view to searching the possible answer to the question, the discussion on social psychology seems to be crucial. It is also confusing to see that in spite of the active participation of the women at all stages of production, the subordination, subjugation and undermining of the position of the women has been a historic destiny throughout the globe. The simple answer to erase this confusion may be the society's endorsement and approval towards such devalued position of the women. But the basic question—why at all society does so and how it comes to impress the whole society, especially the women, for enforcing these negative and retrogressive features in the name of gender socialization as a result of which gender inequality, gender discrimination and gender oppression become almost a stable feature of all societies and across all cultures and as a result of which marginalization of women has been a

---

[1] Jane L. Parpart, M. Patricia Connelly, and V. Eudine Barriteau, eds, *Theoretical Perspectives on Gender and Development* (Canada, International Development Research Center, 2000), 4.

universally settled fact—can only be solved by the impact of social psychology on the behaviour and actions of the people of a given society or a community.

The root of gender study, undoubtedly, lies in the feminist approach which since the beginning of its theoretical germination, has been concerned about the ways the problem of gender inequality is to be resolved. It is also a theoretical rejection of the entire problem of gender inequality. According to Bandana Chatterjee, 'Feminism is the force which has transformed women into self-conscious social category.... In its essence, feminism is the belief that the nature and the worth of a human being, man or woman, should be independent of gender'.[2] Feminism is a theoretical discourse which puts women at the centre of the theory and speaks for gender equality, women's empowerment and gender justice.

> Feminist scholars have argued that knowledge based mainly on male, culturally specific experience represents a skewed perception of reality and is only partial knowledge. The best way to correct this is to take women's daily experiences and their informal theorizing into account and, on this basis, adopt feminist approaches to building theory and knowledge.[3]

Thus feminism, since the beginning, took a woman-friendly stance and put the demand for the right to equality in the eyes of law, right to education and right to vote, and added fuel to different protest movements throughout the globe.

> Feminist theories, though seeking to create a better world for women in general, differ from each other in terms of philosophical overview and methodology. These theories also differ in terms of goals and objectives.... The reason obviously lies in the fact that feminist theories have no monolithic pattern. Rather they have been expressed through a variety of forms. Generally these forms can be divided into three broad categories, i.e. liberal feminism, radical feminism and socialist feminism.... Beyond these three major types, there are also some other forms of feminist

---

[2] Bandana Chatterjee, "Women and Politics in India," in *Politics India: State Society Interface*, ed. Rakhahari Chatterjee, 2nd ed. (New Delhi: South Asia Publishers Pvt. Ltd, 2009), 351–86.

[3] Parpart et al., *Theoretical Perspectives*, 10.

approach.... such as Black Feminism, Postmodern Feminism, Eco-feminism, Gynocentric Feminism, etc.... They differ from each other only with respect to the situation and angle of vision.[4]

Gender study first appeared as the concept of feminism which started its journey with Mary Wollstonecraft's book *A Vindication of the Rights of Women* published in 1792 and gained a strong foundation through 'second wave feminism' started through Simone de Beauvoir's book *The Second Sex* published in 1949. Beauvoir's 'recognition that "one is not born, but rather becomes, a woman" became the basis for the distinction between sex and gender. Her argument that women were defined in relation to men, but unequally, so that "woman" was the negation or "Other" of "man," resonated in later feminist theories. The writings of Kate Millett, Betty Friedan, Valerie Solanas, Shulamith Firestone and Juliet Mitchell echoed the concerns of the emergent Women's Liberation Movement. They drew attention to the varied forms and sites of female subordination male power (from reproductive technologies and socialization practices to laws and cultural representations), and to the ways that marriage and motherhood confined women to the "private sphere." All this prevented women from realizing their potential and contributed to their acceptance and even interiorization of inferiority'.[5] At the primary stage of feminist discourse, gender studies was limited in the discussion of gender inequality and men's domination and oppression over the women and thereby gender studies was necessarily women's studies where women's subordination by men was the universal experience and thereby 'From 1630 to about 1780 feminist writing survives as a thin but persistent trickle of protest'[6] against this appropriation of rights of the women in male-dominated society. According to George Ritzer, 'The record of feminism, however, is not one of steady, uninterrupted development.... The high points in the record of feminist activity and writing occur in the liberationist "moments" of modern Western history....'[7]

---

[4] Chattopadhyay, *Gender Inequality,* 33–37.

[5] John Scott and Gordon Marshall, eds, *Oxford Dictionary of Sociology,* 3rd ed. (New York, NY: Oxford University Press, 2005), 218.

[6] George Ritzer, *Sociological Theory,* 3rd ed. (Singapore: McGraw-Hill, 1992), 494.

[7] Ibid, 451.

Feminist questions had to wait for some more time to be the part of 'university based, academic discourse of professional sociology'. 'Although the term gender is often used euphemistically in sociology for "women," the sociology of gender is, more precisely, the study of socially constructed male and female roles, relations, and identities—a somewhat different subject from feminism's focus on women. This focus on the interrelationship of men and women is not equivalent to a feminist theory.'[8] Women's studies turned into gender studies after the emergence of second-wave feminism and particularly after Beauvoir's clear argument on the differentiation between sex and gender. But since 1970 the feminist philosophy developed as a separate discipline of gender studies following the emergent 'New Wave Feminism' which combined the theory with practice and as such concepts started being applied through the activism, and thereby gave the so-called feminism a matured shape out of which gender studies started its journey as an academic discipline as well as a protest movement in social, political, economic fields or more specifically as an interdisciplinary movement. It is said, 'Gender studies are a field for interdisciplinary study devoted to gender identity and gendered representation as central categories of analysis. This field includes women's studies (concerning women, feminism, gender, and politics), men's studies and queer studies'.[9] The basis for the academic field of gender studies was laid in many countries in the 1970s, when women in academia protested against the ways in which academic knowledge production made women invisible and ignored gendered power relations in society.

> The history of gender studies looks at the different perspectives of gender. This discipline examines the ways in which historical, cultural and social events shape the role of gender in different societies. The field of gender studies, while focusing on the differences between men and women, also looks at sexual differences and less binary definitions of gender categorization.[10]

Gender studies for its development as 'sociology of gender' has strong links to not only feminist ideas and practices but also

---

[8] Ibid, 458.

[9] https://en.wikipedia.org/wiki/Gender_studies

[10] John W. Scott, "Gender: A Useful Category of Historical *Analysis*," *American Historical Review* 91(5) (December 1986), 1053–75.

to women's movements, gender activism, suffrage movement throughout the globe and political work for change in society, science and culture. Gender studies neither limits its scope in women's studies nor only to male–female relation, but rather it is nowadays interested in the study of LGBTQ, that is, lesbian, gay, bisexual, transgender and queer genders. Apart from the LGBTQ, there are cross-dressers, eunuchs (male and female), disorder gender (a male having the feelings of a female and a female having the feelings of a male), effeminate (man as womanish) and termagant (woman as tomboy-type) persons who are also coming fast in the discussion of gender.

Since gender is a social and cultural construction, different social norms and practices and cultural values dominate the formation of gender and the process of gender socialization. Gender, having its root in social events, takes a complicated form by being intertwined with the social, political and economic problems of colonialism, racism, caste system, communalism, dictatorship, democracy and problems of underdevelopment in all situations. Through the process of gender socialization, gender becomes a socially accepted issue across all societies and cultures, and in this process of acceptance many institutions play their role such as the institutions of marriage, property and particularly the institution of patriarchy. So gender studies has to deal with the norms and practices, institutions and the thought process of the concerned society. Thus in true sense of the term gender studies is a really an interdisciplinary subject closely related with religion, history, sociology, geography, economics, political science, physical sciences—particularly physiology, biology and genetics—philosophy, anthropology and literature. So, in all, gender studies, in order to disseminate all the details by which gender formation of a person, male, female or others is influenced, must have to count the social psychology which is also important to understand the nature and functioning of gender socialization. 'As understandings of gender have developed as a complex, multifaceted and multidisciplinary area, involving the study of relationships within as well as between genders, the term "gender studies" has gained currency, albeit not uncontested. Whatever label given to the academic study of gender relations in the twenty-first century, there are a number of features that have endured. First, the study of gender remains resolutely multi- and interdisciplinary and that is its key strength, and has had the most profound impact on contemporary theory and attitudes to the production of knowledge. Second, alongside the more focused, if varied, constellation of texts, knowledge and theorizing on and about gender that constitutes gender studies, gender issues continue to penetrate mainstream disciplines more widely (though not always with ease) and are enthusiastically embraced by students. Third, feminism remains a central perspective for the study of gender relations, reminding us that this discipline emerged from the identification that women as a group were misrepresented—in both the public sphere and in the conception of their "real" natures. As gender relations continue to change and mean different things, so feminism as a political ideology will change and find new avenues to explore.'[11]

From the above-mentioned arguments forwarded by Pilcher and Whelehan, some generalizations can be made. First, gender studies is never a dilution of women's studies but rather a quest for the exploration of new avenues on the perspective of 'third-wave feminism' where women of the late 20th and early 21st century seek to view the world from absolutely their own experiences, knowledge and will of their own. Second, 'Our second generalization is that until 1960, feminist ideas were introduced into sociology only on the margins of the discipline. For example, such ideas came from various male theorists who were marginal to professional sociology, even though their ideas were subsequently influential on sociology. ... the major works of these theorists, the statements that have fundamentally shaped the sociological perspective, give almost no attention to gender as a social arrangement.... The best example of this conventionality perhaps is to be found in the theories of Talcott Parsons.... Parsons argues that for the family to function effectively, there must be a sexual division of labor in which adult males and females play very different roles.... As is self-evident, this sociology of sex roles is essentially, if perhaps unintentionally, antifeminist in orientation and is perhaps the most dramatic instance of mainstream sociology's lack of involvement, down to the 1960s, with feminism'.[12]

---

[11] Jane Pilcher and Imelda Whelehan, *50 Key Concepts in Gender Studies* (London: SAGE, 2004), xii–xiii.

[12] Ritzer, *Sociological Theory*, 455–56.

The evolution from gender-blind sociology to the 'sociology of gender' became possible by the enduring efforts of the new wave feminism, particularly contemporary feminists, with their inputs of the theories of gender difference, theories of gender inequality and theories of gender oppression. Although there is no denying the fact that such evolution owes the debts to all the theorists of first-wave and second-wave feminism. Third, gender studies is basically interested in the classification of genders and their natures. Beyond the widely used categories of male and female and their nature of masculinity and femininity, there are many other genders that have still remained on the margins of gender studies. In recent days, LGBTQ have come under discussion but their nature and links to the process of social and cultural construction of gender are yet to be exposed. Reaction of the social arrangements to them and their counter-reaction to the social process should have been a matter of useful discussion of gender studies. The social and political movement and protest against the existing laws and social norms and practices on the part of LGBTQ throughout the globe is still considered as the movement of some deviated, socially segregated and marginalized persons. The two dominating genders, male and female (in terms of categorization), are always studied both by the social and cultural ways and means and also by the biological signs assigned at birth. But this methodology is not found in case of the study of LGBTQ genders. How, in their case, biological signs operate differently and how their social and cultural choice affects their existence is still a marginal topic of gender studies. It is very unfortunate to see that the discipline of gender studies is almost mum in case of some less-identified genders such as cross-dressers, eunuchs, disorder gender, effeminate, and termagant persons who should also come fast in the discussion of gender studies. Fourth, gender is the result of a long historical process. 'In each stage of history gender is differently defined and this definition depends upon the mode of production in a specific historical situation where males relate with society and with each other according to their role in production process. After the overthrow of women from production, stated by Engels as historic defeat of women sex, family and marriage leave most women in the position of slaves.'[13] According

---

[13] Chattopadhyay, *Fighting Gender Inequality*, 48.

to Flora Anthias and Nira Yuval-Davis, 'The ideology of gender is not universal in form. It is specific to particular historical periods, cultural backgrounds and positions within the hierarchies of class and nationality'.[14] 'So the concept of gender is changing and it means a combination of some socially constructed features by which men and women act and behave different and come to perform sex oriented roles prescribed by the society.'[15] So the discipline of gender studies is always a dynamic subject and is open to all issues ranging from institutions to ideology.

The lesson of gender-specific behaviour is indoctrinated through socialization, imitation of others' behaviour through encouragement and coercive methods. Socialization operates through cultural indoctrination and social regulation, the basic objective of which is to engrave the gender differentiation between male and female in particular and among other genders in general. As a result, the context of gender covers our lifestyle (by norms and practices), institutional formation (by marriage, property and patriarchy) and thought process (by gender ideology). So ultimately language, walking, speaking and laughing style, space, profession and so on everything comes under gendered social psychology, and accordingly women's access in all the spheres becomes gradually restricted. Society approves of the women's marginalization and this is the reason that gender inequality becomes a natural part of the social system. Individual choice is not much relevant here; individual there has no right to challenge. The whole context of gender is the result of social choice as a result of which 'women under the "gendered formulation of identity" are only to subscribe to the norms sanctioned for women gender with a view to becoming a woman in true categorical sense of gender'.[16] Thus in the study of gender, social influence, social approval and role of social norms and practices and, in all, role of social psychology is very much important.

Since the social influence of gender is the established fact, the dialogue between gender study and social psychology has

---

[14] Flora Anthias and Nira Yuval-Davis, "Contextualizing Feminism-Gender, Ethics and Class Divisions," paper presented in Conference of Socialist Economists, Bradford University, UK, 1983.

[15] Chattopadhyay, *Fighting Gender Inequality*, 48.

[16] Ibid, 32.

been accepted by the feminist sociologists as a convenient and pragmatic methodology for the critical investigation and understanding the people, group and social relations and attitudes of a society towards gender. Thus gender studies, being strongly related to social psychology, have contributed to an improving knowledge on gender relations, gender identity and gender socialization, the key matter of discussion of this book. According to Jaqueline Gomes de Jesus, 'Social psychology is the study of the manner in which the personality, attitudes, motivations and behavior of the individual ... are influenced by the social groups'.[17] It should be kept in mind that it is not the case that individuals, always and all the time, are influenced by social groups; sometimes the opposite of the incident also happens meaning thereby that individuals may influence the course of thinking of the social groups as well. So the structure of social psychology and the social influence is a complex combination of the opinion of both the individual and the society. It may be said that social psychology is the understanding of the social dynamics of everyday living of the millions of individuals based on psychological method. 'Within the framework of psychology, social psychology focuses especially on the study of face-to-face social interaction, making considerable use of experimental studies of small groups. There is, however, a more sociological social psychology, particularly influenced by symbolic interactionism, and employing methods such as participant observation.'[18] Social psychology, as a special area of gender study, draws its elements from sociology, psychology and also from feminism. It presents and analyses the issue of gender as the study of different genders, especially male and female genders, in their interactions with one another, and seeks to reveal how such interactions affect the individual's thoughts, feelings, emotions and habits towards the perception of gender society, culture, institutional norms and practices. 'From the psychological point of view, social psychology is concerned with the ways in which personality and behavior are influenced by

---

[17] Retrieved 10 July 2017, from https://www.researchgate.net/profile/ Jaqueline_Jesus
[18] Scott and Marshall, *Oxford Dictionary of Sociology*, 534.

a person's social setting.'[19] From the sociological perspective, social psychology includes any study of social processes which systematically considers how the psychological properties of men and women as the expression of masculinity and femininity or the personality dispositions of other genders, acting in a situation, influence the outcome of the social process. Again from the feminist point of view, social psychology is interested in the process of unfolding the social attitudes as a result of which women's subjugation by men becomes a universal happening. It is also interested in detecting the avenues through which women can be emancipated from the state which has been described by Beauvoir as a 'threatened concept of femininity'. According to Beauvoir,

> For us woman is defined as a human being in quest of values in a world of values, a world of which it is indispensable to know the economic and social structure. We shall study woman in an existential perspective with due regard to her total situation'.[20]

Social psychology is a weapon of disseminating and analysing the issues of gender studies in its totality.

Social psychology is the scientific study of what people think, express and behave about genders and how they act as reacting agents to social stimuli. Thus, it is the combination of the gender perceptions of the people interacting with each other cognitively, affectively and behaviourally, thereby expressing their gender perception through different levels of thoughts, emotions and actions. From the standpoint of individual, social psychology exposes the individual's response to the social stimuli moulded and patterned by the gender ideology of the society and thus becomes identified as psychological social psychology based on the study of the mental behaviour of the individual. From the standpoint of society, there is sociological social psychology that focuses on broader group behaviour or societal variables such as institutional practices, social and cultural norms, approaches

---

[19] D. C. Bhattacharyya, *Sociology*, New 7th ed. (Kolkata: Vijoya Publishing House, 2002), 24–25.

[20] Simone de Beauvoir, *The Second Sex*, translated and edited by H. M. Parshley (London: Vintage, 1997), 83.

to male and female genders and influence of patriarchy. So far as the dialogue between gender study and social psychology is concerned, the major historical roots perhaps lie in the *psychoanalytic theory* and *theory of behaviourism*.

Psychoanalytic theory is based on Freud's (1856–1939) emphasis on unconscious motivation and mapping of the emotional dynamics of personality of the female on the basis of their psychic patterning. Freud claims that there are two parts of mind— conscious and unconscious. Like the portion of the iceberg above the water, the conscious part of mind represents the outer world of information and experiences which have actually their roots in the unconscious part of the mind like the invisible portion of the iceberg below the water. The unconscious part of the mind represents the emotions, desires, instincts, imitation and internal psychic faculties by which women are prone to internalize the traits of femininity and men are prone to express the traits of masculinity. To Freud, the real cause of subjugation of the women by men lies in the psychic structure of the female. The psychoanalytic theory argues that

> the mental features that women acquire have nothing to do with statecraft, public participation or economic profit-and-loss. Rather, these features inspire them to remain under the control of male guardians and to be confined within safe shelters and private areas, i.e. within the family. Thus, gender inequality takes place insidiously in society.... Freud has presented a very complex map of personality development which is basically grounded in the psychological differences between male and female and more accurately on the sexual feelings of the child at the subconscious level which plays a vital role in the formation of gender, and ultimately, gender inequality. ... In later years, some thinkers came forward to justify and complete Freud's perception of the creation of gender inequality. Helen Dayesh is one among them. She remarked that women belong to the substandard consciousness because their sex organ is less satisfying. Childbearing imposes such pressure on them that they do not have the space to develop their personality in the public sphere and, therefore, their confinement within the family becomes their destiny.[21]

[21] Chattopadhyay, *Gender Inequality*, 29–31.

In attempting to use Freud's theories, however, feminists have to undertake a fundamental reworking of his conclusions. For, Freud himself was notoriously patriarchal. He acknowledged gender differences and gender inequality but not gender oppression. Women to him were second-class human beings whose basic psychic nature fit them only for a lesser life than that experienced by men. Feminist theorists, therefore, have had to follow through on directions implicit in Freud's theories while rejecting his gender—specific conclusions.[22]

In order to avoid repetitions we may refer to some aspects of psychoanalytic theory already discussed in this book in the chapters on gender and gender socialization.

Behaviourism is the analysis of learning that focuses on observed behaviour.

The two most significant intellectual roots of Mead's work in particular, and of symbolic interactionism in general, are the philosophy of pragmatism and psychological behaviorism…. In fact, Mead called his basic concern *social behaviorism* to differentiate it from the *radical behaviorism* of John B. Watson[23] (who was one of Mead's students). Radical behaviorists of Watson's persuasion were concerned with the observable behaviors of individuals.[24] Their focus was on the stimuli that elicited the responses, or behaviors in question. They either denied or were disinclined to attribute much importance to the covert mental process that occurred between the time that a stimulus was applied and a response emitted. Mead recognized the importance of observable behavior, but he also felt that there were *covert* aspects of behavior that the radical behaviorists had ignored…. Mead and the radical behaviorists also differed in their views on the relationship between human and animal behavior. Whereas radical behaviorists tended to see no difference between humans and animals, Mead argued that there was a significant, qualitative difference. The key to this difference was seen as the human possession of mental capacities that allowed people to use language between stimulus and response in order to decide how to respond.[25]

[22] Ritzer, *Sociological Theory*, 471.
[23] John Broadus Watson, *Behaviorism* (New York, NY: W. W. Norton & Company, 1925).
[24] Kerry Wayne Buckley, *Mechanical Man: John Broadus Watson and the Beginnings of Behaviorism* (New York, NY: Guilford Press, 1989).
[25] Ibid, 327–29.

Mead's emphasis on language has tremendous influence on gender study in general and gender socialization in particular. Gendered language becomes a forceful method of inculcating patriarchal gender ideology among the people, especially the female of all sections throughout the globe. Behaviourism is sometimes called as *reinforcement theory* that emphasizes the observable behaviour of people inculcated, reinforced and dictated through the prevalent gender ideology of the society. Reinforcement theory asserts that social behaviour is caused both by reward and punishment. People internalize the norms, practices and behaviour pattern that are supposed to be rewarded by society and oppositely people tend to avoid those behaviours that may result in negative punishment or coercion. Thus, reinforcement theory of social behaviour, often related to gender, may also be called as encouragement or discouragement theory of behaviourism. The organization of family often uses this theory of reinforcement of gender behaviour in order to keep their wards in track through reward and punishment.

Another theory of social psychology is *social learning theory* which is often described as a form of behaviourism as the result of social learning. Social learning theory developed by Albert Bandura posits, 'learning is a cognitive process that takes place in a social context and can occur purely through observation or direct instruction, even in the absence of motor reproduction or direct reinforcement'.[26] Social learning theory, which is described as an expansion of traditional behaviourism, argues that social behaviour, especially gender-specific behaviour, results from the complex pattern of social practices, social institutions, social customs and social regulations that influence the process of construction of gender, that is, formation of masculinity and femininity strictly in social and cultural sense. So it is society which, by using the social norms and practices, organizations, institutional support such as family, marriage and, above all, patriarchy, and 'which by using the biological signs of woman trains and shapes her as other and creates the ground for discrimination, inferiority and subordination and in all gender inequality, the sole victim of which is woman'.[27] This process is

---

[26] Albert Bandura, *Social Learning and Personality Development* (New York, NY: Holt, Rinehart and Winston, 1963), 9.

[27] Chattopadhyay, *Fighting Gender Inequality*, 56.

stated by Beauvoir in her famous statement, 'One is not born, but rather becomes, a woman'.[28] The main argument here is that social learning tends to create such a social psychology that results in a unique lifestyle, institutional support and thought process all of which are responsible for the problem of gender inequality in society.

> Through gender construction and through socialization gender inequality has been a part and parcel of the *life style* of the people. Just as habit is the second nature, so the life style is also the very basis of habit through the practice of the same thing, same behavior, and same actions in day to day life starting from morning tea to retiring in the bed at night. The whole day, the month, the year and also year after year thinking and practicing of the same thing along the gendered line and performing of actions following the policy of gender role differentiates fixed by society and culture creates the life style transplanting the very seed of gender inequality i.e. women's inferiority and subordination in it at every moment of practice of social behavior and action. Thus just as practice leads to perfection, so life style also leads ultimately to the assimilation of ideas of gender inequality, gender differences and gender discrimination as very natural and essential. Signs of inequality and discrimination expressed through life style are not only ever challenged but also given *institutional support* in order to continue and reinforce it in a systematic manner without any resistance. The first institution of its kind is family where construction of gender i.e. masculinity and femininity and subsequent inequality between them is created and taught through socialization, coercive and co-opting.... After family the institution of marriage comes next as a cause and effect of gender inequality.[29]

For Beauvoir, 'marriage is the destiny traditionally offered to women by society.... Marriage has always been a very different thing for man and for woman'.[30] It is marriage that ultimately confines woman in 'home', the world of woman, where it is expected for her to acquire and express henceforth only homely or domestic qualities related to femininity.

---

28 Beauvoir, *The Second Sex*, 295.
29 Chattopadhyay, *Fighting Gender Inequality*, 57–58.
30 Beauvoir, *The Second* Sex, 445–46.

The process of the formation of gender inequality against women is again strengthened more and more as it becomes a part and parcel of the innate nature and *thought process* of the members of the society. The process of thinking is also the result of imitation, learning and socialization and again thinking itself shapes the process of gender construction in a society.[31]

Thus social learning theory studies the issue of social psychology about gender as a set of behaviours learned from the environment.

From the social psychological point of view, it is argued that behaviour therapy as the result of social learning is based, like reinforcement, also on modelling which means imitating or copying other's behaviour. Thus *modelling theory* also influences the development and construction of social psychology. Children observe the people around them behaving in stereotypical ways and they pay attention to these people (models) and copy their behaviour most of which relate to socially accepted notion of gender. In course of time, imitation of other's behaviour becomes the guiding force of all observed behaviours, actions and social psychology. When the child expresses himself or herself by copying the action, behaviour and attitude of others is called imitation. According to Mead, imitation is 'Self-conscious assumption of another's acts or roles'.[32] Assimilation of gender, for a child, is mostly the result of imitation of the action, language and behaviour of father or mother. A male child often imitates his father while a female child imitates her mother. Imitation is inspired and restricted by positive or negative sanction. As for example, when a boy conforms to the roles played by his father, he is often eulogized for being the ideal representative of his father. But when a boy or girl fails to conform to the socially sanctioned roles as played by his or her father or mother, he or she is often rebuked as the black sheep. For Giddens,

> These positive and negative reinforcements aid boys and girls in learning and conforming to expected sex roles. If an individual develops gender practices which do not correspond with his or

[31] Chattopadhyay, *Fighting Gender Inequality*, 59.
[32] G. H. Mead, *Mind, Self and Society: From the Standpoint of a Social Behaviorist* (Chicago: University of Chicago Press, 1962), 52–60.

her biological sex—that is, they are deviant—the explanation is seen to reside in inadequate or irregular socialization.[33]

Imitation is limited to material objects such as dress, food or style like walking or speaking style and again it works in respect of non-material items such as thought process, culture, etc. Imitation may be spontaneous or planned. In a strictly gender-stratified society, imitation spontaneously happens most of the time especially in respect of dress, style, language and pronunciation. Social psychology manipulated by gender socialization always extends support for the *dress* which is selected from the viewpoint of gender. Dress, across all cultures and in all societies, bears a gendered significance. Imitation also occurs in case of *make-up*.

> There are a clear gender-biased division of make-up items starting from hair colour and deodorant to jewelry and their imitations. Children assimilate the make-up style through imitation in consideration of their respective gender. ... A child, since his power of judgment develops, sees his or her parents to perform different social roles and to conform to different social norms. Little by little, the conviction that is carried by the child is that father and mother represent different genders and so they do not have to be regarded as identical. ... But soon, as the gender socialization begins, the child comes out of this crisis and starts becoming used to the ideology of gender. The child starts imitation of his or her father or mother from the gender point of view. The example of such imitations are copying the walking, speaking, laughing and looking style. A boy or a girl tries to develop his or her masculinity or femininity also through the imitation of *speaking or laughing* style.[34]

It is almost admitted that male and female genders speak or laugh differently. So it is the viewpoint that a male or female practises and expresses his/her styles differently in a sharply gender-divided society continuously, whereby these styles get gendered dimension almost as a stable feature of society and the boys or girls, generation to generation, come to imitate these styles as their conscious steps to gender socialization. Thus the social psychology, especially in case of gender, is built on

[33] Giddens, *Sociology*, 108.
[34] Chattopadhyay, *Fighting Gender Inequality*, 17–19.

the process of imitating the behaviour of the models of a given society giving birth to a fixed notion of beliefs or stereotypes. Social learning theory draws heavily on the concept of modelling or copying socially accepted behaviour or learning by observing such behaviour.

> Bandura outlined three types of modeling stimuli: Live model in which an actual person is demonstrating the desired behavior; Verbal instruction in which an individual describes the desired behavior in detail and instructs the participants how to engage in the behavior; Symbolic in which modeling occurs by means of media including movies, television, internet, literature and radio.[35]

According to Bandura, modelling or imitation involves a series of cognitive and behavioural processes including

> Attention which means that observers must attend to the modeled behavior; Retention which means that in order to reproduce an observed behavior, observers must be able to remember the features of the behavior; Reproduction which means that to reproduce a behavior, observers must organize responses in accordance with the model; Motivation that means the decision to reproduce (or refrain from reproducing) an observed behavior is dependent on the motivations and expectations of the observer, including anticipated consequences and internal standards.[36]

Role theory is very closely related to the understanding of social psychology. Role theory is concerned with social statuses and social roles. Social statuses are different positions of society such as father, mother, son, daughter, etc. Roles are the expectations for how people in different social statuses should behave. The term 'role theory' points to the 'expansive and variegated body of analyses examining the linkages between the social organization, culture and performances that humans give while engaged in interaction'.[37]

---

[35] Taken from "Social Learning Theory" in *Wikipedia*.

[36] Albert Bandura, "Modeling Theory: Some Traditions, Trends and Disputes," in *Recent Trends in Social Learning Theory*, ed. R. D. Parke (New York, NY: Academic Press, Inc., 1972), 65–77.

[37] Daniel D. Martin and Janelle L. Wilson, "Role Theory," in *Encyclopedia of Social Theory*, ed. George Ritzer, vol. 2 (Thousand Oaks, London, New Delhi: SAGE, 2005), 651–55.

The role theory has from its beginnings the extensive history. Social philosopher George Herbart Mead (*Mind, Self and Society,* 1934), anthropologist Ralph Linton (*Study of Man,* 1936; Role and Staus 1947), a psychologist Jacob Moreno (*Who Shall Survive?* 1934) are considered as the founders of role theory, independently from each other. The significant development of role theory is made by works by Talcott Parsons and Robert F. Bales (1951), Robert K. Marton (1957), Ralph Dahrendorf (1958), Raewyn Connell (1979), Keller, (1997), Martin-Wilson (2005).[38]

Since role theory is not an integrated concept and it is used in various disciplines and different paradigms, it is difficult to describe and define this theory as an understanding of social psychology. This discussion, being a part of gender study in this current research, aims at the impact of role theory in building gender-stereotypical images of men and women and at the social and cultural processes of gender socialization ultimately contributing to the creation and continuation of gender inequality in society. Historically social role theory developed during the 1980s as a gender-related theory. Eagly published a book in 1987 titled *Sex Differences in Social Behavior: A Social Role Interpretation* and exposed the main gender issue as to how role theory as a perspective of social psychology contributed to the justification and continuation of the differences between men and women. Her main argument was that social roles are necessarily influenced by the society in which we live. Social role theory uses a structural approach to sex differences, rather than a cultural approach. The structural pressures coming from family, peer group, school and colleges, other communities and religious organizations have caused men and women to behave in different ways and inculcated the perception in the people that social roles are solely based on gender of the concerned persons and are formed by social norms of the organizations. According to Eagly, 'Social norms, according to social psychologists, are shared expectations about appropriate qualities or behaviors. Social role theory of sex differences promotes a view of social life

---

[38] Martin Beres, "Role theory in the social work—in the context of gender stereotypes" (Slovakia: Faculty of Arts, Institute of Educology and Social Work, University of Presov).

as fundamentally gendered, given current situations'.[39] So the role theory of social psychology opening a dialogue with gender study as well is, in all ways, devoted to the task of helping the individuals to assimilate the ideology of gender constructed by society through various structural organizations and their norms and practices. Thus it is more a curriculum of genderization than socialization of individuals.

Thus, it is seen that through various structures and processes role theory of social psychology comes to ensure an ideological support to gender role performances in particular and gender differences and gender inequality in general. Role theory, perhaps, is 'the vocation which introduces individual male or female with the gender ideology of the respective society and thereby proves the gender difference, gender discrimination and gender inequality as natural as well as important at least judged from the functionalist point of view'.[40]

Symbolic Interactionism is also a relevant theory of social psychology.

> The theories of George Herbert Mead and, to a lesser extent, Charles Horton Cooley and W. I. Thomas provided its initial core, but a variety of different perspectives developed in the ensuing years. ... In Mead's view traditional social psychology began with the psychology of the individual in an effort to explain social experience; in contrast, Mead always gives priority to the social world in understanding social experience.[41]

In the words of Mead,

> We are not, in social psychology, building up the behavior of the social group in terms of the behavior of separate individuals composing it; rather, we are starting out with a given social whole of complex group activity, into which we analyze (as elements) the behavior of each of the separate individuals composing it. ... For social psychology, the whole (society) is prior to the part (the individual), not the part to the whole; and the part is explained in terms of the whole, not the whole in terms of the part or parts.[42]

---

[39] A. H. Eagly, *Sex Differences in Social Behavior: A Social Role Interpretation* (Hillsdale: Lawrence Erlbaum Associates, 1987), 13–31.

[40] Chattopadhyay, *Fighting Gender Inequality*, 39.

[41] Ritzer, *Sociological Theory*, 326–33.

[42] Mead, *Mind, Self and Society*, 7.

To Mead, social psychology is based on the group mentality and behaviour of a social group which expresses its mental state through four stages of act and they are—impulse, perception, manipulation and consummation. In Mead's view a dialectical relationship prevails among all these four stages. Although the act, to Mead, involves only one person, but it is always influenced by the socially earned store of knowledge and herein lies the basic difference between lower animals and the humans. The social act, for Mead, involves two or more persons and gestures are the basic mechanism in the social act. To Mead, 'Gestures are movements of the first organism which act as specific stimuli calling forth the (socially) appropriate responses of the second organism'.[43] Mead refers to vocal and physical gesture by pointing out that the objective of gesture is to develop the social interaction through significant symbols. For him, 'It has been the vocal gesture that has preeminently provided the medium of social organization in human society'.[44] As an example of significant vocal symbol Mead refers to language with which the gestures as well as their meanings are communicated.

> It is only through significant symbols, especially language, that human thinking is possible. ... Significant symbols also make possible symbolic interaction. That is, people can interact with one another not just through gestures but also through significant symbols. This, of course, makes a world of difference and makes possible much more complex interaction patterns and forms of social organization than would be possible through gestures alone.[45]

Mead uses a number of concepts like mind, self and society in his theory and argues that the common attitudes of the community or the society is key to all symbols and interactions and ultimately social psychology prevails over all stages and processes of symbolic interactionism. So far as socially constructed views of the symbols and interactions are concerned, the issue of gender becomes a guiding force behind such symbols and interactions. Gender viewpoint of the concerned society or

---

[43] Ibid, 14.

[44] George Herbert Mead, *The Philosophy of the Present* (La Salle, Illinois: Open Court Publishing, 1959), 188.

[45] Ritzer, *Sociological Theory*, 337–38.

the community influences all the four stages of individual act, social acts, symbols, especially language and the development of mind, self and society radically.

Evolutionary theory asserts that genes govern social behaviour. Through evolution people of a community or a regional area possess some ancestral property of behaviour and lifestyle passing on through their genes. As a result, they belong to some uniform characteristics and traits which direct them towards maintaining and expressing certain socio-psychological orientations which become their anthropological, physiological and biological inheritance in course of time. Evolutionary theory of social psychology drew heavily upon the materials of anthropological school, especially two great works of E. B. Taylor—*Primitive Culture* (1871) and *Researches into the Early History of Mankind* (1865)—and consequently the growth of evolutionary anthropology became possible. 'According to this approach, the similarity in lifestyle and creativity of people of various countries is not the result of mutual influence. Rather, it is the result of uniformity of an organic nature and thought process.'[46] Charles Darwin (1809–82) was the proponent of the theory of evolution through natural selection which, by the natural process of eliminating inferior qualities gradually over time, talks of the preservation of the functional advantage that enable species to compete, survive and reproduce. 'The main contention of Darwin ... was: i) all life has descended from one common ancestor; ii) therefore all are related with a whole; iii) every individual part is integral; iv) scientific naturalism is above theology and thereby non-religious.'[47] Herbert Spencer (1820–1903) is believed to be the most notable exponent of social evolution. According to Spencer, 'all nature, including human society as a part of nature, is bound together as one whole in a universal process of transformation or evolution'.[48] 'Spencer's evolutionary theory of historical development was influenced by the Darwinian view of natural selection and Spencer applied the concept of survival of fittest, to the social world, in the name of

---

[46] Chattopadhyay, *Gender Inequality*, 50.
[47] Sujit Kumar Chattopadhyay, *Revisiting Vivekananda: From Revival to Renaissance* (Kolkata: Levant Books, 2015), 123.
[48] Bhattacharyya, *Sociology*, 867–68.

an approach called social Darwinism.'[49] The evolutionary theory of social psychology is the synthesis of several disciplines like psychology, sociology and anthropology and in India Vivekananda was perhaps the

> first to apply these disciplines in the study of historical evolution which was also a study of social change where individual mind, social movement and ethnic background were tied in a very complicated relationship. To him, every movement first starts in the mind of the individual and then, in course of time, it is applied on the social plane.[50]

According to the evolutionary theory of social psychology, both physical characteristics and social behaviours are the point of focus and persons with better physical ability become more relevant than the persons lacking it. This theory also tends to influence the mating relationship in society. Thus ultimately the evolutionary theory of social psychology champions the slogan of 'survival of the fittest' and accordingly this theory has a tremendous impact on the issue of gender differences, discrimination and inequality. The slogan of 'survival of the fittest' actually turns into the slogan of the superiority of the male gender in society and emphasizes that the concept of masculinity and femininity is the result of social evolution and natural mental, psychological and cultural capital of male and female earned through evolution. Thus as an evaluation of social psychology from the viewpoint of gender studies, it is argued that evolutionary theory ultimately strengthens the idea of male domination, gender role distribution and female subjugation in any society. After the emergence of the practice of evolutionary psychology in 1980s, a new section of researchers concentrated on the study of gender. The roots of this research lie not in feminism but in sociobiological theorizing (Wilson 1975), which in turn emerged from earlier Darwinian theory. The new vocation of research along the line of the theory of evolution included the discussion of evolutionary psychology, theory of evolution, natural selection, evolution and human behaviour, impact of evolution on gender study and all other matters linking evolution with gender.

---

[49] Chattopadhyay, *Revisiting Vivekananda*, 120.
[50] Ibid, 192.

Many feminist psychologists have remained critics of evolutionary psychology because of its emphasis on the differing innate natures of men and women and its lack of attention to active, constructive cultural processes (e.g., Eagly and Wood 1999, 2011; Travis 2003). Despite such criticisms, evolutionary psychology has considerable visibility and has spawned intense debates about how nature and nurture combine in producing the phenomena of gender observed in contemporary societies (Gangestad & Simpson 2007). For example, the journal *Sex Roles* devoted an entire 2011 special issue to evolutionary psychology (Smith and Konik 2011).[51]

Gender study as a discipline and its scope has been continually transformed, not only in terms of its increasing dynamicity, newer development of theories and movement centring around it but also in reaction to the questions involving social influence, social opinion and social coercion and compulsion surrounding the issue of gender—its construction, development, nature and scope. Thus gender study as an academic discipline and feminism as a movement tends to focus a myriad of aspects of gender from the psychological point of view and encouraged the researchers to devote in the study of social action, social behaviour, social realism and social psychology. Accordingly, a new trend of research based on the dialogue between gender study and social psychology began. Gender, basically being a social and cultural construction, has its roots in social psychology of the concerned society and, thereby, it has been argued that the psychology of gender and women has to be investigated within the specific research area of social psychology. So this scholarship has now moved from a mere study of psychological approach to gender inequality to the socio-psychological investigation of gender study.

The prior discussion on gender study and social psychology in this chapter is very much relevant to this book as much as this discussion contributes a theoretical proposition to the whole discussion of gender socialization and role of different agents. First, although gender study gained its primary inspiration from feminism, but in the process of extensiveness of its scope

---

[51] "Feminism and Psychology: Analysis of a Half-Century of Research on Women and Gender," 25. Retrieved 2 February 2014, from http://www.apa.org/pubs/databases/training/class-codes.pdf

gender study has finally escaped and surmounted the boundaries of feminism. In traditional feminism theories of gender differences, gender oppression and gender inequality draw most of the attention of the researchers. It also focuses on gender role distribution, sex role stereotypes, power relations between men and women and issues of violence against women. But gender studies as a broad academic discipline has broadened its scope to include a wide assortment of variables ranging from socially accepted form of gender construction, gender relation and gender identity to the classification of genders and their nature. It is also interested in the study of the institutions that play a vital role in gender socialization such as family, peer group, school and colleges, media, religious institution and, above all, patriarchy. The institutions always act as a faithful structure of patriarchy, and institutional norms and practices encourage or compel the people of all genders to internalize the spirit of gender ideology which again teaches everyone to behave and act in compliance with the biological signs assigned at birth. Second, as of classification of genders, gender studies is not only interested in the study of relation of subordination and subjugation between men and women, but also is eager to include other genders beyond the conventional category of male and female, such as lesbian, gay, bisexual, transgender and queer gender, who are popularly called as LGBTQ. Even within the conventional and unconventional format of genders, there are different mentalities, expressions and identity crisis. The existence of third gender has been recognized in many countries in the field of voting rights, right to gender identification, mate selection and even right to marry a partner by one's own choice of gender. In feminist discourse, the scope of discussion could not overcome the traditional relation between male and female and their nature as masculinity and femininity. Feminism revolved round basically women's study and their subordination, subjugation and devaluation in patriarchal society and thus took notes of mainly the patriarchal agenda of confining women in private sphere, that is, home through the concept of inferiority, subservience and domesticity. But gender studies tends to surpass the limitations of feminism and wants to include all the genders beyond biologically assigned men and women. Gender studies also has been a weapon of studying the complexities, so called biological deformity and problems of the third gender and other genders including LGBTQ. Third, But this is never the fact that gender study abandons the scope and subject matter of feminist ideology, rather it may be said that as an academic area of study complementary to feminism, gender study puts the feminist points of discussion in an academically sound theoretical structure. It is never a dilution of feminism but an academic expansion of it.

> Some feel that ... 'gender studies' does fit more easily within the institution and feminist politics ... 'gender studies' also better incorporates not only men and masculinity studies, but also those who take the post-Judith Butler view that gender assignation only takes meaning through performance and iteration. Women's study has had to accept that a monolithical model of 'woman' can exclude and affirm inequality, and gender study is one way of addressing this concern.[52]
>
> Prior to 1970s, the social sciences in general, and sociology in particular, largely ignored gender. The 'people' it studied were mainly men and the topics it focused on were aspects of the social world especially significant for men, such as paid work and politics. Women were almost invisible in pre-1970s' gender-blind sociology, only featuring in their traditional roles as wives and mothers within families. Differences and inequalities between women and men at this time were not recognized as an issue of sociological concern and were not seen as problems to be addressed.[53]

The main-stream sociology was perhaps the male-stream sociology.

> M. Harlambos and R. M. Herald, in their book *Sociology: Themes and Perspectives*, have quoted some anthropologists and sociologists such as Lionel Tiger and Robin Fox, George Peter Murdock, Talcott Parsons, John Bowlby, etc. All of them have emphasized women's traditional role in childbearing and child-rearing and their role in socialization as the chief reasons for gender inequality and the subjugation of women.[54]

There are many a notorious sociological theory that have prepared the ground for marginalization of the women. 'The

[52] Pilcher and Whelehan, *50 Key Concepts*, xii.
[53] Ibid, ix.
[54] Chattopadhyay, *Gender Inequality*, 31.

functional theory of stratification as articulated by Kingsley Davis and Willbert Moore (1945) is perhaps the best known single piece of work in structural-functional theory. Stratification is, in their view, a functional necessity.'[55] Talcott Parsons, a leading functionalist thinker, viewed women in expressive roles providing care and security to children and offering them emotional support. John Bowlby argued, 'the mother is crucial to the primary socialization of the children'.[56] Another sociologist G. Rubin argued, 'women's oppression lies in the way humans have arranged their biological sex-gender system via the kinship structure that rests universally on the exchange of women'.[57] 'Thus, the sociological approach has emphasized the social necessity of gender inequality and every society indulges in sex role-differentiation according to its necessity'[58] and, in this way, sociology, for a long time, took a misogynist stance. In the context of second wave feminism and of the emergence of gender study as a new academic discipline, the issue of gender and all the related matters started getting attention and importance from the researchers of social sciences and sociology. Apart from social inequality, difference and discrimination in general, gender inequality, gender difference and gender discrimination became an issue of sociological concern. Along with sociology other social sciences such as political science, philosophy, psychology, cultural anthropology, economics, demography, history and culture study also included the issue of gender in their curriculum. So in course of time gender study became an area of interdisciplinary research and discussion. Sometimes the science of hormones, genetic engineering, physiology, neuroscience and biological science have been relevant to the discussion of gender. Accordingly many a concepts from social science as well as from the science of hormones or genes have been addressed in the vocation of gender study. As for example, we may refer to the book by Jane Pilcher and Imelda Whelehan titled *50 Key Concepts in Gender Studies* (2004). In this book,

---

[55] Ritzer, *Sociological Theory*, 235.

[56] Giddens, *Sociology*, 113.

[57] Rinita Majumdar, *A Short Introduction to Feminist Theory* (Kolkata: Anustup, 2001), 33.

[58] Chattopadhyay, *Gender Inequality*, 32.

the authors have taken a wide range of diverse materials such as androcentrism, body, citizenship, class, domestic division of labour, essentialism, family, gender, heterosexism, identity politics, lesbian continuum, masculinity, patriarchy, pornography, postmodernism, queer theory, race/ethnicity, reproductive technologies, sexuality, socialization, stereotype, violence and women's studies. The inclusion of so many diverse materials proves the enormous scope of the discipline of gender studies.

The discussion of gender study has a great relevance to the current book. Two chapters of 'gender' and 'gender socialization' are structured thematically from the point of view of the academic angle of gender study. The construction of gender, identification of gender and its consequences are never to be understood without a proper knowledge of gender study. Placement of sex-gender matrix is also done in compliance with the vocation of gender study. Since gender studies today has a wide scope of interdisciplinary discussion and analysis, the current book uses this scope in different discussions of sociocultural and cultural anthropological nature. The institutional and structural influences towards the formation of gender and towards the implementation of gender socialization have been examined through the lenses of gender study which basically flow from the inter-disciplinary approaches. The role of family, peer group, school, media and religion in successful operation and transmission of the vocation of gender socialization among the women in particular and men in general also is possible to explain only with the help of other social sciences such as sociology, anthropology, psychology, ethics and theology.

The discussion of social psychology is also strongly relevant to this current book. First, gender socialization is always done with the consent and approval of society which is basically patriarchal in nature. There is no denying the fact that the worst victim of the gender socialization is the women who are our sisters, daughters, wives and mothers. So basically the puzzle which we cannot solve is that how and why the society goes against the women in order to marginalize them? The answer lies in the exposition of social psychology of a society or a community. Renowned Marxist theoreticians Antonio Labriola, Agust Bebel, Rosa Luxemburg and Plekhanov have supplied enough of clues about the impact of social psychology. All of them in general and Plekhanov in particular described social psychology as 'social inclinations and customs' or 'social emotion and mental structure'. B. Porshnev has referred to Plekhanov in his book, *Social Psychology and History* and opined that in order to understand the courses of evolution of social history, the knowledge of economics is not sufficient. For the purpose of exposition of social mentality, inclination or tendency, we are to shift our practice of knowledge from economics to social psychology. Plekhanov very clearly stated that all thoughts, social and cultural, are produced from a common source of social psychology. The Marxists do not believe in the non-changeability of human mind. It has been an established fact that the effectiveness of human brain is not determined by natural force or environment; rather it is controlled by social history, social and cultural environment, norms and practices. Social history, social and cultural norms and practices create a sort of uniform reaction in the mental configuration of the society. The society then internalizes the basic spirit of such mental configuration and act according to their self-imposed dictates which virtually come from the social pressure exerted by the gender ideology of the patriarchy. These so called self-imposed dictates are called, in the field of psychology, as 'Auto-suggestion' which may be positive and negative. In case of positive auto-suggestion, people of a society or a community involve in good works and ideological struggles against all odds collectively. But in case of negative auto-suggestion, people come to exploit, marginalize and subjugate a definite section, race, or gender automatically guided by what is happening in the society. They do not dare to go against the conventional teachings of the society especially in case of gender related issues and they conform to the principles of status quo. All members, men and women, internalizes the gender education through auto-suggestion and form a common social psychology that lead the women, especially, towards their own victimization.

Thus, Through gender construction and through socialization gender inequality has been a part and parcel of the *life style* of the people. Just as habit is the second nature, so the life style is also the very basis of habit through the practice of the same thing, same behavior, and same actions in day to day life starting from morning tea to retiring in the bed at night. The whole day, the month, the year and also year after year thinking and practicing of the same thing along the gendered line and performing of actions following the policy of gender role differentiates fixed by society and culture creates the life style transplanting the very seed of gender inequality i.e. women's inferiority and subordination in it at every moment of practice of social behavior and action. Thus just as practice leads to perfection, so life style also leads ultimately to the assimilation of ideas of gender inequality, gender differences and gender discrimination as very natural and essential.[59]

Every agent of gender socialization ranging from family to religion as discussed in this book is guided by an implicit dictates of social psychology. Family, for its descent obsession, the system of gender-biased nomenclature of its members, controlling the mating relationship, exerting control over the institutions of marriage and property, is, at all levels, influenced by the social psychology and by all of its spoken and unspoken parameters. Peer group, which is often termed as relatively free and independent of the conscious watch of the society, is also consciously and unconsciously ruled by the blood-shot eyes of the social psychology. The matter of reward and punishment acts as the main drive behind their all relatively free actions and behaviours. The impact of social psychology is also relevant to the nature and all the functions of the educational institutions that serve virtually as the mirror of social psychology and act as the medium of enforcing social norms and practices either through textbooks and references or through classroom lectures and behaviours of the teachers inducing the ideas and practices of gender discrimination and gender inequality among the boys and girls. Media influences over all people ranging from infant to the adult and old are significantly visible especially in case of gender socialization. Media influences society as well as it is true that society influences media. The social attitude towards the women is reflected in media either through advertisements or through audio-visuals and feature wrings. Several times it is experienced throughout the globe that reporting of gender related crimes or incidents in both the print and electronic media is also gender-biased and straightway misogynist. The patriarchal society is always intended to portray the women as an object of sexual pleasure and attraction and media serves this purpose

[59] Chattopadhyay, *Fighting Gender Inequality*, 57.

of patriarchy, directly or indirectly, all over the world. The representation of women as fragmented, objectified and dehumanized through media is a global experience. Unless we study the social psychology behind such portrayal and representation and unless we understand the modes of gender socialization as the means of justifying such humiliating projection of the women, we will surely face a theoretical inconsistency in explaining and analysing all the aspects related to gender, be the socialization, anti-socialization or differential socialization. Religious sanction towards the social attitude, social mentality and social psychology is by far the best possible reason of the surrender of individuals to the feet of social dictates. So in order to understand the hidden curriculum of social psychology behind the religious texts, interpretations, norms and practices, this chapter, especially the section on social psychology, will surely carry relevance.

So far as the main theme of this book, gender socialization, is concerned, this chapter has significant bearing upon all the subsequent chapters of this book. Gender socialization and role of various agents is a matter which is closely linked with the two concepts, namely, gender and socialization. For an in-depth analysis of what the gender is and how does it take its form gradually but steadily and also for knowing the consequential application of the idea of gender, the discussion of gender studies is crucial. How the process of socialization is reversed and is converted to the notion of differential socialization, especially for the women, is a matter of understanding which is only possible through the dissemination of the description by social psychology. Social psychology not only exposes the hidden curriculum of gender socialization, but it also enlightens us about the conscious and unconscious store of thoughts we have about ourselves and the society.

2

Gender: Meaning, Formation and Effects

It is a general tendency to equate the meaning of gender with the meaning of sex. For a long time in sociology and also in other social sciences, the term 'gender' was used to be discussed as an alternative word of 'sex'. But with the development of feminist sociological discourses and with the growing academic pressure of defining gender inequality from a scientific, sociological as well as psychological viewpoint, it was felt necessary to discuss gender as a separate broad category and the process of bringing out the concept of gender from its overlapped meaning meshed with sex began. Thus, today separate tools and indexes are used to define sex and gender.

At the outset, it is necessary to study the difference between sex and gender in order to have the discrete meaning of gender. From the viewpoint of *biological approach,* sex is considered as the biological feature of the being, human or animal, expressed through physical feature or mental instinct in a potentially provocative situation. Biological approach emphasizes the biological activities for sexual satisfaction. For Giddens, 'in general, sociologists use the term "sex" to refer to the anatomical and physiological differences that define male and female bodies'.[1] As a biological fact, sex is closely related to chromosomes, hormonal profiles, anatomical configuration of internal or external sex organs and instinctive potency which together determines the intensity of the sex drives in a being, that is, individual and which makes the difference between man and woman and male and female. From the biological point of view body organs (vagina or penis), chromosomes (XX or XY) and hormones (testosterone or oestrogen) of the male or female play a very vital role in displaying and channelizing the sexual drives. But the problem of identifying sex from the biological and organic point of view is not fairly neat and clean. It is argued that the sets of biological characteristics that define humans as female or male

---

[1] Giddens, *Sociology*, 107.

are not mutually exclusive, as there are individuals who possess the features of both sexes.

> [Sex] in human beings is not a purely dichotomous variable. It is not an evenly continuous one either.... A fair number of human beings are markedly intersexual, a number of them to the point where both sorts of external genitalia appear, or where developed breasts occur in an individual with male genitalia, and so on.[2]

Thus, the organic approach to the study of sex cannot cover the whole space of those who participate in sexual behaviour without accepting the standard biological pattern. Here comes in the *identity approach* which intends to identify many a non-conventional sexual form such as lesbian, gay, bisexual, queer and asexual and argues that liberty of choosing sex partners is the only solution of establishing and expressing the sexual identities of the so called other sex. In that case convenient social atmosphere is also needed for the easy expression of the sexual identity and for the satisfaction of the sexual urge thereof. We believe that it is indispensable to deconstruct the binary sex/gender system that dominates the Western field of gender studies absolutely, and in most cases the binary system goes unnoticed. For 'other sexualities to be possible' it is indispensable and urgent that we stop governing ourselves by the absurd notion that only two possible body types exist, male and female, with only two genders inextricably linked to them, man and woman.

> We make trans and intersex issues our priority because their presence, activism and theoretical contributions show us the path to a new paradigm that will allow as many bodies, sexualities and identities to exist as those living in this world might wish to have, with each one of them respected, desired, celebrated.[3]

Thus, the question of the other gender, apart from male or female gender, becomes inextricably related with the social,

[2] Clifford Geertz, *Local Knowledge: Further Essays in Interpretive Anthropology* (New York, NY: Basic Books, 1983), 81 (parenthetical insertion mine).

[3] International Gay and Lesbian Human Rights Commission [IGLHRC], 2005, Institutional Memoir of the 2005 Institute for Trans and Intersex Activist Training, 8, Retrieved 10 July 2017, from http://www.iglhrc.org/files/iglhrc/ LAC/ITIAT-Aug06-E.pdf

cultural and also legal milieu and comes within the broader purview of gender study. *Instinctive approach* to the study of sex can supplement here. This approach judges sex as an urge, a mental and psychological response to the call of another male, female or even other sex. Sex, being biological in nature, is best understood from the angle of instinct. It is argued that

> Since sex is a body related matter, its nature is basically biological. Biologically we, human beings, inherit and carry several types of instincts such as appetite, sleep, anger, fear, greed, jealousy and other impulses. Sex is one like them. Any individual, man or woman, may feel hunger, sleep as well as sex at any biologically impulsive situation. But what situation and method individual would prefer to satisfy his or her sex drive or how, is a matter of social learning and imitation of other's behavior. Here comes the question of gender when sex also comes under social control and social regulation.[4]

Gender, in sociology, does not represent a biological category. It is a combination of socially and culturally constructed concept of masculinity and femininity in addition to biological concept of sex identity and since it is society and culture specific it has no uniform standard. According to Maria Miss, a feminist theoretician, gender, that is, masculinity or femininity is the result of a long historical process. 'In each stage of history gender is differently defined and this definition depends upon the mode of production in a specific historical situation where male relates with society and with each other according to their role in production processes.'[5] According to Flora Anthias and Nira Yuval-Davis, '[t]he ideology of gender is not universal in form. It is specific to particular historical periods, cultural backgrounds and positions within the hierarchies of class and nationality'.[6] So the concept of gender is changing and it means a combination of some socially constructed features by which men and women act and behave different and come to perform sex-oriented roles prescribed by the society.

[4] Chattopadhyay, *Fighting Gender Inequality*, 44.
[5] Chattopadhyay, *Fighting Gender Inequality*, 47–48.
[6] Anthias and Davis, "Contextualizing Feminism," 1983.

Within a society at particular point of time, individuals come to adopt gender-specific behavior, attitudes and dispositional traits through process of socialization and allocation that perpetuate gender role differentiation. Through the process of socialization individuals internalize gender stereotypes that buttress existing gender differentiation and stratification.[7]

Gender describes the characteristics that a society or culture delineates as masculine or feminine. Sociologically, gender means a category to which different societies and cultures attribute different characteristics and behaviours to different sexes. In this sense, the concept of 'real man' in any culture means the male sex plus what that culture recognize as masculine qualities. Similarly, the concept of woman means always the female sex plus the recognized feminine qualities of that culture. Each society has a unique history and culture on the basis of which gender roles are distributed and in course of this distribution gender inequality as a persistent form of society is created. While sex is based mainly on external bodily characteristics, gender is the internal sense of a person as man or woman or other sex and in perfect tune with this internal sense a person responds to the stereotype role performance set by the society and culture. Gender refers to the categories within which socially constructed roles, behaviours, patterns and attributes are distributed according to the norms and practices of a given society. This is the reason that in most of the societies male genders are considered hard working, aggressive, dominating and powerful. This is a gender-biased notion of masculinity. Likewise, in most societies female genders are expected to be faithful, virtuous, emotional, softhearted and self-effacing. That is why females are considered to be most suitable for the job of nursing, teaching and homemaking. This is also a gendered notion of femininity that is formed and developed through a long process of socialization since the birth of a female child. Each society according to its historical legacy and cultural background makes a social division of power, roles, behaviours and attitudes among the male sex and the female sex and moulds their personality and perception in the direction of conforming completely to the social

[7] Edgar F. Borgatta and Karen S. Cook, eds, *The Future of Sociology* (Newbury Park, CA: SAGE Publications, 1988), 134.

division of the given society as a result of which the concept of masculinity and femininity or the notion of masculine gender or feminine gender emerges. Thus, ultimately it is society that makes the gender. That is why Beauvoir argued,

> One is not born, but rather becomes, a woman. No biological, psychological, or economic fate determines the figure that the human female presents in society; it is civilization as a whole that produces this creature, intermediate between male and eunuch, which is described as feminine.[8]

According to Food and Agricultural Organization of the United Nations (FAO), 'It (gender) is a central organizing principle of societies, and often governs the processes of production and reproduction, consumption and distribution'.[9] Foucault also observes that the ideology of gender has a great role in the distribution of power in any society. It is the matter of historical experiences in all societies and across all cultures that the ideology of gender is taken up and applied with the premise of inequality among sexes as taken for granted and male gender gets the priority as dominant gender. In contrast to the position of male, the position of the female becomes comparatively weak and subordinate as a result of the assignment of gender in any society. Accordingly, either in the matter of distribution of values, roles, attitudes or in the matter of distribution of power or property among male and female the ideology of gender always stands beside the male or isolates the female from all possible sources of power and domination and also from the control of the process of production of the given society. Thus the notion of weak, soft, childish, emotional, homely, self-effacing and tolerant woman is developed and applied in the interest of patriarchy and results in the birth of the concept of femininity and women become the worst victim of all sorts of inequality in course of time. On the contrary, the notion of strong, tough, rational, matured, aggressive, dominant and powerful is developed for the male gender and these qualities form together the notion of masculinity in a given society. So in the long run the meaning of gender becomes inextricably bound

---

[8]   Simone de Beauvoir, *The Second Sex*, trans. and ed. H. M. Parshley (London: Vintage, 1997), 295.

[9]   Retrieved 3 March 2014, from www.fao.org/sd

to the agenda of supplying a sexual justification of inequality between male and female.

The difference between sex and gender is briefly illustrated in the following table:

Sex	Gender
1. Sex is biological and physical.	1. Gender is cultural and mental.
2. Sex is body related and that is why it is mostly external.	2. Gender is related to personal sense of representation of one's self and that is why gender is internal.
3. Sex is universal and does not vary substantially between different human societies.	3. Gender is regional and since it is society and culture specific and since society and culture is not uniform in nature, the concept of gender may vary from society to society.
4. Sex is characteristic of all beings, human and non-human.	4. But the ideology of gender is the characteristics of only the human society.
5. Male and female are sex categories.	5. Masculine and feminine are gender categories.
6. Sex is expressed through organic activities.	6. Gender is formed and expressed through inorganic activities dictated by society and culture.
7. Sex is instinctive in nature and expression.	7. Gender is socialized and practised through cultural norms and customs.
8. Sex is a characteristics of human or non-human beings usually expressed in a sexually impulsive situation.	8. Gender is a category to which persons assign themselves on their own or by others or by the pressure of society on the basis of sex signs.
9. Sex refers to the inborn physical differences between men and women.	9. Gender refers to the socially constructed and culturally moulded differences between the sexes.
10. Sex is difficult to be changed since it is inborn.	10. Gender can be changed if the society or culture permits and it can be changed even by operation.

(continued)

(continued)

Sex	Gender
11. Across all societies and cultures, sex differences exist.	11. In each stage of history, gender is differently defined and it is specific to particular cultural backgrounds of a given society.
12. Sex is the result of biological process.	12. Gender is the result of socialization process.
13. The notion of sex is closely related to chromosomes, hormones, reproductive organs, and so on and all other bodily features.	13. Gender is closely related to behaviour, attitude, feelings, social roles and responses to all other directions from society.
14. Sexual identity is based on genetic and anatomical features.	14. Gender identity is always acquired identity which is learned through a long process of gender socialization.
15. Sex is functional since it is stimulated only when the biological organs and other sex and sense organs work.	15. Gender is relational since it not only refers to just men and women as sex category but to the relationship between them.
16. Sex identifies man or woman as to how or what he or she is.	16. Gender explains as to what a man or woman does.

The formation of gender is very important in so far as it ultimately affects the very spirit of the gender ideology of a given society. If the formation becomes erroneous it seriously hinders the philosophy of gender in general and the process of gender socialization and gender identity in particular and results in causing also a threat to the development of the children who have been the victims of the wrong process of the gender formation. Gender formation is the process of achieving the gender identity at the age between two and three years of a male or female infant by the way of separation from or individuation of mother's or father's sexual identity and by way of responding to the stereotyped sex role expectations of the society. According to modern sociologists, 'within a society at particular point of time, individuals come to adopt gender-specific behavior, attitudes and dispositional traits through process of socialization and allocation that perpetuate gender role differentiation',[10] and the process by which the gender

[10] Borgatta and Cook, *The Future of Sociology*, 134.

consciousness of the child are shaped in the expected way are termed as gender formation. The process of gender indoctrination starts since birth of a child who with his/her growing up is encouraged to behave like a boy or a girl as suitable and as will match perfectly with the biology of their genders. So the formation of a male or female infant in tune with the stereotyped sex role and their ultimate acquisition of the role of father or mother are termed as gender formation. In short, gender formation is the process of the subjective experience of one's own gender. When children of both the male and female sex reach the age of two and start labelling their own sex and gender as compared to each other and also with other people within their known social setting, the process of the formation of gender identity is generally called as gender formation. At the age of seven, their sense of gender becomes stable and this is called as gender consistency. And when these children are grown up they sometimes behave in ways not absolutely accepted by social norms because they are granted relaxation of norms as a reward of persistently conforming to the gender ideology and accordingly because their gender formation has been so stable that ultimately they will not make any harm to the stereotyped gender ideology of the given society. Thus, the process of acquiring gender identity works through the formative years, the age of consolidation and relaxation. Although it is a matter of great controversy as to whether gender is inborn or acquired attribute, the recent studies have shown that if not all, but the most of the perception of gender impression are the result of bio-social, social and sociocultural setting where children tends to acquire stereotyped sex roles as expected by the society. According to Zebrowitz, impression formation is 'the process of forming descriptive and evaluative judgments about a target person',[11] and when such judgments are applied with a gender bias with a view to achieving gender differences between the sexes then it is called gender formation.

Different factors play in the process of gender formation and factors ranging from biology to psychology through social settings are included in the list. These factors are identity, role and

---

[11] L. Zebrowitz, "Impression Formation," in *The Blackwell Encyclopeadia of Social Psychology*, eds A. S. R. Manstead and M. Hewstone (Oxford: Blackwell Publishers Ltd, 1995, 1999), 309–14.

expression. The *identity* factor is very much a dominating point in the process of the construction of gender. Primarily, sense of identity develops from the biological signs of the child, male or female, especially through his/her penis or female genital. At the age of two, children start becoming conscious of the significance of the difference of the sex organs of both sexes and thus sexual identity of their own are established in their mind. Infants of both sex look at each other which raises a curiosity about the difference between them and this sense of difference grows with their association with other children in the outer social setting, the influence and the intervention of which also add incentive to their sense of identity. This is primarily through consciousness about the biological sign of the male or female infant that gender identity comes to be expressed and subsequently it is shaped by all other social and cultural norms of gender socialization. Gender identity is always caused by the sense of difference and similarity with the persons of the broader social setting. A male infant looks at his mom's body, takes the breast milk of his mom and is caressed by her in a unique way as felt by the infant, and all these prompt him to think of the difference between his own body and the body of his darling mom. In contrast to his experiences with mom, the male infant discovers the similarity of biological signs with his dad and comes to follow the dad in matters of orientation building unknowingly. He also discovers the parental sex role as different and this also makes him inquisitive about the identity of his own. The male infant separates himself from his mother in a very subtle way of calculation of the gender differences between him and his mother and works very consciously towards the individuation of his father's traits. A girl child also proceeds for the formation of her gender identity in the reversed way of the male child. The female infant is prompted for separation from her father and is encouraged for the individuation of the traits of her mother in course of her association with the outer setting of the world. Thus the matter of difference–similarity and the notion of separation–individuation play a very dominant role in the formation of gender identity primarily at the beginning of the process. At the age of six or seven, the sense of gender becomes stable in the mind of the child and he/she becomes active in acquiring and expressing the sociocultural norms of gender and stereotyped sex roles as fixed by the social setting of the given society. This is the stage of gender consolidation when all the questions of the formative years relating to sex or gender are solved and a speedy development of gender gets priority to the boy or the girl. The chief object of the age within the purview of the consolidation of gender is to show or manifest one as the ideal representative of his/her gender and to perform the stereotyped sex/gender roles by occupying the space as early as possible in perfect conformity with the ideology of gender. As the boy or the girl grows up and becomes teenagers the gender consistency achieved in the mid-time span of the formation of gender identity often receives a blow from the teenagers consciously or unconsciously by their so called inconsistent behaviour of breaking the social norms of gender. In all societies sometimes the teenagers of both sexes are seen to be displaying the behaviour diametrically opposite in manner in terms of his/her gender. They are seen to be exchanging and practicing the language, space, time and the life-style of each other in terms of their sex. The young girl may indiscriminately use the *language* of what is called in a gendered society as the 'male language'. The young boy may decorate him by the ornaments and the clothes by what is called as 'female fashion'.

> The context of gender has also temporal dimension i.e. a dimension related to time. In agricultural and semi-industrial society, women are not allowed to move freely at any time of their choice at day especially at night. The safe time for women's movement has been notionally fixed by the patriarchy as the day time i.e. from 6 AM to 6 PM and a woman is never allowed to stay out of home at a stretch for this time slot.[12]

But when the young girl dares to break this rule and wish to move freely in the society in a time what is generally called as 'male time', that is, late at night, the behaviour is generally termed as deviant of gender norms. Similarly, a young girl or a young boy may feel temporarily convenient and comfortable in the space opposite to their sexes. The context of gender has also a spatial dimension in the sense that some spaces are considered for men's free movement and those are not open to women as their access

[12] Chattopadhyay, *Fighting Gender Inequality*, 51–52.

to all spaces is not permissible, and some spaces are very much restricted for women. Bar, local club, football ground, street tea stall, coffee house, beer pub, night club, etc., are considered male spaces where women's presence is not socially recognized. On the other hand, kitchen, space attached to house well, temple, lad's compartment, etc., are considered female spaces where a relative sovereignty of female is permitted. But when such conventional notion of gender space is temporarily broken by a young boy or girl then a problem of conformity arises in society. The situation may arise when the young boy may choose to move in the so-called space of women and similarly a young girl may choose to move in the so-called space of the male. Such behaviour is not punished by the society as the persons associated proved their persistent conformity to the social norms over the years. Society thinks it prudent to leave the matter of conformity to them as it is accepted that the so called deviated persons have already successfully crossed the formation and consolidation stages of gender identity and now owing to certain temporary problem they have been hostile for the time being and after the crisis is over for them they will again come back to their sense of identity. So for the time being, the young boy or girl may be granted relaxation and in all open societies and across all dynamic cultures the point of relaxation is accepted as an important component of gender identity. Thus gender identity is shaped through the stages of formation, consolidation and relaxation over the first 15 to 18 years of human life and in the next 50 to 60 years of the life cycle gender identity cause to manifest and implement the gender ideology of the given society. *Gender role* acquisition is a very important element in the construction of gender. Gender role is the expectation of the society for appropriate male and female behaviour as suited to their biological sexes. By the age of two or three both the male and female infants become conscious of their sexual as well as gendered identity and they prepare themselves for acquiring their gender role in society. Through the process of socialization or by means of reward or punishment the male or female children in each society are prompted to assimilate or imitate the appropriate male or female activities identified as suitable to their sexes almost since their birth. Public and private jobs, family role or parental sex role determine the system by which the gender ideology works in a society. Role in a gendered society is always stereotyped and distributed according to the sexes. So, in almost every gender-divided society segregation of role takes place in almost every important sector such as education, public work, homemaking, etc. So far as the educational curriculum is concerned, gender ideology operates through the differential education system for the boys and the girls. The stereotypical gender role argues that schools should inculcate the lesson that girls are caring, nurturing, quiet, helpful, considerate of others and place others' needs before their own. In contrast, the school curriculum should represent boys as biologically strong, powerful, aggressive and fit for outer and hard jobs. The students who question much and participate in academic criticism are favoured by the teachers whereas the girls are not. The stereotyped role presents that boys are fit for science education while the girls are fit for arts education. All public works, political, administrative and other outer jobs are considered fit for male. In a patriarchal society, the differences between public and private is very cleverly made with a view to offer the male all important public jobs on the one hand, and on the other, with a view to earmark some private jobs for the female so that the position of the female can be undermined and they can be easily subjugated to male domination. In contrast to the society's allocation of public jobs for the male, homemaking is allotted for the female. In all gendered societies, it is a common belief that females are more caring, virtuous, self-effacing and tolerant. So in addition to the natural job of child producing, the job of childrearing should also be vested in the hands of female. Thus when the man or woman admits fully of the stereotyped role as fixed by the society and comes to acquire and express these roles in reality, then the gender role acquisition becomes an important factor in the construction and the perpetuation of gender. *Expression* factor also plays an important part in the construction of gender. Gender expression is the external manifestation of one's response to gender formation process of a society usually through masculine–feminine behaviour, clothing, mannerism, haircut, style and all such gender-variant behaviour. Gender expression is how a person publicly presents their gender through internal and external appearances. Internally, it is the spontaneous urge for the presentation of one's gender perception and externally it is the effort of receiving the attention of others in order to make them endorse his/her gender perception. The degree of expression may vary in different situations. Some boys may try to be over-masculine whereas some may come out as passive. Some female may express over-feminine traits whereas some of them again may express normal or tomboy attitude. Again, in between the two stereotyped concept of male or female there is androgynous (not exclusively masculine or feminine) gender where the expressions not only vary in degree but also in kinds. The first thing that the boy or a girl, since their infancy, adopts as the expression of their gender is clothing and dress appropriate to their sexes. Through dresses male or female or even the persons under gender blending try to motivate the society with a view to have the acknowledgement of their gender and they also satisfy their ego in respect of their sense of gender. Haircut also is taken as a conventional presentation of one's gender to which the society grants its consent and thereby encourages the respective gender to be formed in alignment with the sex assigned at birth. Style and mannerism also is the easiest way of gender presentation. They are always expected to be developed in conformity with the stereotyped judgment of gender perception. The mode of speaking will also have to be in compliance with the notion of gender in vogue. It is expected in a gendered society that the voice of a male will be louder and hoarse and the mode of speaking will be confident, courageous and strong. Whereas the reverse of it is expected from a female who is expected to be soft, low, submissive and obedient under all circumstances. Thus through the shaping and reshaping of the factors like identity, role and expression, the process of the formation of gender gains a stable, perpetual and socialized character. The effort of everyone for attaining the gender identity actually increases the strength of the ideology of gender and creates the culture in the persons so that they smoothly accept the philosophy of gender as a way of life in society. Spontaneous role acquisition of the persons indicates that the society is free from any danger that can hurt the gender ideology of the society and thus can harm and restrict the functioning of the formation of gender in any way. The factor of gender expression in conventional gender line also proves that the formation of gender is being done with the desired objectives towards the cherished goal of the gendered society.

Different factors encourage the development of gender smoothly in a variety of ways. There are a number of theories that explain the formation of gender from many angles. They are psychoanalytic theory, social learning theory, cognitive development theory and gender schema theory. Sigmund Freud, the father of *psychoanalytic theory*, asserted that two instincts motivate human behaviour—the life instinct (which includes the sex drive, labelled libido) and the death instinct (labelled 'thanatos'). Freud believed that society and individuals can and do sublimate or redirect the sex drive, the libidinal energy. The direction taken by this energy is influenced by their components of the human personality: the id, the ego, and the super ego. In the age two to three the child feels attraction to other sex and in their age of five to six the children feel guilty over their attraction towards other sex. However ultimately with their relatively better mental alignment with same sex of father or mother the child proceeds towards the formation of gender identity smoothly. To feminists, Freud's theory is inadequate because it is basically male-centric. According to *social learning theory*, children learn their gender roles through different procedures. First, they learn through the system of reward or punishment of the society. Those who observe the social norms in full are rewarded by the society and those who break the social norms and deviate from the norms are punished by the society. Those who are rewarded for their conformity to the social roles are also applauded by the social setting. In contrast, the deviated persons are hated by the social setting. Second, the children watch and imitate the behaviour of other persons of the social setting and try to assimilate them in himself/herself. Third, children learn the gender roles through differential socialization system as a result of which male or female fit themselves into different roles according to their sexes. Fourth, children are encouraged to learn stereotyped sex roles from different mediums of instruction such as family, school and media. *Cognitive development theory* argues that it is primarily the child's cognition and perception of reality that is responsible for the gender-role development of the child. This cognition is first achieved in the family which can influence the child due to the reason that the child is born in family which also takes every care of him/her. *Gender schema theory* argues that children use their gender as schema to organize and guide their view of the world. Children learn how the society or culture defines the gender role and then they internalize the lesson as schema. So the gender perception of the child is the interaction between schema and experiences about the social setting in respect of gender. Thus they learn to accept the role as they deem fit for the development of their gender. Their own thought process encourages them to develop their gender in the stereotyped sex pattern. Above all, the social learning theory motivates them to acquire gender-specific behaviour. *Evolutionary theories* of gender development are grounded in genetic bases for differences between men and women. Functionalists[13] propose that men and women are biologically different and these differences play a great role in the formulation of their sexual identity. In conformity with their sexes men and women play their roles differently in family, public life and everywhere. As their sexes are different so their functions are also different and these differences are necessary for survival as well as for the smooth functioning of society. According to symbolic interactionism developed by George Herbert Mead, sexual behaviour is not just an expression of biological instincts, merely a response to stimuli, nor simply imitation of the behaviour of others, but a product of interaction and communication between people of the society. Another socio-biologist approach argues that behavioural differences between men and women stem from the different sexual and reproductive strategies by which the biological differences are passed on genes causing the development of sexual identity, and further the sociocultural influences motivate the people to move towards the development of gender.

Thus several theories play their role in strengthening the gender bias in the mind of the children. Gender formation or gender development is a long process although it starts operating at the birth and almost takes a complete shapes before teenage. The theories explain the process of gender development which, by no means, is the result of the theories. It is the society and culture of a given society that constructs gender through gender socialization, various coercive measures and arrangements of rewards. So from its initiation to maturity gender is developed by practical application of the basic tenets of gender ideology.

---

[13] For example, Stephanie A. Shields, "Functionalism, Darwinism and the Psychology of Women: A Study in Social Myth," *American Psychologist*, 30 (1975), 739–54.

Theories just observe the development and put the observation before us through models, framework and propositions.

The issue of gender has many implications in society. Since the issue of gender is socially and culturally constructed and since it bears no natural identity of human being it is always artificially planted in society in order to impart the social and cultural code implicit in gender ideology of any given society. The formation and development of gender always strengthen the patriarchy in view of the fact that under the gender question only two ideal types of human sex come and they are male and female, and of these two sexes male in all societies and across all cultures get the predominance. Thus the question of gender, by projecting male as the first sex, ultimately undermines and devalues the female and that is why Beauvoir described female under the patriarchy as the second sex. By reaping all the benefits from the genderization of the society, male sex becomes the declared controller of not only the society but also the life of the female sex. In all important sectors of society the domination of male sex is established and in proportion to the growing domination of the male, the position of the female becomes inversely undermined in society. This section of the paper examines the implication of the gendered society on human being and the issues of development in general and on the life of female in particular. The concept of gender has a philosophical implication in so far as of the view that gender issue directly hits the notion of equality, natural or social, and horizontally divides the society in two sexes, male and female. Sociological, economic, educational, domestic and professional implication of the constraint of gender is not to be neglected. Experiences record that the development of gender has created so many problems that deserve to be examined and discussed in proper perspective which has not been done so far in the existing literature of gender.

The effect and implication of gender in human society is far-reaching. Since the birth of a child many mediums come to play an important part in the socialization of the child and among all of their roles gender socialization is the first and foremost. To a number of sociologists, socialization is the spontaneous process of learning by which individual, men or women, conform to the basic social norms. As Gillin and Gillin state, 'By the term "socialization" we mean the process by which individual develops into a functioning member of the group according to its standard, conforming to its modes, observing its traditions and adjusting himself to the social situations'.[14] Gender socialization is the outcome of the concept of sociology of gender.

> Socialization when conceived in view of gender perception is called gender socialization. Under socialization programme society in general is the goal of all discussion but under gender socialization all discussions revolve round the concept of gender in particular. The process of gender socialization works with the purpose of moulding the social understanding and social consciousness from the gender point of view and ultimately the process acts for legitimizing and justifying gender bias in all relation, role acquisition and work performance and also sharing of works. Gender socialization is the continuous process by which men and women are socialized into different sex roles and accordingly it is ultimately an inequality of socialization of gender.[15]

As Giddens has pointed out, 'Through contact with various agencies of socialization, both primary and secondary, children gradually internalize the social norms and expectations which are seen to correspond with their sex'.[16] Thus, by the techniques of gender socialization, by the system of rewards and punishments and through the measures of coercion the society teaches the notion of gender perception, distributes the gender values among the members of society and ultimately helps forming the gender identity within them. The task of creating a gendered society and creating the perception of gender within the members of the society is never an unplanned and short-term programme, but rather it is a very much planned and a long-term programme. Over the years this plan of action in respect of creating gender perception is implemented and many important social, political, cultural and religious mediums participate in the task of such implementation.

Since almost all the mediums of different sectors of the society remain engaged in imparting the gender bias within the members of the society and since that also is done over a long span

---

[14] Gillin and Gillin, *Cultural Sociology*, 11–17.
[15] Chattopadhyay, *Fighting Gender Inequality*, 12.
[16] Giddens, *Sociology*, 108.

of time, the gender perception is intensified to that extent as to influence the philosophy, psychology, ethics and the functioning of all the important mediums of instruction of the society. Mediums such as family, school, media, etc., participate in the task of gender formation and again they themselves are affected and influenced by the ideology of gender. So the elements ranging from the philosophy to different mediums of the society create gender as much as gender creates them. Gender, remaining at the centre of this process of creation and recreation, exerts far-reaching effects over the society at large. The effects are far-reaching in the sense that they are even capable of moulding the philosophy, ethics and the roles of different mediums of a given society to the tune of the ideology of gender. The effects of gender over different matters can be discussed in the following way.

First, the worst affected area of society is the *philosophy and style of thinking*. The most negative effect that gender ideology produces is that it changes the philosophy of the society at large. Here by the term 'philosophy' it is meant that how do we see or view the society or social questions or how our brain insists us to see in a fixed and pre-planned way. Since our perceptions of viewpoint or parameters of brainwork are drawn exclusively from the reality, it will not be exaggeration to state that it is ultimately the experiences of the world that make our philosophy of life and society. When the experiences of the reality are set in a theoretical and abstract format then it is termed as philosophy. So philosophy is the abstract configuration of the reality and accordingly philosophy represents reality as well as the reconstruction of the reality. Thus society and culture create philosophy as much as philosophy shapes and reshapes them. In the role of doing so, philosophy becomes the invisible dominator of human thought and actions in respect of gender. This role of domination comes with a negative effect on the society when philosophy becomes the theoretical supporter of the idea of gender segregation in the society. It is the philosophy of gender that influences the thinking of the people in respect of gender, especially male and female. People learn to think that there are only two sexes, that is, male and female, and they are bound to choose between the two and are to act according to their choice of sex subsequently. Through various theories, philosophy of gender preaches that the jobs of the world are naturally branded as 'male' or 'female' and in conformity with these brand the values and qualities have been naturally divided into two dual sets which are necessarily the binary oppositions of each other. Male–female, strong–weak, dominating–subjugating, brave–timid, active–passive, up–down, aggressive–submissive, public–private and appearing–disappearing, etc., are such binary oppositions which makes the male a competitor of the female and vice versa. Gender is the one of the earliest social categories that divides society on the basis of gender and in view of the oldest proverb 'united we stand, divided we fall', it may be stated that gender division between male and female is an unwelcome arrangement in human society.

There are theories that come to strengthen the gender philosophy of a given society through the abstract presentation of the reality and also supra-reality of the social setting. Some theories attribute development of gender role identity to biology, role models and cognitive processes while others focus on the functional aspect of the society. The most controversial theory of gender development is Freud's psychoanalytic theory although there are other theories such as social learning theory, bio-social theory, cognitive development theory, gender schema theory and functional theory of gender development and gender discrimination. These theories play a very effective role in limiting the people's consideration and thinking as they preach in some way or another the difference, hatred and discrimination between male and female and justify them. Thinking power is the most potent weapon of human being and the effect of gender philosophy is viewed in restricting the smooth expression of this thinking power. People are used to believe and think that gender division is natural, and accordingly the message of discrimination inherent in the gender ideology is to be justified and implemented. The concept of gender gives birth to some derogatory social practices that hinder the spontaneous development of the women and that shape or restrict the decisions, choices and behaviours of groups, communities and individuals in respect of gender treatment. Social practices and cultural beliefs set the parameters of decisions, choices or behaviours in a society and therefore play a key role in defining and influencing gender roles and relations. Discriminatory social norms and practices based on gender can directly influence women's social and economic role which ascribes greater social value to male over female and thus results in underinvestment in the health and education of the female. Gender division, gender discrimination and gender inequality exerts a great influence both directly and indirectly over social thinking which again is shaped and reshaped by the different theories in support of the gender ideology. So the most negative side effect of the concept of gender is thus manipulating the social thinking of a given society and social thinking subsequently controls all other actions and expressions of the society towards the pre-settled conclusions in tune with the gender ideology of that society.

Second, the idea of dividing society on the basis of gender especially male and female and thereby to apply the notion subsequently in other working areas of society exerts a tremendous negative effect on the *workplace*. One, since the concept of gender discrimination is planned for undermining the position of woman it always supports the idea of offering preferential treatment for men over women in the workplace. It is a common experience that male worker gets better wages than female worker as it is believed that male are hardworking and efficient by nature and also can be fitted in all types of jobs. In contrast female workers are commonly believed to be inefficient and less diligent than male. In the workplace women still do not receive equal pay for equal work, do not enjoy the legal protection afforded to men, and domestic workers—especially migrants—often fall outside the scope of labour laws. Two, cases of sexual harassment of female workers in the workplace are often reported to be happened as it is preached by the gender outlook that female are the matter of sexual enjoyment and they, especially working female of the unorganized sectors are cheap and thereby the cases of sexual harassment in the workplace have been a repeated event. Three, the gender discrimination creates hostile working conditions for women resulting in reducing the productivity. Fourth, thus gender discrimination create an economic inequality that prevents the women from being financially self-sufficient and independent. Their gender prevents them from getting better education and thus their lack of education places them in unskilled section of the workplace and accordingly they get less payment which again results in their poverty. This is a vicious circle of gender due to which they are forced to be disadvantaged in the workplace where they are treated more as female than worker and all such constraints they face only due to being female.

Third, gender discrimination excludes women from *quality health care*. Studies by the World Health Organization and other social service agencies show that gender plays a very vital role in receiving quality health care and medical attention. In all gendered society female get less medical attention in their family. In the families of rural society of a poor and developing country female are mostly ill-fed and malnourished. So a considerable part of female population of those countries suffers from iron deficiency throughout the year and also throughout their life. Accordingly, their undernourishment often becomes the cause of miscarriage and many post-delivery problems. Forced pregnancies, unintended pregnancies, forced abortion, threatened abortion, early marriage and female genital mutilation, etc., are the common symptoms of a discriminated society and all these seriously affect the health of women.

> Many girls in Africa undergo female circumcision, otherwise known as female genital mutilation (FGM). At least 130 million girls and women are affected worldwide, and another 2 million are at risk every year, according to UNICEF.... Female foeticide is the selective abortion, based on gender, and made a large emergence in the 20th century, this is mainly due to the ability to determine sex through the use of ultrasound.'[17]

Higher infant mortality rates of the underdeveloped countries also force their women to conceive and carry in a short gap which also affects their health considerably. Above all, the occurrences of domestic violence leaves a drastic effect on women health.

Fourth, the most negative effect of gender discrimination is viewed in media presentation of the female. Often the hypersexualized images of women on television programmes, advertisements, journals and magazines and, above all, in the mainstream movies of every country creates an undercurrent sexual feeling within the people especially male causing female to be turned into the easy prey of male perpetration of violence. Media in every country presents women as an object of sexual enjoyment and in course of doing so media causes objectification,

---

[17] Cassandra Clifford, *Are Girls Still Marginalized? Discrimination and Gender Inequality Today*. Retrieved from https://foreignpolicyblogs.com/2007/05/29/are-girls-still-marginalized-discrimination-and-gender-inequality-in-today's-society/

fragmentation and dehumanization of the women. Certain generalizations can be made about the process of degradation of women portrayed in media, electronic and print, 'following Fischer's observations of the inner ideological contradictions of art and culture that cause decadence of society—

1. *Objectification of women*: In a patriarchal society women are forced to be alienated from all creativity. They are compared to things and are considered the most impotent, the most contemptible of all objects.
2. *Dehumanization of women*: Dehumanization is the process of depersonalization of women which presents women as no person, no human. The dehumanization of woman, especially in riddles and proverbs, can manifest itself not only in the disappearance or distortion of woman, but also in an anti-humanist attitude which sometimes assumes the character of brutally harsh social criticism of women.
3. *Fragmentation of women*: It is a conventional conspiracy of patriarchy to portrait women as fragmented and alienated from totality. This is an important symptom of decadence of culture. These devaluation processes have recurrently worked in riddles, rhymes and proverbs with a view to undermining the position of women'.[18]

Like all sectors of society, media also is controlled by the representatives of the patriarchy which does not leave the chance of manipulating the thinking and culture of the people by using the tremendous influence of the biggest means of social and cultural communication, that is, media for keeping the women under strict social control. In order to enforce the social control media portray certain visual images that impart the norms within the people in respect of ideal woman, duties of women and other instructions for encouraging women to take the stereotyped sex roles. The media also teaches how the ideal women are supposed to speak, look and do in perfect tune with their gender. Thus the effect that gender ideology exerts through media results in the marginalization of the women in society.

Like media, the cultural product especially the folk products of the rural areas also play an effective role in the objectification,

---

[18] Chattopadhyay, *Gender Inequality,* 137.

fragmentation and dehumanization of women in the society. Women have been seriously undermined in the riddles and proverbs of the folk society. Riddle is an important folk literature since the ancient time.

> Through these riddles various social viewpoints have been reflected. One such view-point is gender-inequality. Through the riddles women have been seen as a thing of sexual enjoyment. There are so many riddles which are suggestive of sexual-undermining the position of women. That is why slang and vulgarity have been used at random in the linguistic formation of the riddle expressed through a sexually associated metaphor. Such type of riddles often undermines the position and honour of women.[19]

'Certain objects may predominately be found in the riddles of a certain geographical region because of its abundance and importance in a particular area.'[20] Thereby imposition of woman-hood on the material objects is a basic feature of the riddles of the rural society. These features have made some riddles gender biased where women have been humiliated in a number of ways. Red chilly has been compared with the beloved wife of the house. Woman has been metaphorically compared to the essential commodities like onion, garlic and turmeric, banana tree and jackfruit. Thus imposition of womanhood on different things has just turned woman into an inanimate object devoid of any originality and autonomy so far as the cultural product of the folk society is concerned. Proverb is the popular store of knowledge of the rural society of all civilizations across all countries and across all cultures. Being the traditional posses-sion of the rural folk, it is regarded as a most important section of folk literature throughout the world. Milner has noted 'the nearly universal distribution' of proverbs throughout the world, 'almost irrespective of time, place, level of technical and economic development, language or culture'.[21] Because of the central role

---

[19] Ibid.
[20] Barun Kumar Chakraborty, *Bangla Lok Sahitya Charchar Itihas* (Calcutta: Sahityasri, 1977), 162.
[21] Quoted from Noor Sanauddin, "Proverbs and Patriarchy: Analysis of Linguistic Sexism and Gender Relation Among the Pashtuns of Pakistan," PhD thesis Scotland: University of Glasgow, March, 2015), 16.

of the proverb in the manipulation of male–female relationship, family bonding, gendered division of household work, exercise of male power over female, control of property along the gender line and gendered concept about the continuation of the descent or lineage, gender role distribution and formation of gender stereotypes proverb has been of much interest of study to the scholars. According to Mineke Schipper,

> Proverbs have been defined in many ways. A proverb tends to be seen as more generally than a saying applicable in a large variety of contexts. Proverbs close discussion, make up for a misunderstanding, disguise ignorance, or put a good gloss on a bad cause. Although no satisfactory all-embracing definition exists, proverbs are quickly recognized as such by users and listeners. One might describe them as short, pithy sayings, ingeniously embodying an admitted truth or cherished belief.[22]

Yuksel asserts that because of some popular features of proverbs, such as simplicity and completeness, traditionalism and coded nature, etc., they attract the attention of the rural folk from one generation to another, and accordingly proverbs create certain attitudes towards gender which again are internalized by the rural folk through the method of gender socialization; the resultant impact is the devaluation and degradation of women not only locally but also globally. So Yuksel opines, 'Almost every proverb that touches on women contains a severe negation of the value of women in society'.[23] Describing the features of proverbs through the eyes of gender lens is perhaps a task often overlooked by the proverb scholars. The proverb scholars either study the proverb from linguistic viewpoint or from uncritical functional viewpoint emphasizing the didactic or other positive social aspects of the proverb. Under this perspective, the most important point here is that misogynist attitude has been the essence of social psychology and social experiences portrayed in the proverbs throughout the world and across all societies and cultures. By making a socially approved differences between son

---

[22] Mineke Schipper, *Never Marry a Woman With Big Feet* (New Haven, CT and London: Yale University Press, 2003), 9.

[23] Wolfrang Yuksel, *Women in Proverbs* (Oxford: Oxford University Press, 1993), 66.

and daughter or male and female, by undermining the position of women in their in-laws' house, by supporting the polygyny and by causing a sexual devaluation and by presenting women as things of sexual enjoyments through proverbs, folk literature in general and proverbs in particular have come to enforce the overt and covert agenda of gender socialization guided by the patriarchy. Thus riddles and proverbs play an important part in the formation of gender as well as in leaving a deep impact on the women's life.

Fifth, gender bias in education is also an important area of study for calculating the negative effect of gender ideology in a society. In a gendered society it is commonly believed that girls are less intelligent than boys. It was the common practice at a time in Europe to judge the brain level of the girls in terms of their height and since most of the women are of lesser height due to purely physiological reason it was easy for the agents of patriarchy to preach that the low height of the girls come from the cause of their less intelligence. So they need not be educated in science education such as mathematics and physics, chemistry, etc. It is the reason as to why the participation of girl students in the developing countries in science education is as low as 25 per cent as compared to the participation of the male students. In order to highlight the men's position in society the gender ideology always preaches that men/boys are by nature intelligent and gifted whereas the intelligence of the girls is the result of hard work and fortune. By strictly segregating the gender role in public and private area and by opening the public area for the male and by limiting the women in the private area the gender ideology often deprives the women of all the benefits of exposure in the outer world including education. The main task for the female is believed to be childbearing and childrearing in a gendered society and accordingly the question of their educational development is set aside. If any argument is accepted for their education at any time, it is for getting them educated for social science and homemaking. The theory of opposing duality of the qualities and values also calls for the compartmentalization of the roles of the male and female. Through various theories philosophy of gender preaches that the jobs of the world are naturally branded as 'male' or 'female' and in conformity with these brand the values and qualities have been naturally divided into two dual sets which are necessarily the binary oppositions of each other. Male–female, strong–weak, dominating–subjugating, brave–timid, active–passive, up–down, aggressive–submissive, public–private and appearing–disappearing, etc., are such binary oppositions which makes the male a competitor of the female and vice versa. All the qualities such as strong, active, brave, public, aggressive, etc., are taken as male qualities and in contrast to them the qualities and values such as weak, timid, passive, soft, obedient, etc., are taken as female qualities which are best suited in the private atmosphere like family and home. So if they are sent outside for a long time in the name of education that will be contrary to their basic nature. Thus in all countries gender ideology has done an irreparable loss to women's empowerment through the private–public concept and through the theory of opposing duality of the qualities and values and that has caused the girls lagging behind in respect of educational development.

Teacher's conscious and unconscious gender bias can produce discriminative practices in the class room. Teachers, being the product of gender ideology, often tend to take the domination of the boys as typical masculine behaviour and they are inspired to be the target students of the class. In contrast, the girls are always expected to be mute and silent and they are less attended for their level of development to come in a visible state of expression and thus they lag behind gradually.

> Teachers often give girls less meaningful and less critical praise than boys. Boys' work is described as unique or brilliant, while girls' work is often undervalued, critically ignored, and praised for its appearance. This aspect of teachers' behavior is particularly detrimental to girls because it means they do not receive feedback on their work that could help them develop deeper understandings of concepts.[24]

Thus the gendered behaviour of the teachers leaves a negative impact for the education of the girls. 'Teachers are critical components in challenging gender bias in schooling, but they also can be major contributors to it as well, through their

---

[24] F. Liu, "School Culture and Gender," in *The SAGE Handbook of Gender and Education*, eds C. Skelton, B. Francis, and L. Smulyan (Thousand Oaks, CA: SAGE Publications, 2006), 425–38.

pedagogical practices, curriculum choices, and assessment strategies.'[25]

So gender bias leaves a negative impact in education for the girls. The gender bias always divides the society into male and female who emerged as competitor, one against another. Education, being the most potent weapon of empowerment of women in true sense of the term, becomes the target of the patriarchy for the implementation of all its hidden agenda of marginalizing the women at any cost. So in a gendered society the girls are always denied and deprived of accessibility, acceptability and adaptability in respect of education.

Thus the philosophy of genderizing the society always creates a sort of gender bias which encourages male to become the dominant gender in society and to stand against the female gender in all possible spaces of importance. Gender ideology and gender socialization are aimed at marginalizing the women in possible ways by limiting their thoughts and activities in all fields. The myth that the female gets priority in the family is completely broken against the background of the growing incidence of domestic violence and the fact of deprivation of the women from the family property such as land, bank account, etc. It is only due to the fact of their gender the women are denied access in education, workplace, politics and all other important fields of empowerment. The implication of genderization is not only limited to the deprivation and marginalization of the women but also it is directed to the hidden and sometimes overt agenda of eliminating the women physically. The growing incidence of domestic violence, wife battering, dowry death, trafficking, rape and murder and many other forms of violence against the women prove that the matter of gender is not at present the case of conflicting interests or competitive attitudes of the male and the female but it has been a provocation to war between male and female. Similar to the warlike situation, male and female have come in a state of hostility and since the gender ideology favours male gender in this hostile situation, female have been the worst victim of the war in all society. Gender bias has been so strong that the class of women has come to the point of

---

[25] Retrieved 10 July 2017, from www.education.com/reference/article/gender-bias-in-teaching/

extinction. If the whole situation is allowed to reign for some years more, the civilization will perhaps come to an end. So the situation is so grave that it requires immediate attention of the policy makers, statesman, activists and all thoughtful persons. Gender equality does not happen by chance or accident but it is the result of human endeavor and planned effort of the sensible persons of the society. The process of gender equality and gender equity as well must be started right now and this is the only easiest way for the eradication of the negative implication of the gender bias in shortest possible time.

3

Gender Socialization: Meaning, Nature and Scope

The uniqueness of human beings lies in the fact that humans, in spite of being the result of biological evolution, are not solely guided by the instinct which motivates the animal world and its functions. In contrast to the animal world, human being learns how to regulate and control the instincts and how to express his/her behaviour in a planned way mostly approved by the society. So the humanness has necessarily two segments—one is physical which is the result of biological evolution and the other is mental which is socially created. It is the mental attributes of the human being that ultimately differentiate them from the animal and leaves a clear impression of planning and programming over their thoughts and activities. In this way, they are encouraged to be engaged in the interaction with the other people and accordingly they come to behave like a social creature. Thus, 'our humaneness is a social product and it arises in course of what sociologists call socialization'.[1] According to the *Oxford Dictionary of Sociology*, 'socialization is the process by which we learn to become members of society, both by internalizing the norms and values of society, and also by learning to perform our social roles (as worker, friend, citizen and so forth)'.[2] When such process of internalization and learning is guided by gender ideology of a given society and aims at re-enforcing the stereotyped gender roles according to sexes, then it is called as gender socialization. 'Socialization when conceived in view of gender perception is called gender socialization. Under socialization programme society in general is the goal of all discussion but under gender socialization all discussion revolves round the concept of gender in particular.'[3]

---

[1] Bhattacharyya, *Sociology*, 144.
[2] John Scott and Gordon Marshall, eds, *Oxford Dictionary of Sociology*, 3rd edition (New York, NY: Oxford University Press, 2005), 621.
[3] Chattopadhyay, *Fighting Gender Inequality*, 12.

Everything that human being performs as a member of society is the result of social learning or socialization. So when men are inspired to form their attitudes, express their behaviours and play their social roles according to their sexes then that is also caused by a specific type of socialization and that is gender socialization. The process of gender socialization works with the purpose of moulding the social understanding and social consciousness from the gender point of view and gender socialization is the continuous process by which men and women are socialized into different sex roles.

> So the socialization process which teaches men and women gender identity and differences and which inspires individual to adopt the social role corresponding to their gender through various agencies like family, school and media and through various religious and cultural activities is called gender socialization. Socialization as such conceives of society as a composite of social being irrespective of gender but gender socialization is the concept of indoctrinating gender bias in the whole map of social relationship, division of labor and social role acquisition and accordingly, unlike socialization, gender socialization conceives of a society that is absolutely stratified by gender. So gender socialization is a theory of depicting a fragmented picture of society based on gender and it champions the theory of differential socialization of male and female.[4]

The meaning of gender socialization can best be understood from three points of views: differential socialization, differential gender identity and differential gender role distribution.

From the point of view of *differential socialization* it can be said that gender socialization is the key to the imparting of the notion of gender to the members of society of all ages especially the children and accordingly, it results in the formation of the gender consistent attitudes within them. The spirit of gender ideology, in all societies and across all cultures, focuses on the point of two genders—male and female—as virtually existing and operating in reality. There may be other genders such as transgender, gender queer, cross dresser, etc., often described as so called third sex in society and the academic discussion is

---

[4] Ibid, 12.

also going on with a view to address their practical problems but the persons under the so called third sex are also included in the curriculum of gender socialization as the deviants of the norms of gender socialization. The gay, the lesbians, the eunuch and all non-standard persons under the so-called third sex come to be often described as result of the failure of gender education, gender acculturation and gender socialization. As for example, when a boy conforms to the roles played by his father, he is often eulogized for being the ideal representative of his father. But when a boy or girl fails to conform to the socially sanctioned roles as played by his or her father or mother, he or she is often rebuked as the black sheep. For Giddens,

> These positive and negative reinforcements aid boys and girls in learning and conforming to expected sex roles. If an individual develops gender practices which do not correspond with his or her biological sex—that is, they are deviant—the explanation is seen to reside in inadequate or irregular socialization.[5]

Thus, by limiting and mostly restricting the freedom of choosing the genders, expressing the non-standard behaviours and performing beyond the stereotyped sex roles, the society actually punishes the persons under the so-called third sex for their audacity of going beyond the conventional male–female format of gender. So, socially accepted and culturally enforced standard norms of gender are prepared in view of two genders—male and female—chiefly operating in almost all societies. Thus, gender ideology always views the society divided chiefly between two sexes and they are man and woman. Gender socialization is the process of imparting this notion of conventional male–female format of gender division within the children and accordingly it results in the creation of a fragmented picture of society based on gender. Children come to accept the view that they are either male or female and the question as to actually what they are is often solved by linking the issue to the basic identity of their biological sexes. Differences of sex predominate the differences of gender. So gender socialization is the process by which the biological sex division is transformed into a social sex division on the basis of

---

[5] Giddens, *Sociology*, 108.

which the gender roles are distributed among the members and accordingly they are performed in compliance with the stereotyped norms of the society. In the way of the transformation of the biological signs of the sex to the social signs of gender a number of means are used such as religion, culture, narratives and different institutional codes and infrastructures which together build a complicated network of gender socialization. Thus ultimately by creating the social division of gender the ground of differential socialization is prepared and the system is ensured so that a child is born with the innate idea of gender division and comes to adopt the gender-specific behaviour accordingly.

The process of differential socialization starts since the birth of the child and even before the birth of the child. When a woman remains in a carrying stage, the surrounding always expects from her a male child and she is provoked and inspired to pray and wish for the same. It is tried to guess the sex of the forthcoming baby from the physical changes and signs of the pregnant woman. In the areas of urban background people are seen to use the technological means of ultrasound in order to know in advance the sex of the forthcoming baby. In an extreme male-biased family the pregnant woman is forced to abort the baby either through any traditional means or through modern medical system in case the forthcoming baby is a female. In a comparatively liberal situation, the family members and the expecting mother devote themselves to plan for the decoration of the room of the baby in conformity with the gender of the baby. If the baby is supposed to be a male then the room is coloured red or blue and if the baby is supposed to be the female then the room is coloured pink or white. The playthings and dolls supposed to be supplied to the newborn baby bear also a sharp signs of discrimination between the sexes. The parents especially the father of that child plans for the future of the baby in conformity with the gender of which either they have guessed or known. Thus the atmosphere of differential socialization is created for the baby before the birth and other lessons of gender socialization starts just after the birth of the baby.

In the beginning phase the child views and reviews the environment and situation and captures data which are scanned and processed in the brain and mind of the child through his/her experience, observation and inference. The child watches father to speak in a comparatively harsh and louder voice whereas the child views mother to speak in a very submissive and silent voice. The child experiences 'power' in every primary and secondary activity of father ranging from caressing him/her to pass commands for others and he/she also watches that the target of father's power is mother and other female members of the family including her in case the child is a girl.[6]

The point of the male–female format of gender division and the ideology of male domination in the society over the female becomes of utmost importance for the curriculum of gender socialization with a view to enforce the differential socialization through a structural framework. For this purpose, all arrangements are made for the female baby so that she can easily assimilate the motto of gender ideology very smoothly and can internalize the dictum of male domination taught through the gender socialization in all societies and across all cultures. From her experience of the reality and from the cognition and mental perception she gains from her observation and inference, the female baby collects data for shaping her future destiny of gender. The situation for a female baby is clear from a passage of Beauvoir,

> she will never be the sovereign father ... if her father shows affection for his daughter, she feels that her existence is magnificently justified.... The historical and literary culture to which she belongs, the songs and legends with which she is lulled to sleep, are one long exaltation of man ... children books, mythology, stories, tales, all reflect the myths born of the pride and the desires of men; thus it is that through the eyes of men the little girl discovers the world and reads therein her destiny.[7]

Thus the female child becomes not only conscious of the hard reality of the existence of the two sexes—male and female—but also comes under compulsion to believe that male gender is much above the female gender and the world she lives in is actually guided and controlled by the male gender. Gender socialization is the process by which the domination of the male gender in

[6] Chattopadhyay, *Fighting Gender Inequality*, 33–34.
[7] de Beauvoir, *The Second Sex*, 314–16.

society is represented and legitimized through various means of religion, culture and social norms dictated by the patriarchy. So if the meaning of gender socialization is to provide the systematic support to the notion of the existence of two sexes—male and female—in societies then another meaning of gender socialization is to create the infrastructural support for the domination of man over woman in society. Thus the condition and the necessity of the differential socialization of the two sexes—male and female—is created and accordingly men and women are socialized differently in conformity with their respective sexes. Gender socialization is the cultural process of the enforcement of such differential measures and thereby they are the 'processes through which individuals take on gendered qualities and characteristics ... and learn what their society expects of them as males or females'.[8] Thus, by treating the boys and the girls differently gender socialization places them in different learning environments where 'they develop different needs, wants, desires, skills, and temperaments; in short they become different types of people— men and women—who hardly question why they are different or how they ended up that way...'.[9] Thus by developing their own needs, desires and skills the boys and girls are inspired to form different types of identities for facing the society.

From the point of view of *differential gender identity* gender socialization is the process by which a boy or a girl is inspired to form their gender identity differently and obviously in conformity with their biological sex. As Giddens has pointed out, 'Through contact with various agencies of socialization, both primary and secondary, children gradually internalize the social norms and expectations which are seen to correspond with their sex'.[10] Gender identity is the personal and subjective understanding of one's own gender. This understanding is very much innate and mentally configured and so gender identity is based on the psychological identification of person's gender which may or may not correspond to the assigned sex at birth. But gender socialization always prompts the individuals to

[8] A. S. Wharton, *The Sociology of Gender: An Introduction to Theory and Research* (Malden, MA: Blackwell Publishing, 2005), 31.

[9] Retrieved 10 July 2017, from www.public.iastate.edu/~f2004.soc.327

[10] Giddens, *Sociology*, 108.

develop and express their gender identity in a stereotyped way of socially accepted perception of masculinity or femininity in strict conformity with their sex assigned at birth. So from the point of view of differential gender identity, gender socialization is the method of assigning a definite but different style of speaking, dress, mannerisms, etc., for man and woman and thus the external expressions and behaviours of man and woman in conformity with their biological sex are the result of gender identity formation process. Thus through the internalization of sex role, sex behaviour and sexist viewpoint of society, in general, stakeholders are encouraged to develop gender identity—masculinity and femininity—which creates gender differences and ultimately gender inequality in society.

> So the socialization process which teaches men and women gender identity and differences and which inspires individual to adopt the social role corresponding to their gender through various agencies like family, school and media and through various religious and cultural activities is called gender socialization.[11]

The formation of gender identity is very important in so far as it ultimately affects the very spirit of the gender ideology of a given society. If the formation becomes erroneous, it seriously hinders the philosophy of gender in general and the process of gender socialization and gender identity in particular and results in causing also a threat to the development of the children who have been the victims of the wrong process of the gender formation. So far as the gender identity from the conventional viewpoint of gender expression is concerned it is always expected to shape one's identity in conformity with one's biological sex and social perception of gender. 'Gender identity is a person's private sense, and subjective experience, of their own gender. This is generally described as one's private sense of being a man or a woman, consisting primarily of the acceptance of membership into a category of people: male or female.'[12] Although apparently

---

[11] Chattopadhyay, *Fighting Gender Inequality*, 12.
[12] Neil R. Carlson and C. Donald Heth, eds, *Psychology: The Science of Behaviour* (Toronto: Pearson, 2010), 140–41. Adopted from Wikipedia, the free encyclopedia.

it is believed that gender identity is the private matter of the individual, but in reality the process of identity formation is seriously affected by social interactions, norms, regulations and other person's feelings in a broader social setting. That way the influence of the conventional attitude towards gender, the impact of the stereotyping of the gender role and the effect of parental domination can never be ignored in respect of the formation of gender identity of the child. Thus ultimately the matter of gender identity becomes also the result of gender socialization. Gender socialization always aims at imparting a sense of difference and discrimination within the child based on his/her gender. So gender identity within the purview of gender socialization leads always to the formation of differential identity. Generally gender identity includes beyond man and woman the other genders such as intersex, transgender and all others termed as the so-called third sex. But gender socialization always inspires individuals to consider themselves as cisgender that is belonging to either man or woman gender corresponding to their assigned sex at birth. According to modern sociologists, 'Within a society at particular point of time, individuals come to adopt gender-specific behaviour, attitudes and dispositional traits through process of socialization and allocation that perpetuate gender role differentiation'[13] and the process by which the gender consciousness of the child are shaped in the expected way are termed as gender formation. The process of gender indoctrination starts since birth of a child who with his/her growing up is encouraged to behave like a boy or a girl as suitable and as will match perfectly with biology of gender. So the formation of a male or female infant in tune with the stereotyped sex role and their ultimate acquisition of the role of father or mother are termed as gender identity formation. Thus, it may be argued that gender socialization is the method of imparting the notion of differential identity formation within the child by which the gender ideology of a given society is legitimized.

From the point of view of *differential gender role* distribution, gender socialization is the method of presenting the functional

---

[13] Borgatta and Cook, eds, *The Future of Sociology*, 134.

necessity of acquiring different social roles corresponding to biological sex. Gender role acquisition is a very important element in the construction of gender. Gender role is the expectation of the society for appropriate male and female behaviour as suited to their biological sexes. By the age of two or three the male or female infant become conscious of their sexual as well as gendered identity and they prepare themselves for acquiring their gender role in society. Through the process of socialization or by means of reward or punishment the male or female children in each society are prompted to assimilate or imitate the appropriate male or female activities identified as suitable to their sexes almost since their birth. Apart from activities, gender role theory also preaches the importance of adopting specific attitudes, movements and expressions. The boys are inspired to be hard, tough, louder, aggressive and strong when the girls are inspired to be caring, virtuous, soft, domesticated and submissive. Different mediums such as family, school, peer group and media also come to play their role in enforcing the motto of gender socialization in respect of building the gender role attitudes. The tradition of popular culture and the narratives and the language also play the role in reinforcing the gender role attitudes. Gender socialization always preaches that different gender roles are necessary for the proper discharge of all the functions of the society. So man and woman should separately prepare themselves for performing their roles in proper way. Gender socialization is the training for the man and the woman of that preparation for the performance of their roles in society.

Thus gender socialization offers a complicated meaning of differential socialization, differential identity formation and dif-ferential gender role distribution. The concept of gender as such is very complicated in view of various opinions as to whether gender is naturally selected or it is socially constructed. Although psychologists and sociologists have come to the conclusion that gender is basically a social and cultural product, the influence of biology can never be ignored. Keeping the nature versus nurture debate in calculation it will not be an exaggeration to conclude that gender socialization is the result of a complicated interwining of psychological expressions, social expectations, cultural and religious instructions.

Gender socialization is comparatively a recent topic of academic exercise in sociology as well as in feminism. According to the feminists, there are a number of matters related to various social processes that influence, control and regulate the gender behaviour in all societies and across all cultures. The complicated intertwining of these processes, practices and norms create a gendered notion of behaviour and expressions in society or, in short, a gendered society that ultimately divides the society between male and female. The genderization of the society virtually calls for the entire social system and the social processes to work in such a manner as they can come to enforce the gender ideology of a given society in a very smooth manner. The study of the construction of gender and the impact of the social practices and norms over gender links the issue of gender to the sociological investigation. Thus the whole empirical problem of describing, analyzing and explaining gender through sociology resulted in the emergence of the new topic of discussion and that is gender socialization.

From a broader perspective, gender socialization is the way of imparting the sense of gender, basically the male–female notion of gender, within the members of the society. From a narrower angle, gender socialization acts for the subjugation of woman in society. Thus it means that ultimately gender socialization causes social stratification based on gender which limits the space of the women in reality. Thus gender socialization actually aims at justifying the gender basis of power in all institutional sectors of society and thus providing an organized set-up for its expression which finally favours the male counterpart of the society. So for probing the role of gender socialization in power structure and for exposing the different dimensions and the features of gender socialization from organizational as well as from functional and operational viewpoint, it is very much necessary to deal with the nature of gender socialization from an academic as well as pragmatic perspective. The nature of gender socialization can be explained through the difference between socialization and gender socialization, through the nature versus nurture debate and through the power approach which ultimately strengthens the patriarchy.

Differences between socialization and gender socialization can be presented through a table:

Socialization	Gender Socialization
1. Socialization is a very old process in sociology.	1. Gender socialization is a comparatively newly developed technique and process.
2. Socialization is the process by which the individual turns into a social being.	2. Gender socialization is the process by which the individual turns into a gendered category.
3. Socialization aims at teaching and creating the social identity of the persons in the society.	3. Gender socialization aims at creating the gender identity of the individuals of the society.
4. Socialization starts during the birth of the child and continues throughout the life.	4. Gender socialization may start even before the birth of the child and often is completed by the age of six or seven.
5. Socialization does not result in stereotyping of roles in society. People are free to choose their role in society.	5. Gender socialization directly leads to the creation of gender role stereotypes and boys and girls are expected to act differently.
6. Socialization is the way culture is transmitted and the individual is fitted into organized social life.	6. Gender socialization is the way by which gender ideology is transmitted and individual is fitted in gender category of male or female.
7. Socialization works for the assimilation of all persons and hence it is inclusive in nature.	7. Gender socialization works for dividing the society into male and female and so it results in exclusion in society.
8. Socialization is basically spontaneous.	8. Gender socialization is basically planned.
9. Deviation from socialization may result in rebuke or punishment.	9. Deviation from gender socialization often leads to the fatal punishment especially for the women.
10. Socialization is the process by which individuals are informed and taught about the norms and practices of society in general.	10. Gender socialization is the process by which individuals are informed about the norms, practices and expectations associated with their sex.
11. Social differences are not the result of socialization although they are legitimized by the socialization.	11. Gender socialization always directly leads to the gender differences and discrimination.
12. Socialization is aimed at preserving the society in general.	12. Gender socialization is aimed at creating the notion of gender and the gender ideology of a given society in particular.

Gender socialization can also be understood from the point of view of which is popularly called as 'nature versus nurture' debate. There are opinions which argue that gender is the product of biology. Again, there are views that tend to study gender as the product of environment. Nature refers to heredity or genetic traits. Some researchers agree that heredity or the biologically assigned sexual traits determine the psychological differences in male and female as a result of which boys become aggressive, hard, power-oriented and more focused than girls, and the girls become submissive, soft, home-oriented and self-effacing. Some biological signs are present at birth which make a sharp difference between girl and some differences occur during puberty making the differences sharper. Nurture, on the other hand, refers to the environment and artificial process of imparting the gendered values in boy or girl through cultural norms and instructions. The view that gender is a social and cultural construction is based on the theory of nurture. It is perhaps the influence of the nurture factor that prompted Beauvoir to conclude, 'one is not born, but rather becomes, a woman. No biological, psychological or economic fate determines the figure that the human female presents in society; it is civilization as a whole that produces this creature, intermediate between male and eunuch, which is described as feminine'.[14] By remarking that women are made by the civilization Beauvoir actually indicates the methods and techniques of socialization by which male–female differences in society are created and induced within the members of the society and they are inspired to adopt appropriate roles in accordance with their genders based on their sex assigned at birth. Thus in course of time the women are forced to adopt the stereotyped role in society and they are thrown in a world where they are marked as 'women'. The environment of gender socialization is created and operated by a number of agents like the family, school, peer group and the media. In family, the primary socialization in respect of gender is done through the parental influence and teaching basically. It is in the family that the child steps for developing the gender identity by individuation and separation of the attachment of the parents. The baby learns for the first time the physical and biological signs of gender in the family and

---

14 de Beauvoir, *The Second Sex*, 295.

learns the primary ideas of gender roles in society. The school, through the textbooks and also through the practices, creates a gender difference between boy and girl. The school also plays an important role in inducing the emotional and expressive traits within the girls so that they can appropriately perform the role of running the home. The influence of the peer group is also important for directing the child to take the stereotyped gender roles. The peer-group members often ridicule the child who fails to conform to the socially sanctioned gender role on the one hand, and on the other, the peers pose a positive support to the child who takes the gender-appropriate role. The media also plays an important role in influencing and perpetuating gender stereotypes not only in respect of roles but also in respect of attitudes and traits. By causing the objectification, fragmentation and dehumanization of the women, the media often plays a negative role in the socialization process. Thus it is the cultural codes by which the women are turned into a definite gendered category and they become the 'other' of the male in course of time. So in view of the importance of the nurture factor, gender socialization is considered as a tremendously effective process of creating a gendered notion of the basic personality development of the individual as well as the society.

The nature of gender socialization can also be understood from the view-point of patriarchy which is an institutionalized social structure working for the justification of the male domination over women in society. Patriarchy is the system of the monopoly of power of the male in family, politics, and economy and in all social and cultural spheres.

> Feminist Theory defines patriarchy as a social system that is (1) male dominated (i.e. primary positions of power are occupied by and/or encouraged for males rather than others), (2) male identified (i.e. what is defined as valuable or normative in society is associated with men or masculinities), and (3) male centered (i.e. the cultural focus of attention, whether media, scientific, religious or political based, is on men and the things men do).[15]

[15] Retrieved 10 July 2017, from https: www.boundless.com/definition/patriarchy/

Thus as a result of every role ranging from bargaining to decision-making being male centric and being legitimized by patriarchy, gender socialization in a patriarchal system is always a socialization preaching the power of the men as natural, desirable and systematic and thus results in gender inequality, gender difference and gender discrimination. So gender socialization under patriarchy is the process of undermining the position of women in society. So every instruction passed either from one generation to another or from society to individual is actually dictated by an abstract collective male authority, that is, patriarchy. It is with this view of strengthening the factors of male domination in society that gender socialization comes to allocate the emotional, expressive or functional traits and values between male and female according to their gender based on biologically assigned sex at birth. According to social standards, sex and gender must match, and so according to S. Rowan Wolf, 'people with male anatomy must be male in gender identity and gender role and people with female anatomy must be female in gender identity and gender role'.[16] Beyond the male–female binary, any relationship or gender is considered unnatural or unethical in society. In conformity with the notion of gender binary, gender socialization under patriarchy always portrays masculinity as strong, authoritative, aggressive, power-oriented and louder. In contrast, the same patriarchy portrays femininity as weak, submissive, home-oriented, soft and loyal. The manner of the distribution of attitudes along the line of gender binary is essential for the performance of gender roles and for upholding the flag of patriarchy. LGBTQ people, that is, lesbian, gay, bisexuals, transgender and queer gender people upset the dominance of patriarchy and thereby heterosexuality is taught and upheld through overt and covert forms of gender socialization all the time in all societies and across all cultures. Heterosexuality, being the fundamental element of the structure of patriarchy, is promoted and practised through family, school, media, narratives, popular culture and all other religious and cultural norms. Gender socialization is the process by which these promotions and practices are legitimized as a result of which gender power of the male gets the scope of being consolidated in a very normal manner.

---

[16] S. Rowan Wolf, *The Dialectic of Social Inequality*, PhD thesis, 2008, 37–60.

Judged from the angle of power it can be said, 'the major concern of gender socialization is to justify the gender power exercised by the male counterpart of a society and thereby to legitimize patriarchy. Gender power is generally exercised from top, that is, male and the terms of directions are passed to bottom, that is, female. But the problem is that this top-bottom power relationship moulded by gender does not always go unchallenged because power, of any nature and form, necessarily involves resistance. According to Foucault, 'where there is power, there is resistance'.[17] What Foucault meant by this is that resistance is present everywhere power is exercised. To him, 'resistances' constitute 'irreducible opposite of power relation'.[18] So first, 'it becomes an important agenda of the power operating process to look at the matter so that the bottom part, that is, the female counterpart spontaneously admits of the legitimacy of gender power at the top, that is, patriarchy. It is a fact that power remains power so long as it is accepted and tolerated by the section over which power is applied. Acceptance of power is the foundation of legitimacy. The more power is accepted, the more it gains permanence'.[19] So gender socialization is a process by which the gender power, that is, male domination over women is established. For the smooth expression of the male power, it is necessary to restrain 'different areas of women's lives for bringing them under the patriarchal control and and accordingly women's access in all the spheres becomes gradually restricted'.[20] Men control women's productivity both in the family and outside. In the household, the women do not get the remuneration for their work and they are thrown in a situation where they become dependent on their husband for subsistence. Outside the home the fruits of women's labour are appropriated by the male members of the family and even all the terms of payment ranging from amount of wage to environment of work are dictated by patriarchy. That is why feminist writer Sylvia Walby calls this

---

[17] Michel Foucault, *The History of Sexuality*, Vol. 1 (New York, NY: Vintage, 1980), 95.
[18] Barry Smart, *Michel Foucault* (London and New York, NY: Tavistock, 1985), 132–33.
[19] Chattopadhyay, *Fighting Gender Inequality*, 15.
[20] Chattopadhyay, *Fighting Gender Inequality*, 49.

system as 'patriarchal mode of production'.[21] 'Institutions aimed at preparing the grounds for gender inequality will always support every effort and practice to exploit the reproductive power of woman in male interest. The question as to when she will conceive and how many times, etc., are determined by male guardians in most cases in traditional societies. So, the reproductive power, in spite of being her exclusive power, is controlled by the other while this very power has caused her in bearing the most painful task of pregnancy which imposes so many physical, social and medical constraints in her aspiration of being free and equal with male.'[22] Women's sexuality, mobility and economic property are controlled by the patriarchy very strictly so that the domination of the male over the female becomes easier. In all these agenda of controlling the female, gender socialization acts as the faithful agent of the patriarchy. Gender socialization, by preaching the institutionalized notion of home-running as the most virtuous job of the female, the reproduction of male child as the most desired for the family, the institution of marriage as the most standard expression of sexuality, the control of movement of the female by 'purdah' or various religious sanctions and through enforcing the system of dependence of women over their husbands and thereby by preaching the control of the property of the women by their husbands as most natural, actually implements the agenda of patriarchy.

The nature of gender socialization can also be understood and judged from the angle of conflict management, social order and participation. Gender socialization is, in a way, a process of management and resolution of conflict among diverse genders, specially, male and female genders, because resolving and controlling conflict and coordinating the conflicting genders is the condition for the achievement of social order. Gender socialization is successful only when it can ensure social order through resolution of conflict. When conflict remains unresolved then socialization ends. Gender socialization, being a more focused form of socialization, is concerned with the reinforcement of social order and receipt of obligation to recognized social norms, particularly, from the end of female counterpart of the society.

---

[21] Sylvia Walby, *Theorizing Patriarchy* (Oxford: Blackwell, 1990), 74.
[22] Ibid, 58–59.

Gender socialization is concerned less with the causes of the distribution of gender power but more with the patterns of legitimization of such power, especially the male power. So, a sort of spontaneous participation in the process of gender socialization is always required for ensuring such legitimization of male power. According to many, participation of the female in the process of gender socialization is never spontaneous but dictated. It is also told, 'gender socialization is a process of committed socialization and, in a way, fragmented socialization. Unlike socialization, in general, or unlike political socialization, in particular, the process of gender socialization disapproves the open participation of the members in social processes. Participation, here, is also gender-biased and it is the ideology of gender which determines as to how much of right to participation is granted for male and female and as to how much of this right will be restricted. The public–private debate is very much relevant in this regard and this debate has offered logic of fragmented participation. As for a number of political thinkers and sociologists the public space is basically a domain of male and private is exclusively a domain of female'.[23] So male participation in public area and female participation in private area is positively sanctioned and openly preached by the theory of gender socialization. So gender socialization is a closed idea in respect of participation. That is why it is termed as the constrained socialization.

'So the gender socialization is, in all ways, devoted to the task of helping the individuals to assimilate the ideology of gender constructed by society through religion and culture and some other activities. Thus it is more a curriculum of genderization than socialization of individuals. The aim of gender socialization may be summed up in the following way'[24]—

1. To stratify the society on the basis of gender, that is, male or female.
2. To fix and sanction specific role for each gender—male or female. A male may opt for being an entrepreneur engineer while a female should opt for a being a teacher or nurse or something like that.

---

[23] Chattopadhyay, *Fighting Gender Inequality*, 16.
[24] Ibid, 28–29.

3. To allocate the values, that is, behaviour, attitudes, thought process, role acquisition and role performance among the members of society according to their gender. It is argued that different genders must have different set of values. The behaviour pattern and attitude which fits a male should not be imitated by female or vice versa.

4. To present and justify the imaginary gender-biased division and classification of work and roles of society such as physical-mental, public–private, hard–soft, professional–domestic etc. and to locate the gender, that is, male or female in such classified division and to pass a passive direction for each member for performing their roles as specific to their gender.

5. To teach and propagate the views that some roles are only for males and some are for females and no inter-sharing of roles is socially sanctioned.

6. To teach the lesson that male is superior and women are inferior and accordingly roles performed by male are more important than the roles performed by female. It is the duty of female to accept this position of status for the ideal management of society and to perform their role as sanctioned by society without a protest.

Gender socialization is the process of the socialization based on gender and carries with it both the features of sociology as well as feminist study. As the study of interdisciplinary matters, the scope of gender socialization has been complicated. The complication of gender springs chiefly from the fact that gender is the product of so many social, cultural, political and economic variables that do not work always straightway rather their mode of operation enables these variables to interact in an overlapping manner. Thus the intertwining of several factors and variables of different natures and subjects has made the scope of gender socialization complicated on the one hand and on the other hand, variegated in view of its concern with the discussions of many subject matters. The scope of gender socialization may be studied from two angles—theoretical and practical. The theoretical angle deals with different approaches that explain the operation of the process of gender socialization theoretically. These theories are mainly concerned with the reply to the question as to how and in what manner gender socialization operates in a society and in course of its operation how it comes to legitimize the gender ideology of that given society. The practical angle deals with the process of operation of the ideology of gender through gender socialization, formation of gender identity, sex role distribution, formation of stereotypes, construction of gender norms, study of gender and different agents of gender socialization, gender segregation and different types of gender socialization. There is also the influence of institutional approach which deals with the functions of patriarchy, marriage, property etc.

Theoretical angle chalks out the scope of gender socialization through different theories. Different factors encourage the development of gender smoothly in a variety of ways. There are a number of theories that explain the formation of gender from many angles. They are psychoanalytic theory, social learning theories, cognitive development theory and gender schema theory. As these theories are already discussed in the earlier chapter, only some outlines, those are suitable for this chapter, are presented here very briefly in order to give the clue of easy and smooth reading to the readers. *Psychoanalytic approach*, founded by Freud, emphasizes the unconscious processes that influence gender identity and issues directions for gender socialization. For Freud, due to the castration complex of the boys or the penis envy of the girls the gender identity is formed under threat or compulsion. *Social learning theory* is an outgrowth of the behaviourist tradition, which defines learning in terms of stimulus and response. According to this perspective, children are reinforced—both positively and negatively—for gender appropriate and inappropriate behaviour. According to social learning theory, children, through imitation, dictation and observation, assimilate the ideology of gender of a given society and come to internalize the social norms and expectations in respect of gender-consistent behaviour. So ultimately it is the social training that formulates the basic pattern of gender identity and gender socialization is just the process of introducing the child with those trainings, dictations and instructions of the society. In this way, social learning theory leaves a wide scope for understanding the role of gender socialization. Social learning theory is also criticized for its passive characterization of the child. *Cognitive development theory* argues that it is primarily the child's cognition and perception of reality that is responsible for the gender role development of the child and this theory emphasizes the child's own cognitive process of mental development and perception by which they become convinced about the role of gender in acting as the most important organizing principle of social rules and behaviour. *Gender schema theory* argues that children use their gender as schema to organize and guide their view of the world. Children learn how the society or culture defines the gender role and then they internalize the lesson as schema. Gender schemas are the cognitive structures that inspire children to collect and organize information, observe the role of that information in respect of gender and to take the decision in respect of gender construction and identity formation. *Evolutionary theories* of gender development are grounded in genetic bases for differences between men and women.

Thus, several theories play their role in strengthening the gender bias in the mind of the children. Gender formation or gender development is a long process although it starts operating at the birth and almost takes a complete shape before teenage. The theories explain the process of gender development which, by no means, is the result of the theories. It is the society and culture of a given society that constructs gender through gender socialization, various coercive measures and arrangements of rewards. So, from its initiation to maturity gender is developed by practical application of the basic tenets of gender ideology. Theories just observe the development and put the observation before us through models, framework and propositions. Gender socialization is the process by which the observations of the theories of gender come to be tested and implemented very smoothly. So, the scope of gender socialization includes invariably the study of the theories and their influence on the development of gender.

Judged from the practical angle gender socialization has ample scope to study the issue of *gender identity*. Gender identity is the feeling of one's own individual and psychological feeling and identification by which he or she considers him/her as male or female or some other gender. There may be different types of gender but gender socialization always promotes and preaches the cisgender attitudes. Cisgender is the conventional model of male and female based solely on the sex assigned at birth. There is also the idea of transgender which indicates the group of people whose sense and perception of gender does not match with their sex assigned at birth. Cross-dresser is the term for the people who prefer to use the dress of the opposite sex. Gender mismatch is present in them due to the conflict between the apparent and real perception of gender. Third gender is also a category of gender between male and female. 'The term third gender has been used to describe hijras of India, Bangladesh and Pakistan.'[25] The different types of human gender that become almost a challenge to the implementation of the agenda of gender socialization are identified in an abbreviated term 'LGBTQ'. L means lesbian, G means gay, B means bisexual, T means transgender and Q means queer. The problems of and challenges coming from these genders are also the subject matter of gender socialization. In connection with the discussion of gender identity some other discussions are also important. Within the scope of gender socialization gender expression is a very useful topic. Gender expression refers to the external behaviour that is socially defined as masculine or feminine. Such behaviours include dress, body language, style of speaking, walking style and other physical mannerisms. The expressions which are not compatible with the norms and codes of society in general and patriarchy in particular may be discouraged from early childhood. Since gender socialization is basically devoted to the enforcement of status quo, the formation and regulation of sexual orientation is also a serious issue for discussion. Sexual orientation may be expressed through heterosexuality, homosexuality and bisexuality. Gender ideology of a society, being basically patriarchal in nature, always considers sex in association with the binary notion of purity–impurity, just–wrong, fair–unfair, virtue–vice, etc. The main objective behind this is to keep the women abstained from indiscriminate practice of sex. So, gender socialization always favours heterosexuality as the best practised form of sexual orientation. Gender roles are very important areas of discussion involving gender socialization. If the aim of gender socialization is to collect and provide support for the functioning of gender ideology sponsored by patriarchy, then the discharge of functions according to genders and performance of their roles is also equally important for the gender socialization to be successful. Gender role is the functional

---

[25] Taken from Wikipedia, the free encyclopedia.

representation of gender ideology and gender norms. Through gender role distribution, the practices of gender discrimination and gender differences come to be implemented in reality. Gender role is the choice of behaviours, attitudes, emotional representations and works that are suited to their sex assigned at birth, and these roles are supported by socially and culturally defined norms. So, gender role is the performance of the roles as expected by the society. Generally, the training of gender role is given by the family, school, peer group and the media. So the scope of gender socialization is very much related to the study of gender roles. Gender stereotypes are also an important matter of discussion in the area of gender socialization. Gender stereotypes are the fixed, generalized and oversimplified images of gender, that is, man and woman, and axiomatic ideas about the traits and capabilities of man and woman on the basis of which they behave or act in society. Gender stereotypes influence the issue of gender roles in a gendered society. Since stereotypes formulate the innate ideas of gender, the discussion of gender socialization must include it as a matter of study. Stereotypes may be positive or negative. When we say that boys have natural aptitude in politics and girls have natural aptitude in housework, then it is positive for the boys and negative for the girls. Negative stereotyping is the result of gender discrimination and gender differences in society. Stereotyping seriously hinders the progress of women and restricts their access to diverse fields of activity. So, the study of gender socialization has an ample scope to expose the true nature of serotypes in respect of gender. Moreover, the other factors like sex and gender, different agents of gender socialization and different types of gender socialization are also analysed in the discussion of gender socialization. Gender socialization has also ample scope to study the distinction between conformity and deviation, reward and punishment and gender consistency and gender inconsistency.

Institutional approach highlights the role of patriarchy, marriage and property in the working of gender socialization. Gender socialization has shown considerable interest in the analysis of these institutions and social systems through which the gender ideology of a given society operates. Patriarchy, remaining at the top of these institutions, provides the basic philosophy and curriculum of gender socialization. Patriarchy is a social system in which males dominate women in all sectors of power and decision-making. The term 'patriarchy' literally means 'the rule of the father'. According to Sylvia Walby, patriarchy 'is a system of social structures and practices in which men dominate, oppress and exploit women'.[26] Walby, in order to expose the complicated nature of patriarchy, 'has composed six structures that are independent but interact with one another'.[27] In the words of Walby, 'At a less abstract level patriarchy is composed of six structures: the patriarchal mode of production, patriarchal relations in paid work, patriarchal relations in the state, male violence, patriarchal relations in sexuality, and patriarchal relations in cultural institutions'.[28] Through the first structure women's household labour is expropriated by their husbands or cohabitees. The second structure argues that female is systematically excluded from getting access to paid and skilled work. As regards third structure, Walby holds, 'the state has a systematic bias towards patriarchal interests in its policies and actions'. As of the fourth structure, according to Walby, 'male violence against women are systematically condoned and legitimated ... through the practices of rape, wife-beating, sexual harassment etc.' The fifth structure reveals that sexuality of women is controlled and dictated by the male, and heterosexuality is, accordingly, compulsorily imposed. The sixth structure presents women in a derogatory form through cultural representations of religion, education and media. So through all these six structures patriarchy comes to undermine the position of women in society. The role of gender socialization is very much instrumental in view of its cause and effect relation with patriarchy. Since gender socialization is the process by which patriarchal modes of thinking and actions are implemented, the curriculum of gender socialization must include patriarchy as the basic institution of passing commands, enforcing norms and regulating behaviour.

Gender socialization process has much to do with the institution of marriage. Under patriarchy marriage is the institution which only protects the interest of the male sex. Patriarchal culture emphasizes that marriage is the only destiny of woman.

---

[26] Walby, *Theorizing Patriarchy*, 20.
[27] Giddens, *Sociology*, 116.
[28] Walby, *Theorizing Patriarchy*, 20.

The pursuit of education and or job is encouraged so long as they do not hamper the institution of marriage. There have many attempts of undermining the position of female and of upgrading the position of male in patriarchy through several norms, institutions and systems. Marriage is just one of those proving its time-tested viability over the centuries in all societies and across all cultures. There are many implicit messages in marriage that serve as the basic means of serving the interest of patriarchy. One, patriarchy presents woman as 'naturally modeled' upon domestic sphere and so they should remain confined in the private area of home. Marriage is the means of expressing their natural traits and performing their natural roles of home management. Two, the reproductive power of woman is brought under control through marriage. The act of childbearing and childrearing can only be possible through marriage. Three, patriarchy always associates purity–impurity binary with sex. Sex for pleasure is considered impure. Pure sex can only be oriented through marriage which is devoted to the sacred purpose of causing reproduction. Four, only heterosexual marriage is encouraged under patriarchy as reproduction is almost guaranteed here and the traditional notion of male domination can be smoothly expressed and implemented here. In patriarchal culture, there are two roles within heterosexuality: one is penetrator (male) and the other is penetrated (female). So in the very sexual position and act of the most accepted form of heterosexual marriage, the myth, 'man is dominating the woman' is subconsciously expressed and that is why patriarchy favours the heterosexuality. Gender socialization is aimed at decoding these messages dormant in marriage and at indoctrinating the persons (male and female) with their respective gender roles through marriage.

The institution of property is also an important subject matter of the study of gender socialization. In patriarchal societies, women do not enjoy any property rights in true sense of the term. Gender ideology, chiefly modelled upon the patriarchal cultural viewpoint, hinders women often from getting the property rights of their own. The link between gender ideology and women's property rights can be unfolded in the following logical ways:

One, male, being the dominant gender in patriarchy, often influences the public policy and law of a country in general and gender perception of the state in particular. So, it remains a matter of male choice whether female of that given society would be granted property rights or not and if yes, then, how much of it will be given. Two, it is to be kept in mind that

> Property advantage stems not only from ownership, but also from effective control over it … in most countries, men as a gender exercise dominance over the instruments through which their existing advantages of property ownership and control are perpetuated such as the institutions that enact and implement laws, the mechanisms of recruitment into bodies which exercise control over (private or public) property, the institutions which play an important role in shaping gender ideology and so on.[29]

Three, women are socialized into stereotyped gender roles since early infancy as a result of which they are more motivated for the practice of the traits of femininity such as seclusion, self-effacement and sacrifice than the pursuit of financial potentiality through property and job. Gender socialization teaches them how to be a good woman which means to be indifferent to the property. Four, it has been historically experienced by patriarchy that women without property are more vulnerable for male domination than the women with property. Five, gender ideology preaches that women are by nature inefficient for managing and controlling their property as compared to male. Gender socialization always comes to justify this position through its curriculum. Thus, the gender perception of patriarchy and the property rights of the women have an essential contradiction in their relationships. Patriarchy, for its open and implicit agenda of subjugating the women, can never grant enough of property rights either in terms of ownership or in terms of control. Since gender socialization is aimed at implementing the philosophy of patriarchy smoothly through cultural norms and instructions, it always plays a role in curtailing the capability of women in respect of property effectively by changing the mental profile and viewpoint of the women. So the study of gender socialization is also partly related with the institution of property.

---

[29] Bina Agarwal, "Gender and Command Over Property: A Critical Gap in Economic Analysis and Policy in South Asia," *World Development* 22(10) (1994), 1455–78.

Thus, the theoretical, practical and institutional approach chalks out the scope of gender socialization exhaustively. At the theoretical level, gender socialization uses the different orientation point of view of gender identity formation and construction of several gender-related notions. The theoretical highlights demarcate the primary layout of the plan of gender socialization in so far as it can work successfully on the empirical level. At the practical level the major empirical problem of gender socialization is the description, analysis and sociological justification of the peculiar social structure called the gender. Gender, being the most complicated social category as well, calls for probing every details of its origin and development for being shaped, moulded and justified for social interaction judged from patriarchal point of view. At the institutional level, gender socialization is concerned with the social basis of male gender power which is the driving force of gender socialization. Actually it is believed that the scope of gender socialization can be addressed properly through many dimensions of the entire social order under patriarchy. Considered from the broader perspective the scope of gender socialization involves the study of all simple and complicated, open and dormant issues related to gender with their linkages to theoretical, empirical and institutional structures and frameworks.

PART II

Perspectives: Agents of Gender Socialization

4

Role of Family

Gender socialization is a process through which one develops
gender awareness and gender identity of his/her own from early
childhood. Sex is considered as a biological construction. But
in contrast to sex, gender is considered as social and cultural
construct and it is shaped by many social and cultural norms
and orientations which are practically enforced through many a
groups and organizations that influence the gender orientation
and its shaping over the years. It is important to study the role
played by these groups and organizations in the development
of gender orientations of man and woman. These groups and
organizations are known as agents of gender socialization. There
are three main categories of socializing agents that play their
role for the internalization of gender norms. They are primary
groups, secondary groups and reference groups. Family is treated
as primary group, the school and peer groups are considered as
secondary groups and political parties and media are treated as
reference groups. It is through these diverse groups and organizations that the curriculum of gender socialization is imparted
in the minds of the child, and judged from this angle the role of
these agents is as important as the gender socialization itself.
At a glance, there are at least four contributions of these agents
that make the curriculum of gender socialization so potential
and effective. One, it is due to these diverse agents that the curriculum of gender socialization has been so planned, focused and
organized in its style and pattern of operation. Two, the agents
cover almost the entire life span of a human being. A man or a
woman has to pass through either this or that agent in every
stage of his/her life. So the message of socialization is not only
received in early childhood but also is carried forward in almost
all the stages of life thereby making gender socialization a life-
long process. So it can be rightly stated that gender socialization
is the process through which the gender ideology is transmitted
from generation to generation. Three, the real concern of gender
socialization is the stability and maintenance of the gendered

system of the society. So in all models, irrespective of ideologies, gender socialization acts for maintaining status quo in respect of construction and functioning of gender. But, in the face of so many challenges from the outside world gender ideology needs to be adjusted time to time keeping its major aspects intact. This task of gender socialization is only possible with the active participation of different agents that allow change in gender behaviour without violent disruption and handle the challenge of technological advancement, modernity and globalization in a very smooth, gradual and peaceful manner, so that gross gender inconsistent behaviour does not occur in society. Thus, the different agents provide a sort of legitimacy to the concept of gender socialization on the one hand, and on the other, these agents work as safety valve so that gender expression of the child as well as the adult can be adjusted with the changing nature of time. Four, dimension and the intensity of gender socialization can be measured only with the degree of participation of these agents in the process. The more the participation of the agents will be spontaneous, the more will be the degree of penetration. So in this way the agents of gender socialization, that is, the family, the school, the peer group and the media are tied with the process through an inextricable relationship.

As of different agents of gender socialization, the role of family is the most important as 'the family is by far the most important primary group in society'.[1] The term 'primary group' was first used by Cooley to refer to groups 'characterized by intimate face-to-face association and cooperation. They are primary in several senses, but chiefly in that they are fundamental in forming the social nature and ideas of the individual'.[2] Family is considered as primary group because it is based on primary relations and due to its small size and close-knit feature succeeds in giving emotional support to the individual. Family has some unique features that have given it a unique position in the role of transmission of social qualities. 'It is the group through which … we first give creative expression to our social impulses. It is the breeding ground of our mores, the nurse of our loyalties. It

[1] R. M. MacIver and Charles H. Page, *Society* (London: Macmillan, 1965), 238.
[2] Charles Horton Cooley, *Social Organization* (New York, NY: Scribner's, 1909), 23.

is the first and generally remains the chief focus of our social satisfactions'[3] and in these respects the family is the most important primary group in our lives as well as in our society. In the family the child is born and brought up, in it the child forms the basic values and attitudes and in the family the child learns the speech and language which give the child social eligibility, ability to interact and adaptation. In respect of the role of family in the life of a child it can be said that there is no denying the fact that family plays an important role in socialization in general and gender socialization in particular.

The contribution of the family in the life of the child may be described from three specific aspects: *physical, mental and cultural. Physically* the child is completely dependent on the family. The child is born and brought up in the family and the family takes every care of the health, food necessity and other requirements of the child. The family also bears the burden of expenditure towards the education of the child and all types of financial security under its jurisdiction. So the physical protection that the family ensures for the child makes him/her loyal to the family as a result of which it becomes often very difficult for the child and even for the adult member of the family to go against any decision, instruction and norm of the family in respect of gender socialization. The child is also dependent on the family in respect of *mental development.* Emergence of the self is only possible in the family. The open, intimate and spontaneous environment of the family becomes altogether positive for the cognitive development of the child in respect of gender and also other matters. The formation of the gender identity starts in the family with the help of many elements which psychologically play an important role in the formation of 'self' based on gender. These elements are imitation, suggestion and identification. Through imitation the child adopts the proper gender behaviour and expected gender role. The child looks at father or mother and imitates their mode of speaking, their role–performance and position in the family, all of which are based mainly on the gender formed in alignment with their sexes assigned at birth. Suggestion is a form of communication method through which different information, proposal and data in respect of gender are

---

[3] MacIver and Page, *Society*, 219.

supplied to the child who generally accepts them with confidence and without any resistance. There is a power element in the suggestion because it is never directed to the effort of influencing the child through logic or consent formation, rather it acts through force, dictation and coercive instruction. Suggestions of the family can easily motivate the child to the task of gender identity formation, adaptation of gender consistent behaviour, responding to the curriculum of gender socialization and to the task of assimilating the gender ideology of the society. But there is a difficulty in enforcing the suggestion in case of the adult members who have already matured in their opinion and activity. Identification is the method through which the child internalizes the necessary concepts, behaviours and activities in order to meet his/her demand and requirements for easy adaptation with the broader outer setting or society. In this way the child develops the cognition and mentally prepares him/herself for the proper gender role, gender behaviour and all other responses to gender in order to set him/her in the conventional gender format of the society. Family is also responsible for the *cultural development* of the child in the society. For the proper initiation of the child to culture, the family inspires the child to have education both formal and informal. Formal education makes the orientation of the child towards gender more sharp and enlightened. Informal education teaches the child about the religion, norms, rules, and festivals through which the family as well as the child under it gain social and cultural identification which again shapes the gender identity of the child.

Thus, all cultures bestowed by the family are likely to be gender biased in the sense that the family itself is a gendered organization. Judged from the functionalist viewpoint the family is a necessary organization for the discharge of the various sex based functions of the society. There are many functions in the society which are different for the male and the female. Childbearing and childrearing, home management and nursing, etc., are the natural functions of the female whereas bread winning, public jobs, war, etc., are the natural functions of the male. The natural difference between the jobs of male and the female gave birth to the public–private debate. So since from the functionalist viewpoint family is a gendered category of organization, the cultural parameters created by it must have to be gender biased. Judged again from the feminist perspective, family is an organization led by patriarchy and family works on patriarchal terms. So it is the basic duty of the family to preach the patriarchal agenda of male domination and female subjugation and to shape the culture of the child in tune with this basic agenda. The value theory preaches the necessity of assimilating the values, attitudes, traits, behaviour patterns and different styles in respect of gender and also the role of family in their construction and implementation. It is the value theory that provides an ethical, psychological and ideological support to the stereotyping role and gender role enforced by the family. Keeping Bordieu in mind, the contribution of the family can also be described as *social capital, economic capital and cultural capital,* all of which are formed and generated along the gendered line of approach. Social capital indicates the social connections, settings, relationships and different systems of communication among the members of the family. Social capital protects the child from unseen dangers and gives shelter in bad days. Economic capital is the combined volume of income, property and assets coming primarily as the result and consequence of education. Cultural capital is the composite form of religion, rituals, norms, mores and taboos that establish the fact what the members of the family actually are. Culture is the ideological expression of the sense of identity and orientations of the members of the family. In respect of all three contributions, the family works as the representative of patriarchy and thereby the male gender reaps almost all the benefits of these contributions. So the gender socialization caused and transmitted by the family is obviously the indoctrination of the curriculum by which the child and the adult members of the family, especially the female members of the family are taught to accept the domination of the male and at the same time the subjugation of the female as natural and functionally important. Thus the strength of the gender ideology under patriarchy lies in the fact that it is nourished and nurtured through gender socialization by none other than the most important primary group, named family.

If the nature of the family is studied carefully then it is seen that within the very structure of the family and within the very features of the family the cause of its gender-biased character is located. According to the *Oxford Dictionary of Sociology*, 'the family is an intimate domestic group made up of people related to one another by bonds of blood, sexual mating or legal ties. It has been a very resilient social unit that has survived and adopted through time'.[4] For Giddens, 'A family is a group of persons directly linked by kin connections, the adult members of which assume responsibility for caring of children'.[5] Functionalists attempted to define the family on the basis of the functions that it performs. In 1949, George Peter Murdock defined the family as 'a social group characterized by common residence, economic cooperation and reproduction ... family includes adults of both sexes, at least two of whom maintain a socially approved sexual relationship and one or more children'.[6] According to Murdock, there are four important functions of the family and they are sexual relationships, economic cooperation among members, reproduction and socialization of infants and children. According to MacIver and Page, 'The family is a group defined by a sex relationship sufficiently precise and enduring to provide for the procreation and upbringing of children'.[7]

Following MacIver and Page, at least some important points about the nature of the family can be drawn from all the definitions about the family. These significant points are 'mating relationship, a form of marriage through which such mating relation is established and maintained, a system of nomenclature, mode of reckoning descent, childbearing and childrearing and a common habitation, home or household'.[8] An open analysis of these points will certainly expose the gendered nature of the family and will also make it clear as to why family serves as an important medium of gender socialization and will also highlight the exact nature of this socialization as inculcated by the family.

As of the discussion on *mating relationship*, what comes first is the selection of mates which is strictly controlled by the male authority of the family in almost all societies and across all cultures. The right to select mates is never usually left to the

---

[4] Scott and Marshall, *Oxford Dictionary of Sociology*, 212.

[5] Giddens, *Sociology*, 173.

[6] George Peter Murdock, *Social Structure* (New York: The Macmillan Company, 1949), 1.

[7] MacIver and Page, *Society*, 238.

[8] Ibid, 238.

hand of the individual. It is almost a prerogative of the male guardians of the family and thereby authoritative relationship dominates the mating relationship. Second, family system does not normally allow exogamous relationship. 'It may be socially compulsory to marry within a group to which one belongs (endogamy).'[9] In spite of very many changes in the family system due to industrialization, technological change and globalization the very stand about the selection of mates has remained almost the same. The growing occurrences of honour killing prove that even in 21st century the family is not ready to hand over the right from male guardians to individual. Third, there are evidences where it is seen that male partners are relatively freer than the female partners in respect of endogamous selection of mates. In contrast, experiences record that female virtually has no right to select mates even within the group to which they belong. Fourth, there are attitudes in the society both from the end of male and female for the selection of mates and these attitudes prove that almost in every family in all societies and across all cultures selection of mates are dominated by the patriarchal values. To begin with the evolutionary psychology or natural selection theory, it is noticed that men are attracted to women who are able to bear healthy children and can rear them. In contrast, women are attracted to men who are in a position to provide the family with all material resources needed. According to social homogeny theory, individuals are attracted to those who come from a similar social and cultural background. Social exchange theory views the attitudes of mate selections from the angle of profit and benefit. Long ago William Goode wrote, 'all courtship systems are market or exchange systems'.[10] Goode's claim is supposed to be the reflection of the attitudes of mate selection today. 'More recently the influence of the market, exchange and the utility maximizing theories of the family have increased as the new economics of the family has gained more adherents.'[11] One form of exchange theory predicts that men with

---

[9] Ibid, 239.

[10] William Goode, *World Revolution and Family Patterns*, 2nd ed. (New York, NY: Free Press, 1970), 8.

[11] Michael J. Rosenfeld, "A Critique of Exchange Theory in Mate Selection," *American Journal of Sociology*, 110(5) (March, 2005), 1284–1325.

high status and earnings should marry women of great physical beauty[12,13] and thereby exchange happens between financial resources of male and the physical beauty and attractiveness of the female. In a second form of exchange theory, men with excellent labour market skills are predicted to marry women with especially strong domestic skills.[14] Following some sociological observation [15,16,17,18] it can be said that the third kind of exchange theory works when men with low socio-economic and cultural background marry women of higher socio-economic background just for profit. Here racial caste position is exchanged with financial resources. The third type of exchange exists in many forms in many societies. It is to be argued here that in all the forms of exchange theories women have practically nothing to do with the mode of operation of the exchanges that are all the time made for the gain of the male. Women, on account of their gender, remain always at the bottom of the power structure of the bargaining for the exchange. According to the conflict/feminist theory the financial resources of an old man may be exchanged with the necessity of the financial security of a younger woman. In the families under patriarchal values age gap between the male and the female is very strictly maintained in respect of mate selection. Patriarchy favours marriage between the higher aged man and lower aged woman. Feminists argue that age difference is maintained for ensuring the dominant status of men in patriarchal marriage. So the starting point of the family's mode of operation, that is, mate selection does not include women as an independent variable. Thus, gender ideology controls and

[12] Glen H. Elder, "Appearance and Education in Marriage Mobility," *American Sociological Review*, 34(4) (August 1969), 519–33.

[13] William J. Goode, "Family and Mobility," in *Class, Status and Power: Social Stratification in Comparative Perspective*, 2nd edition, eds Reinhard Bendix and Seymour Martin Lipset (New York: Free Press, 1951), 582–601.

[14] Gary S. Becker, *A Treatise on the Family*, expanded ed. (Cambridge, MA: Harvard University Press, 1991).

[15] Kingsley Davis, "Intermarriage in Caste Societies," *American Anthropologist* 43(3) (1941), 376–95.

[16] Robert K. Merton, "Intermarriage and the Social Structure: Fact and Theory," *Psychiatry* 4(3) (1941), 361–74.

[17] Zhenchao Qian, "Breaking Racial Barriers: Variations in Interracial Marriage between 1980 and 1990," *Demography* 34(2) (1997), 263–76.

[18] Vincent Kang Fu, "Racial Intermarriage Pairings," *Demography* 38(2) (2001), 147–59.

watches the matter of mate selection at its every stage. The system of the vigilance is so strong that it will not be exaggerated to state that the patriarchy itself actually selects the mates both for men and women. Under the patriarchal values it has been customary to judge the physical beauty, domestic skill, physical signs, body language, reproductive health and financial strength of the family of the bride during negotiation. From this trend it is clear that the attitudes of mate selection formed by the process of gender socialization is absolutely male-biased and anti-women. It is known from a number of records and from the narratives in almost every language in India in particular and Asia in general that during the formal occasion of interviewing a prospective bride for selection women (the prospective brides) were used to go through a number of physical tests openly before the aged male and female guardians of the bridegroom and these tests ranged from measuring the length of hair to pulling of hairs to confirm whether they are original or not, through the examination of footsteps and walking style of the prospective bride. Thus, the basic approach towards the women gender were to be formulated and taught by family during the starting of mate selection and the process was to be operative during all the subsequent stages of the journey of family.

The institution of marriage is the next important ingredient of the construction and continuation of the family. It is through marriage that new family grows and the mating relationship and the function of reproduction get a social support and setting. The relation between marriage and the family may be termed as cause and effect relationship in view of the fact that marriage results in expansion of family through reproduction and family is the agent through whom marriage is executed and is given a viability and legitimacy. But the problem is that like family as a gendered association marriage is also a gendered institution. By association we mean 'a group organized for the pursuit of an interest or group of interests in common'.[19] But by institution we mean 'the established forms or conditions of procedure characteristic of group activity'.[20] As the form always follows the essence so the marriage always follows the family. It is almost unbecoming of the fact that nature of association is one and the

[19] MacIver and Page, *Society*, 12.
[20] Ibid, 15.

nature of institution is another. So necessarily the gendered nature of the family is faithfully reflected in the nature and functioning of the institution of marriage.

'Marriage can be defined as a socially acknowledged and approved sexual union between two adult individuals.'[21] There are many aspects involved in marriage that widen the route of gender socialization. First, the institution of marriage is modelled upon the patriarchal agenda of regulating and restricting the sexual behaviour especially of the women. History records that women's sexuality was the headache of the patriarchy irrespective of country and culture. In the Middle Ages, in Europe the custom of compelling the women for using 'virgin guard' and the system of enforcing 'burkha' compulsorily for the Muslim women in the Middle East and in many Muslim countries of Asia was the effort of controlling the sexuality of the women. The chief reason behind these methods was to fix the paternity of the child born out of the sexual intercourse of a woman. In order to make the matter of paternity very clear, it was necessary to confine and to keep the women under strict control under the family and necessarily the women were pushed into the prison of marriage. Second, many forms of marriage are evidenced in the history of sociology. Of them, two are most relevant in our discussion here. Prior to industrialization the form of marriage that dominated almost all societies was polygamy. 'There are two types of polygamy: polygyny, in which a man may be married to more than one woman at the same time, and polyandry, much less common, in which a woman may have two or more husbands simultaneously.'[22] Out of these two forms, the first one of male polygamy, that is, polygyny was to be commonly experienced in all societies. Polygyny was practically the custom which turned the women into mere commodities through the institution of marriage and thus through a long time in history marriage was treated by males as a method of confining women and keeping them under control in the name of institutional legacy. In case of polyandry, evidenced in some epics such as the Mahabharata of India, women were the worst affected since, first, they lost the right to sexuality through this marriage, and second, they had to sacrifice their choice and consent at the feet of patriarchal notion

[21]   Giddens, *Sociology*, 173.
[22]   Ibid, 173.

of unity either of family or of any group whatever. Third, with marriage the matter of reproduction is inextricably attached. Marriage is just a method of giving social and ritual sanction to the matter of reproduction which is indispensable for ensuring the outflow of generation in the family. Since marriage is essentially related to reproduction, women under the institution of marriage will never enjoy freedom so long as the process of reproduction is not completed. Even after the completion of this process rarely women will have freedom as during that time women might have reached the age when their dependence on husband or son will be a compulsion just for subsistence. With the matter of reproduction, son-bias of the patriarchy is very much related. Patriarchy, being basically a male-dominated system of power structure, often cherishes the aspiration of the birth of a male-child and it is seen that just in order to meet the demand of the birth of a son, women are more likely to go through the process of reproduction repeatedly, often once in a gap of two years or sometimes less. Thus under the system of marriage the reproduction is considered successful only with the birth of a son and the birth of a female baby is supposed to be the unsuccessful or unnecessary reproduction. In both the cases, the female is the worst sufferer. In case of the first one, the reproduction goes on at the cost of the physical health of the women and in case of the second one, the women suffer a mental crisis, social stigmatization and also socio-legal harassment. Fourth, married women are expected to be more responsive to gender stereotypes, gender roles and gender norms. The stereotypical traits of domesticity, loyalty, virtuousness, sacrifice, submissiveness, self-effacement and chastity are more expected from the married women. The adult women also are trained and taught the lessons of gender socialization along the line of stereotypes through the marriage. Fifth, the concept of childcare is also indispensably joined with the institution of marriage. In traditional and also modern industrial society, childcare is treated as the primary responsibility of the women, especially mothers. So it is due to the performance of the jobs of childcare that women/mothers are often prohibited to enter into the labour market and they are inspired to participate chiefly in home management. Even in case of the working mother very often she has to take leave to take care of the child whenever the child is sick. 'Women spend more hours per week on household and on childcare than men do. And motherhood is a career liability for women while for men, being married and having children are both associated with higher earnings and being in upper level positions'.[23] The increased participation of women in the labour market has changed the traditional roles of women making the matter of childcare more problematic. So far in the family under patriarchal values the job of childcare is believed to be the job of women (mother) exclusively. So in view of the changes of family in respect of structure and functions it is woman who has to adjust and adopt in order to cope with the pressure of childcare in the changing situation. As a result, the excess pressure compels the working women to reduce their sleep and to cancel their entertainment day after day which ultimately cause strain and stress for them. Sixth, 'childcare is a completely distinct and especially burdensome aspect of household labour'.[24,25] Reproduction is also a job which only women can perform. But in spite of being so important for the continuation of the family these jobs go unpaid in all societies and across all cultures and the institution of marriage legitimize the fact of non-payment and women's sacrifice for these jobs in the package of chastity, femininity and motherhood. So the radical feminist's attack on marriage is not absolutely baseless. Seventh and last but the least, even some decades ago in many countries early marriage was the soft method of women control in the family. Chiefly for the control of women sexuality and for using the reproductive capacity of women to the fullest extent, the concept of early marriage was practised in the families of patriarchal values mostly in traditional societies. Due to very many legal restrictions, the system of early marriage of women has been diluted considerably. 'Despite a worldwide decline in early marriage, the practice remains a huge issue. In countries like Niger, up to sixty percent of girls are married in their teens.'[26] In thousands of villages in India, early marriage is still

[23] Stewart D. Friedman and Jeffrey H. Greenhaus, *Work and Family: Allies or Enemies?* (New York, NY: Oxford University Press, 2000), 9.

[24] Sarah Fenstermaker Berk, *The Gender Factory* (New York, NY: Plenum Press, 1985), 41.

[25] Cinthia Rexroat and Constance L. Shehan, "The Family Cycle and Spouses' Time in Housework," *Journal of Marriage and the Family* 49(1) (1987), 737–50.

[26] *Social Institutions and Gender Index (SIGI)*, 2014 edition (Paris, France: Organization for Economic Co-operation and Development).

a problem to be addressed by the policy makers and activists.
Social Institutions and Gender Index (SIGI)

> Provides an evidence base showing that there is strong association
> between discriminatory social institutions and key development
> outcomes, such as education, employment and empowerment.
> Discrimination against the girl child, such as early marriage,
> limits her education, increases her chances of adolescent
> pregnancy, and restricts her decision making authority within
> the family and her ability to make informed choices about her
> income or her family's well-being.[27]

Thus the institution of marriage is nothing but an agent of
patriarchy and accordingly this institution specially contributes
to the role of family in gender socialization.

As of the *system of nomenclature* of the family, it can be said
that the nomenclature system plays an important role in gender
socialization.

> In the languages of Indian subcontinent, especially in Bengali
> language there are a number of words indicating the names of
> male or female which are completely gender-biased. Male names
> are suggestive of power or intelligence or greatness or nobility or
> bestowed whereas the female names are suggestive of plant, river,
> companion, goddess, worship, dedication, illusion, blessedness,
> affection, kindness and wealth. A boy is named by words that mean
> 'rising' when a girl child is named by a word that means 'the end'.
> A boy is named by words that mean 'sun' and 'moon' when the girl
> child is named as 'moonlight'.... Very recently, especially after the
> advent of globalization, a tendency of coining sex neutral names
> has been started but it is still far away to see its positive influence.
> The problem with these sexist names is that the meanings that
> the names carry become a part of feeling, thought, culture and
> action as a result of their utterance day after day and as a result
> of being heard on regular basis year after year. In course of time
> children start thinking that names have been given with a view
> to set the directions of their thought process and role playing.
> The meanings of names are actually the ideology set for them and
> they should imitate the gender ideology inherent in names. Thus
> nomenclature of human being in Indian subcontinent, especially

[27] Ibid.

in Bengal, is grossly fulfilling the agenda of gender inequality, gender discrimination and gender differences.[28]

The objectives behind this system of nomenclature are chiefly of three types. One, the social difference between son and daughter is highlighted by such names. Two, the differences of expectations of behaviours, attitudes, personality traits from son and daughter are highlighted through such sexist names. Three, the ideological foundation of gender roles stereotyping for women is laid through these gender-biased names.

The mode of reckoning descent is an important point for establishing the separate identity and the functional unity of the family. A careful analysis of this point will expose the gendered objective of the family since the inception up to the modern development. According to *Oxford Dictionary of Sociology,*

> Descent groups are the kin groups who are lineal descendants of a common ancestor.... Kinship systems establish relationships between individual and groups on the model of biological relationships between parents and children, between siblings, and between marital partners.... Kinship system exists in order to allocate rights and duties in societies.[29]

From the angle of general sociological understanding descent can be described as the kinship group which is identified by bond of blood, common culture, common economy, common residence and right to succession. For MacIver and Page,

> Descent may be reckoned through the male line (patrilineal) or through the female line (matrilineal). Both systems have been used successfully, and though there is more difficulty in establishing the fact of biological paternity, many groups have shifted from the matrilineal to the patrilineal form.[30]

Many sociologists supported the theory of Darwin 'that the family took shape from the operation of male possessiveness and jealousy'[31] and the mode of reckoning descent is the reflection of

---

[28] Chattopadhyay, *Fighting Gender Inequality*, 23.
[29] Scott and Marshall, *Oxford Dictionary of Sociology*, 150 and 335–36.
[30] MacIver and Page, *Society*, 239.
[31] Ibid, 244.

such male possessiveness over family, property and society. It is also the cultural transformation of the identity theory of the group based on kinship and implemented through custom. There are evidences that prove the existence of matrilineal societies at the dawn of civilization. Again, there are sociologists who opine, 'despite claims about the existence of matriarchal societies, there is no sound anthropological evidence that such societies existed'.[32] But there is no denying the fact that with the development of agriculture and economic dominance of men the patriarchal set up emerged and male line descent theory started being widely accepted and utilized as a result of which the women suffered what Engels stated as the 'historic defeat of women'.

> This historic defeat became possible for the replacement of hunting and gathering of food by women from nature by herding and agriculture and commodity production resulting ultimately in the emergence of private property. The emergence of private property and ousting women from the control of economic production and consequently confining women in 'family' happened simultaneously which ultimately resulted in what Engels termed as historic defeat of the female sex. Capitalism, for its survival, has utilized from the very beginning three major sources of domination—Family, Private property and the State. Engels has explored the issue of their interconnection and the issue of gender oppression as a corollary in his famous book, *The Origins of the Family, Private Property and the State* (1884). So women's emancipation is not possible without the overthrow of capitalism. The Marxian feminism also argues for the re-evaluation and a critical scrutiny of the family system in the light of these debates.[33]

This debatable role of family system is exposed by the mode of reckoning descent modelled primarily for not only subjugating the women but also for making the women species completely disappearing. After the introduction of the mode of reckoning descent through the patriarchal line, that is, male line the name, title, status, inheritance started being transmitted from generation to generation through the identity of the male

[32] Rae Lesser Blumberg, *A General Theory of Gender Stratification* (San Francisco: Jossey Bros, 1984), 23.

[33] Chattopadhyay, *Gender Inequality*, 36.

guardians of the family. The chief characteristics of patriarchal type descent policy are of four types. One, descent is traced through father, not the mother. 'Generally he presides over the religious rites of the household; he is the guardian of the "family gods," of the sacred hearth.'[34] Two, most often patrilineal descent is associated with patrilocal residence which means that women after being married will be sent to the house of the husband. Three, authority within the family or within the larger kin group is vested in the hands of grandfather, father or some superior male guardian. Four, male baby is considered as one important condition of the continuation of the descent. In contrast female baby is considered as a commodity belonging to other with whom she will be married. The birth of a son is usually cherished as the 'rising of sun' whereas the birth of a female baby is viewed as the sin or debt of father. Women in patrilineal descent are described openly as 'the door to hell'. The ancient law-giver of India named Manu described three types of submission: one, in her infancy she is under the father, two, in her youth she is under the husband and three, in her old age she is under the son. Thus the total life cycle of the woman revolves round the identity of a male who rules and exploits her. The implications of all these features of male-line descent policy have been totally negative for the life of women of Asia in general and India in particular. Primarily such descent obsession (along the male-line) hits the developments of the women from a number of aspects. It hinders very often the access of women to education. Since the daughter is supposed to be the property of her would-be husband belonging to other descent, it is considered futile to bear the cost towards her education. Complete social subordination marked the position of women at every stages of their life. According to the prevalent descent policy, daughters are normally denied property rights. Due to the legal restrictions in almost all countries the situation has slightly changed. But the reality is more or less still the same in almost all countries irrespective of economic or cultural status. A recent case may be cited from which the descent obsession of the family can be understood. It is reported that

---

[34] MacIver and Page, *Society*, 249.

A family of Tribeni town in the District of Hooghly in the state of West Bengal has refused to accept their younger daughter-in-law after five months of her marriage due to the fact of her elder sister being eunuch although everything was informed to the members of the in-law's house during the first session of negotiation at the bride's paternal house of Kalna and although that elder sister was present at all stages of the marriage. Reportedly the family accused the daughter-in-law of defaming and stigmatizing the descent of the in-law's house after the said eunuch elder sister came to meet her sister after getting the news of her illness. But the daughter-in-law has protested against such inhuman discriminative behavior of the members (including her husband) of the in-law's house. The newly married bride is firm on her demand of returning and living in in-law's house with honour along with the recognition of all types of normal relation with her elder sister. Ranjita Singha, the member of the 'Transgender Welfare Board' is of the opinion that this incident is the example of the attitudes towards the 'Third Gender' at the societal and familial level. In spite of the right to vote or education of the 'Third Gender' established by the court of law of the land, the society in general and the family in particular is not still ready to shake off the orthodox gender approach and the traditional social division of gender. The incident has been reported and forwarded to the National Women's Commission, State Women's Commission and S.D.O. of Kalna and S.P. of the District of Burdwan and Hooghly.[35]

Childbearing and childrearing are two important jobs of the family and they are performed by the women. With the development of patriarchy the mothering right has been facing a severe crisis. The natural capacity of mothering lies with the women but the right of handling it is transferred to the hands of male guardians of the family. The situation was obviously bad for the women in traditional societies. But the situation in modern family is perhaps worse. The questions as to when one woman will conceive and how many times she will have to do so are determined either by her husband or by her male guardians of the family. Again, the son obsession of the patriarchy has made the reproduction all the more unbearable for the women because during all the time of her pregnancy a woman remains worried with the thought whether the imminent baby is a

---

[35] Bhattacharya, *Anandabazar Patrika* (Kolkata, 17 February 2017), 6.

son or daughter. Thus the natural joy of motherhood becomes collapsed. Childrearing is also supposed to be the exclusive job of the women especially the mother. In view of the consideration of different elements of childrearing such as love, affection, discipline and physical and mental development of the child, it may be said that childrearing is not a very simple job, rather sufficiently challenging and burdensome job which a woman has to perform almost single handedly. Just by providing the financial support the male ends his responsibility towards the childcare and it has been the culture of the male under patriarchy. In the face of technological changes and in the face of globalization childrearing has been tougher for the women and the problem is graphically increasing with the growing number of women coming into the labour market. Since traditionally it is believed that women are the best caregivers, they have to perform this job mostly without any help from their husbands at the cost of their entertainment, sleep or food time in spite of the fact that they (women) spend a lot of time in labour market for income of the family. So ultimately what is left for the women is the excessive pressure on the women for undertaking the burden of childrearing successfully. 'In two-parents' household, when the child becomes ill, the mother usually stays home whether she is employed full or part-time.'[36] Since it is believed that women are primarily responsible for childcare, today's women remain in compulsion either of leaving the job or of finding a job compatible with the role of childcare (those with less travels, more flexible hours and less occupational risk). Sometimes women employed in corporate sectors adjust with the situation by foregoing some career advancements and wilfully forward their option for transferring them in a section where work is less and accordingly pay is also less. Evidences show that a growing setback is happening for the women as well as the job of childrearing itself even in modern times when childrearing has been much more easy and scientific due to the various inventions and at the same time the job has been difficult for the patriarchal values of the family which, in most cases, have failed to achieve a balance between the tradition and the modernity. Families of the

---

[36] H. C. Northcutt, "Who Stays Home? Working Parents and Sick Children," in *International Journal of Women's Studies* 6 (1983), 387–94.

rural areas of India, as a form of gendered organization, believe that the purpose of childbearing and childrearing can be suitably served through early marriages. The dismal picture of child marriage can be presented by primary data collected through Bikash Society of the District of Bankura in West Bengal.

Bikash Society is a non-government organization working with a holistic approach to the programme of sustainable development of women. Bikash was registered as a society in May, 1996 in Bankura, one of the most backward districts in West Bengal, for the long term development of women and children coming from underprivileged society. With these objectives in its background Bikash is running its women development programmes in 250 villages of five blocks such as: Bankura - I, Sonamukhi, Chhatna, Saltora and G. Ghati block. Before the implementation of the *Integrated Nutrition and Health Programme* (I. N. H. P), a survey was conducted by CARE, W.B. in said five blocks of the district on health and nutrition status of women. Data collected from this survey show an awful presence of child marriage and gender inequality. It was seen that 6 per cent women are married at the age below 15 years. 68 per cent women are marred at the age below 18 years. And 26 per cent women are married at the age of 18 and above. 89 per cent women become pregnant at the age below 21 years. In 73 cases out of hundred, it was detected that male child gets more share of food. In 71 cases out of hundred, male child gets preference in education in these blocks. A gross discrimination between male and female regarding food was also detected. It is seen that in 60 cases out of hundred, male child gets better quality of food than a female child.[37]

Thus the feudal mentalities of the family cause the act of childbearing and childrearing to be a predicament for the women and their development.

The common habitation as one important element of family is treated as a place where gender socialization works completely in tune with the motto of gender ideology. Common habitation, home or household serve as gendered category and do not give the guarantee for a gender-neutral treatment at all due to a number of reasons. One, the concept of 'home' was designed primarily for ousting the women from labour market and for confining

---

[37] Chattopadhyay, *Gender Inequality,* 185–86.

them in a safe place under the watchful eyes of patriarchy. Engels, by exposing the interconnections among family, private property and state, argued, 'women's subordination results not from her biology ... but from social arrangements that have a clear and traceable history'[38] and such social arrangement is the family the important feature of which is the household which is patriarchal in nature since it is headed by male authority. So home is an arrangement done by patriarchy where 'the women have no job outside the house and no economic independence, women are in fact the chattels or possessions of their husbands'.[39] Two, women are trained in home by the definite curriculum set by patriarchy in order to confine them in a world which is private. In contrast, men are considered suitable physically and mentally for dealing the jobs which are termed as public. So clearly for establishing the male domination over women in society the concept of private in the guise of home has been forwarded and executed by patriarchy. Thus the slogan 'personal is political' and vice versa has gained ground and it is argued by the radical feminists that just for leaving all political control of public world to men, the agenda of personal world, that is, home for the women is created. Three, the concept of private for the women has been a setback to their enlightenment, employment and empowerment. They are socialized into the role of home-running, childbearing and childrearing and all other domestic jobs. The concept of home has been politically used against the development of women and they have been exploited with and within their body. With their body the women have been compelled to serve in the kitchen for cooking food for the family members and within their body the women have been forced to have pregnancy under patriarchal dictates and to go through reproduction aspired by the same patriarchy. So all round physical and mental exploitation takes place at home which can actually be termed as prison. Four, the women reside at home but they are not the owner of home. They have no access to the property owned by the household as property in family is passed on always to male members of the family as per the descent policy and the mode of reckoning descent in families

---

[38] Ritzer, *Sociological Theory*, 467.
[39] Ibid.

under patriarchal values is always patrilineal. So, the concept of home or house does not provide any economic security for the women. *Five*, since women are to be sent to their husband's house as per patrilocal residence theory, they are treated in their parents' house as liability and as 'reserved asset of other', that is, the asset of the in-laws' house. Again, in their in-laws' house they are treated as immigrant members, whereas in parents' house they were used to be treated as members ready for emigration. So, what finally happens to the fate of women is that they have their father's house or the house of father-in-law both being temporary in nature, whereas they do not have any permanent house of their own.

Thus, from the above-mentioned discussion the gendered nature of the family is very clear. The origin and development of the family over the centuries had been revolving round the single-point agenda and that is the subjugation of women. So theoretically family is by far the most important primary organization for implementing gender socialization in the society. Socialization, in spite of being a type of indoctrination, left ample space for spontaneous development and expression of mind and thoughts. But gender socialization, being more focused than socialization, does not leave any room for any wilful and spontaneous expression of gender which is supposed to be a social and cultural construct. So, much more influences, compulsions, dictations, suppressions and repressions are attached with the entire process of gender socialization for all genders especially for the women. All of these methods attached either with reward or with punishment are best implemented by the family since some important stages of human life from birth to inheritance of property through marriage are passed by the individuals in the family. The child is born in family and dies in family and remains dependent on the family for every possible way of development up to the adulthood and even sometimes throughout the life. So family enjoys ample scope to influence the child in respect of gender identity formation, gender development and gender socialization.

The role of family in respect of gender socialization is manifold of which the most important is the formation of *stereotypes*. Stereotypes may be described as some fixed beliefs, ideas and notions about gender created by patriarchy and assimilated by the society. 'In fact stereotypes are representative of a society's collective knowledge of customs, myths, ideas, religions, and sciences.'[40] It is within this knowledge that an individual develops a stereotype or a belief about a certain group. Gender stereotypes are the notions of gender that are socially created and practised. So when some fixed beliefs and mental ideas about gender become a part of social knowledge then it is called gender stereotypes. As a result of their knowledge, or lack of knowledge, the stereotype has an effect on their social behaviour. A stereotype is defined as an 'unvarying form or pattern, specifically a fixed or conventional notion or conception of a person, group, idea, etc., held by a number of people and allows for no individuality or critical judgment'.[41] 'Traditional gender roles help to sustain gender stereotypes, such as that males are supposed to be adventurous, assertive, aggressive, independent and task-oriented, whereas females are seen as more sensitive, gentle, dependent, emotional and people-oriented.'[42] The family creates the stereotypes through a number of assignments such as religious, cultural and economic, etc., that family undertakes for the smooth running of all the institutional activities of the society. The family also influences the mental cognition of the child and also the adult so that they come to internalize the perceptions of gender stereotypes in their mind and knowledge and express them as different shades of their activities. So ultimately gender stereotyping is the root of what the male or female do as different expressions of his/her identity.

So the biological basis of the psychological legacy and inheritance of gender notions can hardly be ignored. Actually sex stereotypes are the product of both the biological and social conditioning, and in the field of social and cultural conditioning of the gender attitudes family is by far the best penetrator.

---

[40] Macrae, Stangor, and Hewstone. *Stereotypes and Stereotyping*, 15.

[41] *Webster's New World Dictionary* (Webster New World, 1998).

[42] Isabella Crespi, *Socialization and Gender Roles Within the Family: A Study on Adolescents and their Parents in Great Britain*. Retrieved 10 July 2017, from www.mariecurie.org/annals/volume3/crespi.pdf

The family encourages the boys to internalize and develop the masculine qualities such as aggression, dominance, physical strength, ambitious attitude and public appearance whereas the girls are encouraged to acquire the feminine qualities such as softness, loveliness, righteousness, sacrifice and self-effacement. The initiation to the adoption of gender traits starts early in the family through the toys supplied to the children. It is revealed by a number of literatures that family in all societies and across all cultures is guided by the gender bias in respect of the purchase and distribution of the toys between boys and girls. Boys are often given the toy-gun, truck or football whereas the girls are given dolls, kitchen utensils, teddy bear and toy mobiles. The inner spirit of the game sharing and the segregation of toys along the gender line are slowly injected into the minds of the children and the process of differential socialization starts. It is the toys that primarily motivate the boys to be physically assertive and the girls to be mentally expressive. So boys learn and practise the gender stereotypes spontaneously by the message received through the toys, which after being decoded, are taken as a material representation of stereotypes. Likewise the girls come to decode the toys and search out the implicit stereotypical message of the toys for internalizing their ideological kernel hidden in the toys. Thus stereotypical traits for boys and girls are differently allocated through toys. The second important factor of the formation and adoption of gender stereotypes is the dress which is normally different for the boys and the girls in all societies and across all cultures. At the age of two or three children start becoming conscious about their gender identity which they find out externally in their dresses. The dresses of the girls are usually designed very fashionably and thus the stereotypical myths about the female beauty, charming body and biological destiny of the women are highlighted resulting in the creation of an undercurrent sexual excitement. It is the gender approach to the dresses of the girls that have created a number of negative stereotypes and have made the women just an object of sexual enjoyment. The stereotypical traits associated with the female gender such as softness, emotion, homesickness, caring qualities and charming appearance are all first internalized through dresses. So the dress code set by the society in general and by the family in particular is a major medium of inculcating gender stereotypes in the minds of the boys and the girls. Family also injects the stereotypical values into the minds of the boys and the girls and the value system developed in the institution of family is the major medium of gender socialization in general and indoctrination to gender stereotypes in particular. Girls are often trained for sacrifice, tolerance, home-caring, righteousness and childrearing. In contrast the boys are trained by the family for domination, public appearance, political leadership and material pleasure. The traits that the boys and the girls inherit and internalize have their roots in the value system which is often termed as stereotypes of gender values. One such stereotypical value is the ideal of *patibrata.*

> Devotion to the husband is cultivated among girls of all religions, but it is particularly idealized and firmly institutionalized in the Hindu concept of *patibrata.*... The ideal of the *patibrata* is romanticized through legend, folklore and folksong, and reaffirmed through ceremonies of different kinds. It may be pertinent to illustrate with one of the legends, the legend of Sabitri and Satyaban.[43]

Similarly, many values stereotypically formulated and followed in all the religious and ceremonial practices of the family system, especially of India, are motherhood, womanhood and daughter-hood. All these values are formulated for controlling the women and their power. Sociological and anthropological investigations reveal that gender stereotypes, emerged out of the value system of the traditional families, have been formulated due to a number of reasons. One, Engels found the root of the 'historic defeat of the women' in the complex relation among family, private property and the state. Based on his analysis, it can be remarked that in order to oust the women from the control of economy and in order to ensure the possession of male over it, the concept of family and home were created with a view to implementing the subservience of women and their subjugation by men. Thus, as a corollary of this newer development in human society and economy, the value system was formulated with the design of

---

[43] Suma Chitnis, "Feminism: Indian Ethos and Indian Convictions," in *Women in Indian* Society, ed. Rehana Ghadially, 90.

some specific gender stereotypes especially for the women. The concept of family and home threw women into the confinement of a domestic slave, which fixed for the women a lifestyle out of which again emanated the new economy. Thus, there is a very clear relation between gender stereotypes and the growth of economy from the patriarchal viewpoint. Two, there is no doubt that patriarchy itself as an institution certainly tends to limit the space of women. Ideological techniques are more effective than mere force or any pressure. The value system in which the women gender stereotypes are created and shaped is the result of romanticized representation of the ideology of femininity purely modelled upon the agenda of patriarchy. Patriarchy, being a male-centred authority system, is always prone to keep the women under subjugation and control through various beliefs, norms and value system, and accordingly the stereotypical representation of the women under patriarchy happens. The family plays a great role in enforcing the stereotypes since the birth of a child. So gender stereotypes are the bridge between the patriarchy and the family. Capitalism created and used the stereotypical representation of the women strictly for the economic reasons. But patriarchy used the stereotypes strictly for the cause of male domination and the reasons behind the formation of stereotypes is to create 'laws of thought' which will turn the fact of subservience and subjugation of women by men as a culture of habit through which the matter of male domination and female subordination will be accepted as natural. Sylvia Walby identifies six structures through which patriarchy operates. Of these six structures, patriarchal cultural institutions is one structure which tends to represent women from patriarchal gaze and influences the gender identity of the women and, accordingly, their thought-process and behaviour. Gender stereotypes are the product of these patriarchal cultural institutions which in association with other structures of patriarchy come to idealize the marginalized position of the women. Three, biological characteristics of the male and female worked as a dominant source of gender stereotypes. When women's capacity of reproduction is taken into account it becomes clear that women form a separate category in respect of gender. The body of woman is also much more sexually appealing than the body of man. The hormonal configuration has also given the women a separate standing. In view of this biological uniqueness of the female body, it was considered necessary to control the biological potentiality of the women for preserving the interest of the male authority. Thus reproduction and mothering rights have been kept under control by the male authority. Moreover, the female sexuality was also kept under control by the patriarchy. In most of the cultures, women have been portrayed both from positive and negative angles, and all these have been done due to the biological uniqueness of the female body. If the case of Hinduism is taken for example, it is seen, 'the concept of the female in Hinduism presents an important duality: on the one hand, the woman is fertile, benevolent—the bestower; on the other, she is aggressive, malevolent—the destroyer'.[44] Perhaps the reproductive and the mothering power of women have given them the status of the benevolent, or Lakshmi, the goddess of prosperity, and again the sexuality of the women have turned their position down in the patriarchal gaze. Thus biological presentation of women has been all along contradictory for them and it is the male authority which has reaped all the benefits of their biology. Simone de Beauvoir stated, 'an existentialist perspective has enabled us, then, to understand how the biological and economic condition of primitive horde must have led to male supremacy'.[45]

The family is very much concerned with the *gender role distribution* in society through which the agenda of gender socialization is implemented. Women in every society are socialized and indoctrinated towards a set of roles and since these roles are different for the men and women, they are termed as gender roles. Individual choice does not get any priority usually for the selection of gender roles. Gender (being a social and cultural construct) roles are always fixed by the society through family in conformity with the gender ideology of a given society. So, gender role is the societal expectations of what the man or the woman should do or how should they behave in society in conformity with their sex at birth. Different societies have different sets of norms

---

[44] Susan Wadley, "Woman and the Hindu Tradition," in *Women in Indian Society*, ed. Rehana Ghadially, 24.

[45] de Beauvoir, *The Second Sex*, 97.

for activities of the men and women, and according to the degree of the level of cultural achievement and style of thinking and also according to the economic and technological advancement of that society, men and women are expected to perform their roles in conformity with the gender stereotypes of that society. Most often the men or women choose the roles which are in some way or another related to their genders and their performance of those roles are approved by the gender ideology of the given society. Gender stereotypes and gender roles have a cause and effect relationship meaning thereby that gender stereotypes stem from the empirical experiences of gender roles as distributed in the family and outer setting, and gender roles are the practical outcome of the nurturance of gender stereotypes.

There are a number of reasons and grounds that provoke men or women to adopt gender roles in the society. The *first* ground on which gender roles are distributed is the consideration of masculinity or femininity. To be masculine means to perform such roles as are associated with strength or power and in contrast to be feminine means to perform such roles as are associated with emotion or caring attitude. Masculinity highlights male gender and femininity highlights female gender. 'Boys are encouraged and reinforced to develop masculine characteristics (aggression, dominance, independence, sense of adventure and achievement-oriented) whereas girls are encouraged to acquire feminine characteristics (submissive, nurturance, dependence, less achievement-oriented).'[46] It is expected by society that in tune with the masculine or feminine characteristics the men or women will perform their roles in society meaning thereby that their stereotypical representation will motivate and determine their choice of occupations. Thereby boys will be encouraged to take the professions branded masculine such as policeman, sportsman, soldier, etc., and in contrast the girls will opt for the jobs branded feminine such as the job of housewife, nurse, teacher, etc. Since their birth the children experience the distribution of roles in the family along the line of gender. They see father as breadwinner, decision-maker and public spokesman on behalf of the family and they see mother as childbearer, cook or kitchen manager

---

[46] Das and Ghadially, "Parental Sex Role Orientation and Sex Stereotypes of Children," in *Women in Indian Society*, ed. Rehana Ghadially, 124.

and entrusted with the job of childcare. These experiences create a sort of cognitive schema within the minds of the children and they consciously and in their sub-conscious come to imitate the pattern of gender roles performed by their father or mother. Thus it is clear that parents are the primary socializing agents for the children to learn gender roles. 'They (parents) become role models for the children who emulate similar personality characteristics from childhood through observation learning, imitation and mechanisms of identification.'[47] The *second* ground of the gender role distribution is strength consideration which means that gender roles should be distributed according to the physical strength. And accordingly the roles that need more physical strength should be performed by the male and such roles are the job of hunting, tilling, etc. In contrast, the roles that need less physical strength must be performed by the female and these jobs are homecare, childcare and nursing, etc. Clearly it is seen that the basis of strength consideration of gender role distribution is the biological sex of the man and woman. Like the first one, the strength approach is also learnt and adopted in the family. The *third* ground of gender role distribution is the compatibility approach to role performance. This approach suggests that men or women should opt for such jobs as are compatible with their physical and mental configuration. Judged from this angle some jobs are suitable for men and some are for women. Taken the mental make-up of the men in consideration, it can be told that almost in all societies and across all cultures men are comfortable in public exposure whereas the women are comfortable in private area of home. So women must opt for jobs which are either centring round the home or near the home in respect of distance and thus ensure a better mental alignment. In this way, they will also remain in position to tackle the responsibility of childbearing and childrearing. In contrast to the women's roles the men may remain involved in politics and outer economic activities. The *fourth* ground of gender role distribution is functional theory of stratification. According to this theory, all types of works, private or personal and public or political, work within the home or work outside the home, are

---

[47] Alber Bandura and Richard H. Walters, *Social Learning and Personality Development* (New York, NY: Holt, Rinehart and Winston, 1963).

necessary for the continuation of the society. Again, neither all work pays uniformly nor are they possible for the members of both sexes, male and female. So there has been a segregation of works based on gender and men and women are encouraged to do differently, think differently and behave differently. Thus the differential distribution of works is the basic message of the functional theory through which a functional stratification based on gender is shaped in society where male and female are placed for performing different roles in society. Family is the place where the children primarily learn about the functional difference of roles of male and female through the internalization of roles performed by their father or mother. Thus on the basis of these grounds the family successfully participates in the process of gender socialization and comes to play its role in distributing gender roles between male and female in the society.

From the above-mentioned discussion, the role of the family as an agent of gender socialization is established both from theoretical and practical viewpoint. The dynamics of family is rooted not only in the origin and development but also in its changing structures and functions in the face of a challenge of industrialization, modernization, globalization, urbanization and principles of democracy. All these processes have turned the women participation in workforce or politics into a compulsion and the demand of the day. Corporate economy has caused the corporatization of the family also more or less. Exchange of ideas and lifestyle among the states has been possible owing to the advent of globalization. Democracy and the legal arrangements coming out of it have made possible the representation of women from village panchayat to state politics. Thus the impact of these socio-economic changes has produced liberal attitudes towards sex roles throughout the world. Side by side different variables such as education of the parents, socio-economic status and small size are also influencing the dynamics of the family and its role in gender socialization. But in spite of all these challenges from outside, the family is still serving as the most important primary unit of society. The uniqueness of family lies not in its universal existence but in its flexible capacity of assimilating and accommodating the changes occurring all over the world and still remaining the most trustful unit of gender socialization.

Amidst all the changes the standing of family in respect of gender has remained the same. By creating and recreating the techniques, by shaping and reshaping the modes of operation, the family still carries the flag of patriarchy and is devoted to the implementation of the gender ideology of a given society.

5

Role of Peer Group

'The individual is socialized by his equals as well as his elders. In the peer group the individual associates with others who are approximately his own age and social status'.[1] Different agencies participate in the process of gender socialization of which the role of peer group is worthy of mentioning. Peer group is a social group whose members have social position and age in common. Due to the similarity of age and position, the members share in common some ideas about gender among them and willingly or unwillingly become a part of the knowledge so received in respect of gender through the discussion among the peers. Such knowledge includes ideas about gender relation, gender identity, gender stereotypes, gender norm, gender consistency and gender role. Since the knowledge about different aspects of gender is collectively formed and shared in adjustment with the prior information received in the family and shaped in the school, it often conveys more the message of conformity than deviation. Thus the peer group becomes a part of the system and promotes status quo about the gender. In this way, peer group serves as the one important agent of gender socialization.

A peer group is both a social group and a primary group of people who are similar in interests, age, background or social status. The members of this group are likely to influence the person's beliefs and behaviours. But how actually peer group exerts such influence and when or at what stage are the questions the answers of which probably form the theoretical perspectives of the role of peer group especially in gender construction and expression of the boys and girls. In the argument on the role of peer group in gender socialization the theoretical perspectives are meagre. But still we can sort out some theories that guide us towards the exposition of the role of peer group in gender

---

[1] Leonard Broom and Philip Selznick, *Principles of Sociology*, 4th ed. (New York, NY: Harper and Row, 1970), 102.

socialization. The theories which we may refer here are *development psychological theory, group socialization theory* and *adolescence theory.*

Development psychologists, *Lev Vygotsky, Jean Piaget, Erik Erikson, Harry Stack Sullivan* and social learning theorists have all argued that peer relationships provide a unique context for cognitive, social and emotional development. Modern research echoes these sentiments, showing that social and emotional gains are indeed provided by peer interaction.[2]

Development Psychological Theory

Vygotsky's (1896–1934) socio-cultural theory focuses on the importance of a child's culture and notes that a child is continually acting in social interactions with others. He also focuses on language development and identifies the zone of proximal development. The Zone of Proximal Development is defined as the gap between what a student can do alone and what the student can achieve through teacher assistance. The values and attitudes of the peer group are essential elements in learning. Those who surround themselves with academically focused peers will be more likely to internalize this type of behaviour.[3]

Sociocultural theory is an emerging theory in psychology that is prone to locate the development of the child to the social and cultural interaction. Lev Vygotsky, the father of sociocultural theory, believed that like all other agents of gender socialization, peers are also responsible for the social and cultural development of the child both on social and individual level meaning thereby first at the social level of interactions among the people of the society or interpsychological level and second on individual level that happens inside the child or intrapsychological level (Vygotsky 1978). The root of interpsychological and also intrapsychological interactions among the peers lies in the cultural beliefs and

---

[2] Robert Siegler, *How Children Develop, Exploring Child Develop Student Media Tool Kit + Scientific American Reader to Accompany How Children Develop* (New York, NY: Worth Publishers, 2006), 57.

[3] Taken from *Peer Group.* Wikipedia, the free encyclopedia.

attitudes from which peers, either on societal level or on individual level, draw their strength and accordingly come to enforce the socially approved behaviour pattern especially relating to gender. Vygotsky stressed upon the psychological development of the child by language development and by the zone of proximal development which is considered as the most important concept of the sociocultural theory. Vygotsky's language development approach can be substantiated through some observations on our behalf by referring to some other thinkers in this regard especially as regard to gender. As it is known that language uses us as much as we use language. Language is a very important element of culture and serves as a potent weapon of socialization. Language is capable of controlling the thought process of the individual and this process of control through language starts in childhood. In a gender-divided society language is also gender-biased and plays a role in the construction of gender. Narendra Nath Kalia has quoted Vetterling–Braggin to define sexist language:[4]

> A word or sentence is sexist if ... its use creates, constitutes, promotes or exploits an unfair or irrelevant distinction between the sexes ... and if its use contributes to, promotes, causes or results in the oppression of either sex.[5]

This argument of sexist language is very much relevant in the construction of gender in peer group. Peers often develop their psychological orientation of gender through sexist language and in this regard they very often follow the more capable peer friends. Here comes the theory of the zone of proximal development. According to Vygotsky, the zone of proximal development 'is the distance between the actual development level as determined by independent problem solving and the level of potential development as determined through problem-solving under adult guidance or in collaboration with more capable peers'.[6] To put it more simply, capable peer guidance always results in the enforcement of socially approved rules and thus

---

[4] Mary Vetterling-Braggin, (ed.), *Sexist Language: A Modern Philosophical Analysis* (New Jersey: Totowa, Littlefield, Adams, 1981), 3–4.

[5] Narendra Nath Kalia, "Women and Sexism: Language of Indian School Textbooks," in *Women in Indian Society*, 234.

[6] L. Vygotsky, *Thought and Language* (Cambridge, MA: MIT Press, 1986), 150.

Essentially, it includes all of the knowledge and skills that a person cannot yet understand or perform on their own yet but is capable of learning with guidance. As children are allowed to stretch their skills and knowledge, often by observing someone who is slightly more advanced than they are, they are able to progressively extend this zone of proximal development.[7]

Thus the values and attitudes of the peer group are essential elements in learning. Those who surround themselves with academically focused peers will be more likely to internalize this type of behaviour.

Jean Piaget (1896–1980) is also another theoretician of cognitive development theory and he proposed four stages of development such as: sensorimotor, preoperational, concrete operational and formal operational period. *Sensorimotor stage* is the first of the four stages in cognitive development which 'extends from birth to the acquisition of language'.[8]

Piaget's second stage, *the pre-operational stage*, starts when the child begins to learn to speak at age two and lasts up until the age of seven. During the pre-operational stage of cognitive development, Piaget noted that children do not yet understand concrete logic and cannot mentally manipulate information. The *concrete operational stage* is the third stage of Piaget's theory of cognitive development. This stage, which follows the preoperational stage, occurs between the ages of 7 and 11 (preadolescence) years and is characterized by the appropriate use of logic. The final stage is known as the *formal operational stage* (adolescence and into adulthood, roughly ages 11 to approximately 15–20): Intelligence is demonstrated through the logical use of symbols related to abstract concepts.[9]

This form of thought includes 'assumptions that have no necessary relation to reality'.[10] Through the use of Piaget's theory, it is understood as to how the children can develop

---

[7] Retrieved 10 July 2017, from http://www.verywell.com/kendra-cherry-psychology-expert-2794702

[8] Bruce W. Tuckman and M. Monetti David, *Educational Psychology* (Belmont, CA: Wadsworth, 2010), 336.

[9] *Piaget's theory of cognitive development*, from Wikipedia, the free encyclopedia.

[10] Jean Piaget, *The Psychology of Intelligence* (Totowa, NJ: Littlefield, 1972).

their cognition by the assimilation and accommodation of the information received from the peers. Erik Erikson (1902–94), a German psychoanalyst heavily influenced by Sigmund Freud, 'explored three aspects of identity: the ego identity (self), personal identity (the personal idiosyncrasies that distinguish a person from another), social/cultural identity (the collection of social roles a person might play)'.[11] Erik Erikson's psychosocial theory of development considers the impact of external factors, parents and society on personality development from childhood to adulthood. According to Erikson's theory, 'every person must pass through a series of eight interrelated stages over the entire life cycle'.[12] These eight stages are: Infancy: Birth–18 months old, Toddler/Early childhood years: 18 months to 3 years, Preschooler: 3 to 5 years, School age child: 6 to 12 years, Adolescent: 12 to 18 years, Young adult: 18 to 35 years, Middle age adult: 35 to 55 or 65 years and Late adult: 55 or 65 to death. Erikson believed that children develop their orientation about society through psychological process and they come to implement their sense of understanding throughout their life. Almost in all the stages of development, as mentioned by Erikson, peer group plays a significant role in gender construction.

Harry Stack Sullivan (1892–1949) was basically a psychiatrist who stressed the importance of interpersonal connections and developed the theory of interpersonal psychoanalysis. Much of Sullivan's work centred on understanding of interpersonal relationships and Sullivan's interpersonal psychoanalysis suggests that the way people interact with others could provide valuable clues into their mental health and that mental health disorders may stem from distressing interpersonal interactions. Sullivan also believed in the development of personality across the life span. From infancy to adulthood, different types of interpersonal relations influence the children as well as the adult in internalizing the socially accepted norms of behaviour and in so doing the people of all ages especially the children are influenced by the peer group and all such group behaviours

11 E. H. Erikson, *Identity: Youth and Crisis* (No. 7) (New York, NY: W. W. Norton & Company, 1994), 132.

12 E. H. Erikson, *Childhood and Society* (New York, NY: W. W. Norton & Company, 1993), 88.

that exist to the close proximity of them. Sullivan's argument can very well be applied in understanding the process of gender construction and expression.

Group Socialization Theory

Research shows that peers groups should be considered primary in influencing gender construction among children and adolescents. Many have argued that the family exerts the most powerful influence on the development of a child's conception of gender, their gender identity and how they express gender.[13,14] But the role of peer group seems to be neglected in the discussion on gender construction or its expression. Peer group influence begins in preschool and continues as children progress through school and expand their social world. Social influence or the influences of the other agents in gender construction is somehow widely discussed. As compared to those, the discussion on peer group is scanty. Group socialization theory is prone to throw light on this relatively neglected agent of gender socialization. One of the few approaches that explicitly considered the role of peers in personality development is group socialization theory.[15] The theory posits that with children's advancing age, outside-the-home socialization that takes place in peer groups becomes an increasingly important determinant of adolescents' personality development. Group socialization theory focuses on the development of personality and especially gender concern in childhood and adolescents through their entry in different groups most of which are peer dominated. This theory of group socialization also examines the impact of different groups on the behaviour pattern of each other. Research demonstrated that peers tend to resemble each other concerning individual characteristics. This is called homophily and is captured in

[13] P. A. Kaplan, *A Child's Odyssey* (Saint Paul, MN: West Publishing Company, 1991).

[14] J. Santrock, *Child Development*, 6th ed. (Madison: Brown & Benchmark, 1994).

[15] J. R. Harris, "Where Is the Child's Environment? A Group Socialization Theory of Development," *Psychological Review* 102 (1995), 458–89.

the notion, 'birds of a feather flock together'. In early younger age, peers tend to be homogenous in respect of their individual characteristics concerning, age, gender, status etc. the influence of group behaviour is much more strong at that level. But in late childhood, especially teenage and adolescent, peers tend to be segregated on the issue of gender and status.

> For Maccoby, children and adolescents tend to segregate into group of their own gender and age.[16] This homogeneity decreases from middle adolescence on and in adulthood, peer network becomes much more gender-integrated than in adolescence....[17,18] Group socialization theory proposes that siblings who grow up in the same family become different from each other not only because 50% of their genes differ, but also because they belong to different peer groups (Harris 1995).[19]

According to Harris, group socialization theory explains the impact of peer group on gendered personality development mainly by two processes—assimilation and differentiation. Assimilation is the process of internalization of the group norms, beliefs, attitudes and socially approved values. Group psychology consciously or unconsciously guides the children to adopt the gender-specific behaviour and thus to behave like boys or girls as the case may be through their initiation in masculinity or femininity. Differentiation process works for the cause of within-group differences in gendered personality development. For example, in the same peer group girls may follow a separate vocation of gender socialization and thus may differ with boys of that group. Differentiation is the result of segregated group psychology within a same group.

But the question is how the peer group executes the vocation of group socialization? The answer lies perhaps in the fact that

---

[16] E. E. Maccoby, "Gender and Relationships: A Developmental Account," *American Psychologist* 45 (1990), 513–20.

[17] J. D. Lempers and D. S. Clark-Lempers, "A Functional Comparison of Same-sex and Opposite Sex Friendships During Adolescence," *Journal of Adolescent Research* 8 (1993), 89–108.

[18] P. V. Marsden, "Core Discussion Networks of Americans," *American Sociological Review* 52 (1987) 122–31.

[19] Anne K. Reitz, Julia Zimmermann, Roos Hutteman, Jule Specht, and Franz J. Neyer, "Peers and Personality Development," *European Journal of Personality*, Special Issue, 2014.

like family or school, peer group does not represent the hierarchy of inequalities of power and status.

> The individual higher in the hierarchy is believed to have the right to exert influence by virtue of his or her position in the social system, and the individual lower in the hierarchy is believed to have the obligation to comply with the demands that are made.[20]

But a relative equality exists in peer group as the members are almost of the same age and status. So group socialization becomes easily effective in peer group where the children enjoy an apparent freedom of exerting their choice of behaviour especially in respect of gender. Harris observes that peer groups play a major role in children and adolescents' socialization, which goes beyond dyadic relationships (Harris 1995). But it is never the case that the peer group is always a homogenous unit or equal in hierarchy. Since in all societies irrespective of cultures a strict gender division works at the dictates of patriarchy, the male–female, or boy–girl differentiation never allows the group to be homogenous and equal. Thus ultimately group socialization becomes the vocation of executing the differential socialization between men and women. The group pressure, in the form of social influence, manipulates the psychological pattern of gender construction and expression.

Adolescence Theory

Adolescence theory of gender construction is not a new one; it is the reproduction of the theory of cognitive development and gender schema theory and it has also its roots in various types of child development theories and socialization theories. Adolescence is the puzzling period for both boys and girls that starts at the end of childhood and ends in adulthood. The journey from late childhood to adolescence is an amazing time as they face a number of unique developmental challenges including coping with the abrupt changes in their body, controlling their sudden presence of sexual

---

[20] S. Milgram, *Obedience to Authority: An Experimental View* (New York, NY: Harper & Row, 1974), 189.

drives and adopting with slow but steady changes in psychological orientation, setting or resetting new kind of relationships that are often sex-linked and planning their future role either social–familial, or academic and occupational. Over a long period of time all these changes happen and thus the adolescent period is broadly divided into early adolescence, mid-adolescence and late adolescence. 'Adolescence is a period of transition which involves changes in physiological and psychological dimensions. With growth of cognitive skill, interaction with the environment and socialization experience, the sex role behavior of adolescent children gets more strengthened.'[21] Adolescence development is a broad field, encompassing physical as well as intellectual, psychological and emotional growth. Physical growth and changes are easily noticeable and also measurable whereas the other non-physical changes are very much difficult to measure, calculate and understand and thereby the whole process of adolescence development is really complicated for the individual passing through this stage and also for the society to encourage the adolescents to be co-opted with the social norms and practices. The role of peer group in the life of the adolescents is relevant in the formation of gender identity, execution of the gender differences, internalizing the gender stereotypes and adopting the gender roles.

Gender Identity

After the birth of a child, the process of identification with gender begins. At the very beginning child acts by reflex. 'But very soon the instinctive reflex action comes to be replaced by planned action and child's individual choice start being transformed into social choice either by means of consent or by means of coercion.'[22] When identity is studied in association with gender, it falls in the domain of category of gender and identity becomes a matter of categorical formulation and determination.[23]

---

[21] Das and Ghadially, "Parental Sex Role Orientation," in *Women In Indian Society*, 124.

[22] Chattopadhyay, *Fighting Gender Inequality*, 31.

[23] N. Jayaram, *On Civil Society* (New Delhi: SAGE Publications, 2005), 230.

Individual there has no right to challenge. Generally, gender identity is shaped and reshaped through three stage: formation stage, stability stage and adjustment stage. Beginning from the late formation stage at the age of six to seven to the adjustment stage through stability stage, peer group plays an important role in the formation of gender identity which is virtually the private sense of being male or female. In the peer group, adolescent boys and girls view and review the environment, situation and capture data which are scanned and processed in the brain and mind of the child through his experience, observation and inference. Adolescence invites puberty which brings a tremendous change in body and mind of a boy or a girl. For Beauvoir, 'What is happening in this time of unrest is that the child's body is becoming the body of a woman and is being made flesh ... the crisis of puberty supervenes at about the age of twelve or thirteen'.[24] Same is the case of a boy also.

> Puberty gives a muscular change in the body of a boy and offers him a huge physical power the source of which, as believed by the boy, is his gender which for him is the gift of nature and the construction of society. So during puberty abrupt change occurs and a challenge for maintaining a physic-psychic parallelism comes to both the boy and girl. In conformity with this crisis and crisis management identity seekers of both sexes are given a relative autonomy and freedom to get their identity shaped and reshaped and adjusted.[25]

Peer group gives the scope of such relative adjustment and freedom. But that relative freedom of adjustment is never a denial of the social norms. Gender identity even adjusted is positively the portrayal of masculinity or femininity. For woman, as Beauvoir remarks, 'at any rate she must be also a woman; she must not lose her femininity'.[26] Thus identification of gender is considered as a good step for gender socialization. The more the identification of gender will be smooth for the boys and girls, the more the gender ideology will come to dominate the society.

---

[24] de Beauvoir, *The Second Sex*, 314–16.
[25] Chattopadhyay, *Fighting Gender Inequality*, 35.
[26] de Beauvoir, *The Second Sex,* 309.

Gender Differences

Early occurring biological factors—genes and pre-natal hormones—affect gender differentiation in adolescence in several ways. 'Hormones can encourage aggression among boys'[27] and oppositely can influence the adolescent girls for suddenly being body-conscious and can often lead to inferiority and depression and inspire them to internalize the feminine traits such as sentimentality, subservience, domesticity and submissiveness in order to come out of this awkward pubertal situation. Perception on gender differences first start with physical changes during adolescence but as soon as the adolescents try to combat the pubertal challenge and try to adopt with the broader society in compliance with these changes, the question shifts from physical differences to mental differences such as abilities, interests, attitudes and traits. 'Apart from males' greater physical strength and females' ability to bear children, there are few sex differences in adolescents' abilities.'[28] Adolescent girls, especially due to their continuous effort of being woman as per the standard of the society, are prone to remain averse to competition, choose easier task being secluded in home and engage themselves to relationship activities such as sewing, housekeeping or babysitting, etc., in contrast, adolescent boys prefer public exposure, object-oriented jobs or occupation. Regarding attitudes, adolescent girls prefer same sex peer relationships mainly due to two reasons: one, by segregating and confining them in female peer groups girls want to hide their suddenly appeared inferiority complex and build a self-defence mechanism for combating the possible physical, that is, sexual attacks from the adolescent boys who either by nature or by social and cultural initiation become aggressive, violent, defiant, insubordinate, bold, self-styled and eager for developing intimate relation with the girls; two, same sex peer preferences of girls are also due to the social and cultural compulsion of being 'fully woman' as early as possible. Female

[27] N. L. Galambos, S. A. Berenbaum, and S. M. McHale. "Gender Development in Adolescence," in *Handbook of Adolescent Psychology: Individual Bases of Adolescent Development* (3rd ed.), eds R. M. Lerner and L. Steinberg, Vol. 1 (Hoboken, NJ: John Wiley & Sons), 305–57.

[28] Ibid.

peers work as group counsellors for internalizing the vocation of femininity and help each other for being easily accepted in a patriarchal society. 'Popular boys tend to be athletic, funny, defiant and daring; popular girls tend to be attractive (and thin), snobby and cliquish.'[29,30,31] In short, during adolescence the differences between boy and girl, either in body or mind, become the basis of gender differences.

Gender Stereotypes

Gender stereotypes are the stereotypical (fixed) expectations and beliefs regarding role performances of different genders.

> In a gender divided society there are broadly two genders—masculine and feminine. There may be other genders like gay, transgender etc. which are not included in this discussion as because they are beyond the conventional format of gender division in society. So when a readymade concept of gender role is presented from the viewpoint of gender ideology then stereotypical sex role attitude develops. Learning of sex role is very important for successful operation of gender socialization. So from the very beginning of socialization of the children, sex role ideology is brought before them and they are inspired to learn different sex role in conformity with their biological sex.[32]

Gender role

Gender role, judged from the gender point of view, is father's role, mother's role, husband's role and wife's role and so on. Since the

---

[29] David G. Perry and Rachel E. Pauletty, "Gender and Adolescent Development," *Journal of Research on Adolescence* 21(1) (2011), 61–74.

[30] L. M. Closson, "Status and Gender Differences in Early Adolescents' Descriptions of Popularity," *Social Development* 18 (2009), 412–26.

[31] A. J. Rose, G. G. Glick, and R. L. Smith, "Popularity and Gender: The Culture of Boys and Girls." In *Popularity in the Peer System*, eds A. H. N. Cillessen, D. Schwartz, and L. Mayeux (New York, NY: Guilford Press, 2011), 103–22.

[32] Chattopadhyay, *Fighting Gender* Inequality, 35–36.

birth of the child, he/she is taught to capture the role acquisition theory as soon as possible through internalization of the very spirit of gender ideology. In order to give a sort of legitimacy to gender inequality, stakeholders of the society are socialized into gender roles of father, mother, husband, wife, son and daughter. Male individual at first enters into the role of husband who, after the birth of his children, acquires the role of father. The case of female individual is all the same. So the basic ideology remains the same for husband, father and son or wife, mother and daughter and some basic postulates of such ideology are –

1. Male i.e. man is by nature the master of the family. This role can be properly played by discharging the responsibilities of husband and father or by supporting his wife and family.
2. Again the role of wife and mother is complementary. A woman can claim total development of her personality only by performing the role of wife and mother. Wife again can be complete only by taking care of her husband and children.
3. Woman can only be mother as because power of mothering is bestowed by nature to woman. So being mother is not only a stage of her life but mothering is her fate and her consequence.
4. Woman's primary role is in the home and all secondary roles, by all means, will never be performed at the cost of home and family. So woman's social roles are always determined in conformity with her sex and gender.[33]

Peer group in early, mid- or late adolescence indoctrinates the peer boys and girls to cope up with this gender ideology and thereby play a significant role in transmitting the curriculum of gender socialization. Thus we get a clear picture, through different theoretical models, as to how peer group becomes a weapon of gender socialization and resultant gender inequality. Through the rites, rituals and vows which the female peers practice or perform in a group or through the play and games in which the male or female peers participate separately according to their gender or through the choice of curriculum or stream of education by the boys and girls, peer influence guide both sexes towards the enforcement and conformity to the patriarchal gender ideology as a result of which gender socialization can operate very smoothly.

---

[33] Chattopadhyay, *Fighting Gender Inequality*, 38–39.

Peer group is a unique group included in the list of the agents of gender socialization in the sense that it is formed by the equals and influences the equals. It also enjoys a kind of autonomy and at least apparently a free space which is not possible to enjoy either in the family or in the school. That apart, it works in a domain which is not ruled by any official dictation. The unique nature of the peer group is evident by some unique characteristics of peer group which are as follows:

1. *Impersonal authority*:[34] The child was already introduced with the idea of authority in the family and school through the orders passed by their parents or teachers. The authority was personal there. But now, in the peer group, the child is introduced with such an authority which is not personal and solely based on the rules of the game or the general rules of the discussion. 'In the play group, the child learns to obey the impersonal rules of the game ... and to develop a concept of justice which is applicable to all.'[35] In family and also in school the child was always under the care and watch, but in the peer group he enjoys a type of careful neglect which prompts him/her to form any opinion free of the jurisdiction of the family and school. 'In time he himself becomes a representative of law and order; he conceives himself as a protector of the rules, and exercises social control over playmates who break them.'[36] In family and school the child learns all about gender compulsorily and coercively through gender socialization which is all the more imposed and dictated. Accordingly, the child's response to gender is strictly controlled and no individual choice is accepted there. Connell observes that gender socialization 'invites the child to participate in social practice on given terms. The invitation may be, and often is, coercive accompanied by heavy pressure to accept and no mention of an alternative....'[37] Giddens observes,

---

[34] Ibid, 103.

[35] Jean Piaget, *The Moral Judgement of the Child* (London: Kegan Paul, 1932).

[36] Broom and Selznick, *Principles of Sociology*, 103.

[37] R. W. Connell. *Gender and Power: Society, the Person and Sexual Politics* (Cambridge: Polity Press, 1987).

'[a]ccording to this functionalist view, socializing agencies contribute to the maintenance of social order by overseeing the smooth gender socialization of new generations'.[38] In contrast, peer group does not overlook the independent opinion of the children of new generations regarding gender. The participation of the child through peer group is spontaneous. The learning of gender in peer group is more optional and more or less is based on consensus emerged out of the discussion within the group. 'The peer group provides an alternative to adult standards and adult authority.'[39] So peer group offers a space of individual judgment, rejection or modification of the gender norms and practices. Thus remaining free from the direct jurisdiction of authority of the family and school, peer group gives the scope of independent application of the gender perception to the child and by this way the child is indoctrinated to the gender ideology afresh and independently which turns the process of gender socialization from a regimented to a spontaneous one.

2. *Transmission of adult values:*[40] In the family, the children were under the strict control of the parents or any other senior male guardian. But in the peer group, they are apparently free from any external control which may force them to pass opinion or judgment. The children perform the same socializing role in the peer group. They often criticize their adult guardians freely in the peer group for their role in enforcing gender norms and practices coercively. Different aspects of gender are reviewed there in the peer group which may be apparently taken as deviation than conformity so far as the gender ideology and patriarchal structure of a given society are concerned. 'It is important to remember that humans are not passive objects or unquestioning recipients of gender programming....'[41] In family the children cannot express their discontent and objections

[38] Giddens, *Sociology,* 108.
[39] G. Handel, *Childhood Socialization* (New York, NY: Aldine de Gruyter, 1988), 17.
[40] Broom and Selznick, *Principles of Sociology,* 103.
[41] Giddens, *Sociology,* 108.

of gender norms and practices due to the regimentation and authoritative atmosphere developed in tune with the iron rule of patriarchy. So peer group is the safe place for the children where they can ventilate their anger, agony and desire in respect of gender related issues. It is not the case that the child members of the peer group always tend to be deviated and opt for doing something different than what is going on in the name of gender. Since collective opinion endorses the status quo most of the time, the peer group naturally becomes the positive participant of the process of gender socialization. The peer group criticize the gender norms and practices and at the same time the group also sponsors the support for gender ideology, gender norms and practices and gender socialization. In performing both the roles the peer group proceeds with the judgment and consideration which are expected from the adult members only. Thus through the peer group, the transmission of adult values become possible.

3. *Discipline and loyalty:* In peer group, the children learn the gender related discipline and loyalty to the patriarchy. The group members are acquainted with the 'rules of the game' which infuse a sense of discipline within them. The sense of discipline grown up through the interactions, discussions and participations in different games prompts them to judge the issue of gender from the angle of discipline. Their cognitive sense and experience also inspire them to judge the merit and demerit of the gender norms and practices. Most of the peer group members step to conformity than deviation and offer preferences to status quo than to instability of the gendered structure of society. So the preferences for status quo and adherence to conformity result in accepting the gender norms and practices sponsored by gender ideology of a given society and thus ultimately the role of peer group leads to the reinforcement of gender discipline, that is, the adoption of gendered behaviour and the continuation of the tradition of gender identity formation. In this way, by assimilating the gender norms and practices in a disciplined method, the peer group actually conforms to the rules of patriarchy which always aims at producing loyal members who will

reconstruct them through social and cultural norms of gender learnt by gender socialization.

4. *Rewards and punishment:* Like the family the peer group also tries to control the actions and gender behaviour of the peer members through the system of rewards and punishment. 'Like any other socializing agency, the peer group represents a system of rewards and punishment, of approval and disapproval.'[42] For the perfect expression of gender consistency, the members are rewarded which often is limited within encouragement, accompaniment and complements. In contrast, for the deviation from the conventional gender norms, the peer members are always rebuked, boycotted and socially marginalized. Since the peer group promotes the conventional gender norms and practices with a view to encourage gender socialization and accordingly the status quo in the society, it rejects those gender deviations that disrupt and deny the gender ideology of a given society. With a view to maintaining the status quo in gender norms and behaviour, the peer group encourages the peer members for gender consistent behaviour through the system of rewards. Oppositely, for the expression of gender inconsistency of the members, the peer group resorts to punishment of the deviating members.

5. *Source of information:* The peer group serves as the potent source of information about gender and sexuality. In family, first, due to the age and status gap between the parents and the children, it is not possible to get the age-wise information about sex and gender especially during adolescence. Second, the family is a closed and authoritative organization and henceforth, the system of the exchange of opinion in respect of gender and sex is strictly prohibited there. Third, in traditional society issues related to gender and especially sex is not openly discussed particularly in the presence of the children. So there is a least room to share the experiences of sex with the adults in the traditional family. The peer group fills the gap there very successfully. Among the peers different types of sexual experiences are

---

[42] Broom and Selznick, *Principles of Sociology*, 103.

shared and also their opinion about the gender, its norms and practices, techniques of the expression of gender identity, conventional modes of identity formation, role of family and school and their experiences about them, etc., are exchanged among the peer members. Male–female relation, teenage love, experiences of adolescence, physical changes of boy and girl etc. are the popular items of peer discussion. Since the peer group consists of the members of the same age, status and background, it becomes easy for them to come open with their views during the informal discussion about sex and gender. Patriarchy represents the sex and gender from a specific angle of values, family coercively distributes these values among the members and the peer group independently assimilates these values spontaneously. Thus through the discussion among the peers in respect of sex and gender, some form of gender orientation is achieved which ultimately leads them to shape and reshape their identity afresh, to adopt the gender consistent norms and behaviour and to respond to the agenda of gender socialization. But the problem is that the peer group does not always work for the conformity and for the positive development of gender psychology. Many a negative attribute of the peer group cause severe problems often in respect of sex and gender. First, since the peer group mentioned here is mainly the group consisting of the teenage and adolescent boys and girls, it is quite natural that their opinions and experiences are most often immature and romanticized. So gender feedback received through peer group may not tally with what the gender is in reality. Resultant frustration emerging out of the mismatch between imagination and reality may cause severe problem to the future psychological development of the children especially in the field of sex and gender. Second, information received through the peer members is, in most of the cases, prejudiced, hearsay based and unfounded and speculative in nature. As a result, the self-constructed structure of gender socialization based on that gossip-linked and groundless knowledge about gender and sex results, in many ways, in negative socialization which hampers the smooth running of sex and gender oriented activities and relationships of the society. The interrelationships of gender, the nature and implication of sexuality and the approach to the issues related to both of them become either understated or overstated and as a result peer group as a socializing agency comes in direct conflict with the system of gender socialization of the family and the school. Third, peer group often becomes involved in pressurized socialization. When any member is pressurized to behave in matters of sex and gender against his/her spontaneous consent and participatory attitude, then it is termed as 'pressurized socialization'. In most of the cases, this type of peer pressure does not yield any positive result for gender socialization. The degree and intensity of participation in social processes linked to sex and gender becomes very low and feeble. The resultant frustration may often lead to personality disorder and adjustment problem of the peers against whom such pressure was exerted.

Thus the attributes of peer groups, expose and present the potentiality of the groups in performing the societal role of gender socialization. It is not the case that the role of peer group is uniformly effective in the life of all teenagers and adolescent boys and girls. It is not also the case that peer group is always beneficial or harmful for the members in the same scale. It has also been noticed that due to the lack of influence of peer group in a peer's life, the personality has not been developed in the optimum way and level. Again, the opposite of this has also been noticed to be repeated in a number of ways in a number of cases. So it is finally the conglomeration of the attributes, both positive and negative, in a certain degree and intensity that establish the relevance of the peer group as a socializing agency. With the help of these aforementioned attributes, both positive and negative, the children, that is, the peer members come to play the necessary role in the process of gender socialization. The role performed by the peer group in this regard can be analysed from the three angles: formation of *gender stereotypes, formation of gender identity and gender role distribution.*

Gender stereotypes are the fixed notions about the values, norms and attributes related to the gender and such stereotypes guide the male or female gender to the absorption of these notions in such a way so that the persons belonging to the male or female gender can become the representatives of the collective formulation of masculinity or femininity. Expressions of gender stereotypes are often the over generalizations of the traits and attributes of a group, such as male or female, based on gender since the stereotypes are not usually formed on accurate information of the group, rather they are based on biased information and prejudiced approach to the categories of gender. As a result stereotypes may be negative also and it is these negative gender stereotypes that give birth to gender inequality and gender discrimination. Gender stereotypes are born out of the cultural legacy of a society, its style of thinking and habits and behaviours practised year after year. Thus it is the result of a long process operated and continued by a number of agents such as family, school, media and peer group.

Gender stereotypes, formed and shaped by peer group, are commonly associated with the formation of traits, preferences, habits, behaviours and styles. Masculine traits and feminine traits are the common traits that are shaped in peer group and they are believed to be dominating the other elements of stereotypes. In family, after viewing the expressions of father and mother, the children primarily come to form the notion of masculinity and femininity. When these children join in peer group, they become the agents of these traits and represent them consciously. One of the important attributes of the peer group is that it inspires gender segregation among peers. Boys tend to interact with the boys and girls with the girls. Resultant gender segregation does not keep the peer group coherent, monolithic and uniform in its structure and nature. That the peers prefer for sub-groups emerged as a result of segregation based on gender is due to the fact of inherent feeling of acceptance of masculinity or femininity which are inculcated in the peers in a number of ways. First, in the peer group as a whole, the boys tend to present them through the expression of the qualities of domination, leadership ability, heroism, smartness, ambition and manliness. In contrast, the girls tend to present them through the qualities of submissiveness, softness, sexual attractiveness, tolerance and womanliness. Boys with masculinity are not only applauded by the male peers but also by the female peers. Likewise, the girls with femininity are not only accepted by the female peers but also by the male peers. Masculinity is not always the matter of the boys, that is, male but it is also the concern of the girls, that is, female because it is the masculinity that puts the other version of it before the female which is conceived as femininity. So is the case of femininity which remains a concern not only of the female but also of the male. The clear message of such mutuality of concerns is that the traits of masculinity or femininity are never individual-based but they are social or cultural constructions, and accordingly they are learnt through many social groups of which peer group is one important group. Second, peers learn as well as inspire the mates for the learning of the masculinity or femininity traits simply because of the fact of their cognitive experiences that doing and being gender in tune with the conventional outlook about gender will make their position and existence comfortable and the opposite of it will pose a challenge to the patriarchy, the organized strength of which may dismantle their position and threaten the survival. So from the early childhood the child, at the instruction of the schema, resolves to learn the gender stereotypes fixed for the respective category of gender, that is, male or female. In the primary stage of stereotypical assimilation, the children judge the gender from the viewpoint of the assigned sex at birth. But in course of time, when they come in a position to decode the gender language and gender association involved with the norms and practices, they become acquainted with the social and cultural aspect of gender and this development happens in peer group. Since peer group members are guided by the sociocultural norms and practices of the gendered society as a whole, they emphasize in their interactions more about conformity than deviation. The inner psychology behind this tendency is that conformity to gender norms gives an apparent guarantee of protecting the existing status of gender and deviation to gender may be a threat to this status quo. Accordingly, peers, belonging to male or female, work for the 'retention of gender space' in lieu of getting a romantic and rebellious rejection of their present space. Peer group plays a vital role in preaching the idea of 'retention of gender space' among the peers in accordance with their biological sex at first and also in accordance with their social gender. Third, it has been noticed by the researchers that gender inconsistency is disapproved and discouraged by the peer group. Gender inconsistency is the result of the symptom of the rejection of gender stereotypes. So when a boy is not sufficiently manly or when he disappears from the conventional and major characteristics of masculinity, he is often rebuked by the peers as feminine and thus he is usually secluded so that his feminine characteristics do not influence other members of the group. Likewise, when a girl behaves like a boy, then she is presented as 'tomboy', the association of whom is often avoided due to the threat of punishment by the society in general and by the peer group in particular.

> Since feminine traits are negatively valued it would follow that women tend to have more negative self-concepts than do men. A woman is faced with a contradiction. Since having masculine traits is more desirable in this culture, if she wishes to be feminine she risks being an inferior human being. On the other hand, if she adopts the desirable masculine traits in order to become more acceptable, she gives up being the socially sanctioned nice feminine woman which may damage her self-image.[43]

So peer pressure plays an important role in enforcing the gender norms and practices in general and the traits of masculinity and femininity in particular. 'It is more acceptable among children's peer groups for girls to be tomboys than for boys to be sissies.'[44]

Gender stereotypes also influence the shaping of preferences, habits, behaviours and styles of the boys and the girls. Preference for a value or a job is usually given by the boys and girls in tune with the gender stereotypes they have inherited in the family and faced in the peer group. A boy will give the preference of a football or magic cube as toys whereas a girl will tick for doll or kitchen items. Habit is called the second nature of human being, and accordingly habits emerge out of the innate mental construction of male or female. Gender stereotypes line up the mental construction in conformity with the gender ideology

---

[43] Manisha Roy, "Concept of Femininity and Liberation," in *Women in Indian Society*, 142.

[44] P. Kaplan, *A Child's Odyssey* (Saint Paul, MN: West Publishing Company, 1991), 101.

of the given society. In peer group the boys and girls get a free scope of practising such habits. The habits regarding talking, taking food, mannerism and especially complying with the gender time and gender space, etc., all are governed by the rules of stereotypes. Behaviours are strictly formed in accordance with the stereotypical reality of the traditional society. Gender stereotypes teach the boys to be loud, dominating, practical, and instantly connection-oriented and exposed in public whereas the girls are encouraged to be soft, tacit, submissive, caring, emotional and relationship-oriented and convenient in private area like home. Behaviours are often expressed through the interactions among persons and such interaction is ruled by gender stereotypes. Styles are the functional and expressional representations of gender stereotypes. Stereotypes, meant for boys, are often directed towards a pattern of styles which are different in nature than the styles followed in case of the girls. Styles include fashion which is often expressed through dress. Differences of dress are primarily made on the basis of difference of gender. In almost all the countries of the world, dress has a gendered version and accordingly males are fond of dresses which are not the preferences of the females. The cause behind this is that gender stereotypes encourage the boy or a girl to choose dress in tune with the sex assigned at birth in particular and with the social and cultural codes of gender in general. In this way, stereotypes become a part and parcel of human life and come to influence the shaping of beliefs, values, habits, behaviours and styles with a view to sharply divide a given society into social male or social female. Gender ideology inspires the formation of stereotypes and in turn gender stereotypes lead to the formation of masculinity or femininity. Biological sex makes man or woman but it is gender that makes those men or women as masculine or feminine. Society and culture makes the gender which is reinforced by gender stereotypes. Thus through the system of rewards and punishment, approval and disapproval and sanction and coercion, the peer group creates, shapes and reshapes the gender stereotypes that ease the process of gender socialization.

Formation and shaping of *gender identity* is the next job done by the peer group in order to put its contribution in the process of gender socialization. According to modern sociologists, 'within a society at particular point of time, individuals come to adopt gender-specific behavior, attitudes and dispositional traits through process of socialization and allocation that perpetuate gender role differentiation'[45] and the process by which the gender consciousness of the child are shaped in the expected way are termed as gender identity formation. The process of gender indoctrination starts since birth of a child who with his/ her growing up is encouraged to behave like a boy or a girl as suitable and as will match perfectly with biological sex assigned at birth. So the formation of a male or female infant in tune with the stereotyped sex role and their ultimate acquisition of the role of father or mother are termed as gender identity formation. So it may be argued that gender socialization is the method of imparting the notion of differential identity formation within the child by which the gender ideology of a given society is legitimized. As children develop friendships with both same-sex and opposite-sex peers, they continue to develop new ideas and receive reinforcement of previously learned ideas

The role of peer group starts in the age of gender consolidation when the child is perfectly conscious about the gender. In peer group subjective idea of gender is tested, practised and shared by the peer with another mates. Primarily at this stage the peer members are guided by two distinct objectives: one, testing the strength of gender identity thus achieved prior to their entry in the peer group and two, daring to expose the weakness of such identity by forming their own rules of behaviour in the peer group. In order to proceed for testing the strength of gender identity, the peers often notice that their behaviours towards consistency and conformity are generally approved and applauded by their peer mates. Their habits, values, styles and mannerisms coming out of their sense of gender identity are usually accepted and shared by the peers.

> When children are at play, it may seem as if they are engaged in aimless, unstructured behavior, but there is something much deeper than that going on, as indicated by these functions. The first function suggests that behaviors are tried out on friends, and if they are rewarded, they will continue; if not, they will cease. Thus, the little boy who enjoys having tea parties with his teddy

---

[45] Borgatta and Cook, *The Future of Sociology*, 134.

bears and is jeered at or otherwise discouraged from this activity by friends who call it sissy behavior will probably stop engaging in this type of play.[46]

Opinion of the peer mates is very important for an adolescent boy or girl as peers are of the same age group, same status group and same background and accordingly, unlike the family and school, there is no power element in the opinion passed by the peers. Peers' opinion is spontaneously received by the boys and girls and since at the adolescent age a drastic change occurs in the body and mind of the boys and girls, the physic–psychic parallelism gets disturbed temporarily as a result of which adolescent children suffer from a physical and mental crisis. The support of the peers is considered as a potent sedative by which children come out of the crisis in due time. A child's social interaction with persons of his or her own age is a highly significant socialization factor (Handel 1988). Peers are the representative of their mental situation especially at the time of adolescence. It is deliciously satisfying to children to find that they have control over and input into their world. Through the making up of rules for games and activities, the receiving of immediate feedback from friends, and the understanding that peers have standards which may be different from adults, children move towards a further understanding of self. Taking the role of the generalized other within one's peer group means the child develops an understanding that the views and beliefs of other folks are important and are salient to the child's own sense of self (Handel 1988; Mead 1934). Thus the gender identity which was formed much before the access to peer group is more or less valued by the children since major part of it is endorsed by the peers. 'Feedback from friends on gender appropriate behaviors and attitudes is important to children, and children seek out same sex friends because of their need to establish gender identity.'[47] Thus the positive aspect of the gender identity is reinforced by the peer group and like all other agents peer group also participates in the process of gender socialization as a faithful agent.

---

[46] Susan D. Witt, "The Influence of Peers on Children's Socialization to Gender Roles," *Early Child Care and Development* 162(1) (2000), 1–7.

[47] Beal, *Boys and Girls*, 166.

As the boy or the girl grow up and become teenagers the gender consistency achieved in the mid-time span of the formation of gender identity often receives a blow from the teenagers consciously or unconsciously by their so-called inconsistent behaviour of breaking the social norms of gender. In all societies sometimes the teenagers of both sexes are seen to be displaying the behaviour diametrically opposite in manner in terms of his/her gender. The gender inconsistent behaviour is the result of the child's programme of testing the viability and the weakness of the gender identity so far achieved through other agents prior to the access to peer group. Incidence of gender inconsistency happens especially during adolescence when drastic changes occur in the body and mind of the children of the sexes, male and female and resultant disturbance of physic–psychic parallelism prompts the children to disobey rather than obey the rules. During adolescence and puberty, it is the natural urge for the boys and the girls to locate and relocate them in an ideological setting which will come to channelize their suddenly achieved physical strength and rapture of emotions in the mental field with a better alignment so that they succeed in rescuing the disturbed and lost physic–psychic parallelism. If the gender ideology of the given society is not sufficiently flexible as to deal with these so called symptoms of gender inconsistency, the child members of the peer group tend to judge it as incompatible to their sudden physical and mental change. So, first, the so-called deviation to gender norms and practices is their effort to have a progressive set of gender norms and practices compatible with their physical and mental change during adolescence and puberty. By challenging the traits of gender identity, they actually present them as reviewers of the system of identity formation. Any type of inconsistency can be revised and accordingly gender inconsistency posed by some peer group members can never be a permanent threat to gender identity so far as the psychology of the growing children of drawing attraction of the adult members is concerned. So these incidents may be termed as the representations of 'angry generation' in lieu of gender inconsistency. Second, it has been noticed that gender inconsistency is the result of inadequate socialization of the boys and the girls and they come to express their inconsistent behaviours and attitudes through peer group. Since peer group consists of the members of same age group, same status group and same background, the deviating boys and the girls feel free to disrupt the result of gender identity acquired so far. Inadequate socialization stems out of the misfit psychological situation in which the child was reared in early infancy when the child experienced a bitter relation between father and mother often embroiled with violent behaviours exercised by both father and mother or by one of them, recurrent quarrel with frequent use and exchange of erotic slangs to each other or illicit relation maintained by both or one of them. This unhealthy atmosphere has a serious implication in the psychological development of the child. The child reared in such an unhealthy atmosphere suffers mostly from personality disorder and they fail to be developed with an integrated gender identity. Since the parents of the child could not provide any hints for primary development of gender identity and since they (parents) themselves were a threat to the ideal family situation, the child become confused in developing the subjective perception of what and how he/she is and that is why the child comes to challenge the gender norms and practices in the peer group where he/she is relatively free to express the opinion and where there is nobody to arrest him/her. In such a situation the deviant child needs psychological counseling which is best possible by the peers especially by the peer of opposite sex. Such cases of gender inconsistency noticed in the peer group may be called as the incidents of the patients of 'mental lag'. Third, it has been noticed that often the late-teenage members of the peer group become engaged in such behaviours which suggest that they are prone to revalue and scrutinize their identity by expressing a mixed form of gender norms, attitudes and practices of male and female. Some peer members challenge the prevalent version of masculinity by presenting its content in the structure of femininity. They may be cross-dresser and cross fashioned. The peer male may keep long hair, may use earrings and bracelets and may opt for a dress-style which is primarily meant for female. Likewise, a peer female may present herself all the more in masculine styles. She may wear male dress from top to bottom (this has been already accepted even in traditional societies) or she may move in broad daylight in a free dress like Bermuda or short-shirt. The male peer behaves in this way because of his desire to have a better version of masculinity which does not treat the female as other but accommodates them. In case of female peer the reason is different. Adolescent girls pose a masculine behaviour chiefly because of drawing attraction of other peers. This seems to indicate that masculine behaviours are valued more highly by children. Because masculine behaviours are indicators of higher self-esteem in children than feminine behaviours, this may indicate that the cultivation of an androgynous orientation may be particularly beneficial for girls.[48] News flashed in both print and electronic media report often that late-teenage and adult peers are engaged in kissing and hugging in public either in a fest mood of valentine day or as a mark of protest of over restrictions of gender norms. There may be another reason for this deviant attitude of the peer boys and girls. According to Broom and Selznick,

> Within the peer group the child tests the limits of adult tolerance with reduced fear of parental reprisal. Children in groups often behave more provocatively toward adults.... At the same time, the child tests the extent to which his peers will go in defying the adult world and the degree to which he can rely on peer support.[49]

So this type of gender inconsistency is not actually the complete deviation to gender norms and practices. The peer engaged in such expressions of behaviours may be termed as the preachers of 'a redefined gender identity'.

Gender role socialization is one important function that the peer group performs along with other agents of gender socialization. Gender role is a set of functions and behaviours that are socially accepted as appropriate for the individual of specific sex in tune with level of culture at specific historic periods. Gender roles have two essential elements: sex differences, that is, roles based on biological differences and roles based on sociocultural expectations. Peer group plays an important role in indoctrinating the boys and the girls to these two types of roles. Boys and girls learn the gender roles in the family and school but there the learning was indoctrinated on command whereas in the peer group the gender role socialization is indoctrinated by the friends of the

---

[48] S. L. Bem, "Gender Schema Theory: A Cognitive Account of Sex Typing," *Psychological Review* 88 (1981), 354–64.

[49] Broom and Selznick, *Principles of Sociology*, 103.

same level, same age group, same status and same background. So the role of peer group in gender role socialization is supposed to be more spontaneous than other agents of gender socialization.

The child forms the gender identity much before the time when the child enters in the peer group where the child develops and shares the independent interactive version of *sex differences* between male and female. Peer group is no coherent and integrated whole. It is also constrained by so many matters like sex and gender. Peer members are already conscious about the physical signs of the human body. So on the basis of these biological signs of the body, they come to form sub-group within the peer group. Based on sex differences gender segregation is made in the peer group. Peer group usually breaks into two groups of opposite sexes: boys' group and girls' group. Thus gender segregation makes the peers more alert about the differences of sex which again is established through a number of ways. First, peers perceive the fact of gender differences through sex differences. For them, sex differences are expressed mainly through two diametrically opposed traits: masculine traits and feminine traits. Since roles are closely linked with traits, boys and girls members of the peer group resolve to nourish the traits necessary for the discharge of social functions of the male and female gender respectively. Boys tend to acquire the qualities linked to masculinity and these are aggression, ambition, loudness, toughness, domination and authority. Likewise girls tend to be soft, submissive, loyal, tolerant and caring and all others qualities which are necessary for childrearing and home management. Through sports, gossip and varieties of interactions, the peer group inspire the members to internalize the traits suited for his/her sex role. Segregation of sports on the basis of sex is the important means of indoctrinating traits suitable for gender roles. Second, power approach makes the biological differences an important determinant of gender role distribution. Peer boys and girls face a dramatic change in their body and mind during adolescence and puberty. So far as the change is concerned, boys take it as signs of physical power whereas the girls often take it as a step to mental development. Based on such assessment, boys prefer to choose jobs which are associated with physical power and the girls, in contrast, prefer to jobs which will have a better mental alignment with their sex and physical strength. Third, biological differences come to influence the occupational differences. Peer culture is the potent source of nourishing ambition. Through various discussions, interactions, and opinion-sharing during tuition-taking, class note-sharing and submission of applications, peers come to share information about different occupations suited to their sex at birth and also the social gender. It is noticed that boys tend to opt for being engineers, doctors, sportsman, soldiers and businessman. In contrast, girls tend to be mostly teacher, nurse, house-wife, stenographer and data entry operator. Thus biological differences direct the gender role distribution in a conventional format as dictated by the gender ideology of a given society.

Social and cultural expectations also influence the gender role distribution of a society. Gender is a social and cultural construct. Society and culture is inextricably linked with the concept of gender roles which are all about what society and culture of a given society demands from individuals of different genders, that is, male and female. Peer group comes to shape firstly, the gendered role as male and female. Boys and girls imbibe very clearly their future destination as gender and they start rehearsing the roles of adult male and female as the case may be. With a view to performing the future sex roles, the boys and girls prepare themselves for the role acquisition of good son, loyal brother, dominating husband and authoritative father. Likewise the girls come to adopt the role of caring daughter, loyal sister, submissive wife and tolerant mother. Peer group encourages the boys to adopt a masculine style during their choice of roles and thereby boys tend to be status oriented and focus on roles linked to dominance, instrumental rewards and asymmetry in interactions. In contrast, the girls prefer the connection-oriented roles and focus on personal relationship, cooperation and support during their choice of roles. It is noticed throughout the world that peer boys always prefer to power-related roles or roles linked to physical qualities of power or coercive nature of power especially in traditional societies and accordingly they opt for such gender roles which are linked to the exercise of threats, commands, dictation and domination. Oppositely, the girls do not dare to challenge the power structure of the society. Based on the experiences of the peer girls, gender roles are chosen by the girls. In reality, gender ideology dictates each of the gender to adopt appropriate sex roles in society. So judged from that angle, the gender roles selection is instrumental in nature. Peer girls, in association of their cognitive experiences, come to display the roles that are directed to the nurturance of the values of agreement, cooperation, care and coordination. Since there is always a social pressure exerted from patriarchy for doing and taking gender roles in tune with its rules and norms, peers do not dare to go beyond the patriarchal format in respect of the performing sex roles. Beal argues,

> boys and girls socialize one another into traditional gender role behaviour by punishing those who deviate from gender role-appropriate activities through making critical remarks, abandoning play with the friend who persists in doing something that seems inappropriate, or trying to get the friend to do something else.[50]

Thus through encouragement and discouraging, approval and disapproval and rewards and punishment, the peer group participates in gender role distribution in particular and gender socialization in general.

So from the above-mentioned discussion it is clear that peer group is a potent agent of gender socialization. Based on its attributes, it may be said that peer group is an unique agent as compared to other agents of gender socialization. Since peer group is formed with the members of same age, same status, same background and often same sex, it acts independently and spontaneously. Although it is a fact that under the ideological influence of the patriarchal society, it is hardly possible for any person or any gender to be independent and spontaneous in true sense of the term. Judged from this angle it may be stated that choice and selection of gender role is very much instrumental in nature. But still the relative autonomy of the peer group can hardly be ignored. The independent and relatively free nature of the peer group often poses also a threat to the status quo of the gender position of the society. Peer group is not always directed to the enforcement of positive gender socialization. Very often it comes to enforce the negative gender socialization. Peers' perception of gender stereotypes, gender identity and gender role

---

[50] Beal, *Boys and Girls,* 121.

often inculcates in it biases and assumptions of over-masculinity that results in a blind opposition to the female gender and gender discrimination, gender difference and gender inequality. These negative traits often lead the peer boys to the exercise of physical aggression against the peer girls. The incidents of being sexually harassed, teased, molested and even raped by the peer mates are often reported in both the print and electronic media. It has also been noticed that in the name of challenging the codes and norms of gendered society, the peers (both boys and girls) indulge themselves in promiscuous relationship which ultimately hampers their health both physically and mentally. So it will be wise to study the role of peer group in gender socialization keeping in strict view the positive and negative aspects of the peer group.

6
Role of School

Gender socialization is a process through which the children develop gender awareness from early childhood. There are several groups, organizations and institutions that influence the formation and development of gender awareness and orientations of the boys and girls. They are called the agents of gender socialization. Three main categories of socializing agents are identified and they are primary groups, secondary groups and reference groups. In Chapter 4, the importance of family as primary group has been discussed and it is seen that family is of prime importance in the gender socialization process. But other groups are also influential. School, peer group and media can also shape and reshape the gender perception of the members of the society. The particularities and potentialities of secondary groups and reference groups as other agents of gender socialization should be properly analysed since these agents make the child dynamic in thought and lifestyle and thus influence the gender behaviour. In family, the child forms the gender identity but in the school and peer groups the practical application of the identity perception is made. Since early gender socialization has some benefits and convenience for influencing the mind of the child, the role of school along with the peer groups is certainly worthy of special mention.

Socialization links the individual to collective world and in that sense socialization includes both of the features of individual and collectivity. Gender socialization, being a more focused form of socialization, always manipulates the individual biological feature in order to fulfill the social and environmental expectations. Thereby gender socialization is devoted to the task of directing the differences of biological sex towards the creation of social differences of gender. A preferred definition of gender socialization today is that it refers to 'ongoing, multi-level processes of social expectations, control, and struggle that sustain and subvert gender systems'.[1] In this conceptualization, gender is considered as the characteristic of society, not of individual. Experts agree that nature (i.e., biology) and nurture (i.e., environment) act together in reciprocally causal, interactive ways to produce gender differences.[2] In family, the emphasis is given on biological assignment of sex and the gender identity subsequently developed for interacting in the broader social setting is very much influenced by the sex assigned at birth. Although boys and girls are given the primary training of gender from the angle of social and cultural expectations, the identity and perception of gender formed that way hardly get the scope of practical application in society since the closed atmosphere of the family does not permit much freedom for such practice. But in schools the gender perception so formed can get a scope of wide practical application in a new atmosphere free of the domination of the family. The similarity between family and schools is that both reinforce the gender differences in their own ways. Children learn all gender-related matters such as language, norms, beliefs and values from the parents and other relatives in the family. But

> No modern society can transmit its huge cultural heritage and accumulated knowledge simply on the basis of informal and amateurish socialization through the family and the peer group. Every civilized society therefore has developed highly institutionalized agencies of education which, after primary socialization within the family, take over as the focal socializing agency.[3]

The role of school in socialization is recognized in sociology since the very inception of the discipline. In contrast, the role of family in gender socialization is a new one as a subject. A number of recent sociological studies have revealed that there is ample material and cultural and cognitive factors in the school premise

---

[1] M. Ferree and E. Hall, "Rethinking Stratification from a Feminist Perspective: Gender, Race, and Class in Mainstream Textbooks," *American Sociological Review* 61(6) (1996), 935.

[2] Rebecca Bigler, "The Role of Schools in the Early Socialization of Gender Differences," in *Gender: Early Socialization: Encyclopedia of Early Childhood Development*, ed. L. Martin Carol (Funded by UNICEF, 2014), 14.

[3] Bhattacharyya, *Political Sociology*, 244.

and school systems of education that often serve as a factor of constraint in intellectual development of the students, especially the girl students. The experiences afforded to girls and boys within schools are known to affect gender differentiation both directly, by providing differential skill practice and reinforcement,[4] and indirectly, by providing input that leads children to actively socialize themselves along gender-differentiated pathways. In view of the role of school in creating and reinforcing gender differences between boys and girls, it can be said that school serves as a gender barrier, that is, barrier for the development of the girl students especially. Such gender-biased role of the education may be termed as a gate-keeping function of the educational system which means that it does not allow the access of all but some to education based on gender. The gender-biased role of elementary education has turned the school as a major agent of gender socialization. Schools participate in the process of gender socialization chiefly through three aspects: *formation of gender stereotypes, differential treatment and differential socialization and gender role.*

Gender Stereotypes

Teachers and the textbooks are also sources of learning about various layers and issues of gender. Teachers often present their subjective views and experiences of gender before the students and thus they influence the gender perception of the students. Curriculum materials, that is, textbooks often contain gender stereotypic attitudes and behaviour. 'Children internalize gender stereotypes and prejudices, which in turn guide their own preferences and behaviours.'[5]

Unfortunately, teachers receive relatively little training in recognizing and combating gender stereotypes and prejudices—their

[4] C. Leaper, R. S. Bigler, "Gender," in *Social development: Relationships in Infancy, Childhood, and Adolescence*, eds M. K. Underwood and L. H. Rosen (New York, NY: Guildford Press, 2011).

[5] Bigler, "The Role of Schools in the Early Socialization of Gender Differences," in *Gender: Early Socialization: Encyclopedia of Early Childhood Development*, ed. L. Martin Carol, 14.

own and others—and, as a consequence, teachers often model, expect, reinforce, and lay the foundation for gender differentiation among their pupils. Thus, most schools create and maintain—rather than counteract—traditional gender stereotypes, biases, and differences.[6]

Family is the production unit of the culture and norms as designed by the gender ideology of a given society. But school and the educational institutions as such are the medium of cultural reproduction which refers to the ways in which schools in association with different academic aids help perpetuate social, political and economic inequalities based on gender. Taking the theory of cultural hegemony developed by Gramsci and the theory of cultural reproduction developed by Bourdieu as point of departure, it can be argued that educational system reproduces the ideology of the dominant gender, that is, male gender on the dictates of patriarchy and legitimizes it. So long as the records of the history of development of education are available, it can be stated that the reproduction of gender culture and gender ideology has been the chief job of education, both formal and informal, since their inception and accordingly in all societies and across all cultures education served the cause of patriarchy. Patriarchy always advocates the subservience and subjugation of woman as both natural and functional incident. Education, being the convenient instrument of cultural reproduction, comes to reinforce the message of patriarchy through the formation of gender stereotypes that primarily glorifies the male gender and undermines the position of female gender.

Stereotypes may be described as some fixed beliefs, ideas and notions about gender created by patriarchy and assimilated by the society. 'In fact stereotypes are representative of a society's collective knowledge of customs, myths, ideas, religions, and sciences.'[7] It is within this knowledge that an individual

---

[6] N. P. Stromquist. "The Gender Socialization Process in Schools: A Cross-national Comparison," Paper commissioned for the EFA Global Monitoring Report 2008, *Education for All by 2015: Will We Make It?* (New York, NY: UNESCO, 2007).

[7] Charles Stangor and Mark Schaller, "Stereotypes as Individual and Collective Representations," in *Stereotypes and Stereotyping*, eds C. Neil Macrae, Charles Stangor, and Miles Hewstone (New York, NY: Guilford Press, 1996), 13–44.

develops a stereotype or a belief about a certain group. Gender stereotypes are the notions of gender that are socially created and practised. So when some fixed beliefs and mental ideas about gender become a part of social knowledge then it is called gender stereotypes. As a result of their knowledge, or lack of knowledge, the stereotype has an effect on their social behaviour. A stereotype is defined as an 'unvarying form or pattern, specifically a fixed or conventional notion or conception of a person, group, idea, etc., held by a number of people and allows for no individuality or critical judgment'.[8]

> Traditional gender roles help to sustain gender stereotypes, such as that males are supposed to be adventurous, assertive, aggressive, independent and task-oriented, whereas females are seen as more sensitive, gentle, dependent, emotional and people-oriented.[9]

Social psychologists view that gender is first received in cognition through mind and after that it is externalized through practices and gender stereotypes shape the primary direction of the both. So psychologically stereotypes are the fixed notions of mental aspirations towards which different sexes move for achieving a better mental alignment with both the biological structure of their body and social and cultural approach to gender.

> Sex stereotypes refer to the constellation of different traits, activities, values and behavioural characteristics attributed to and used to describe and differentiate two sex groups in a socio-psychological set up. For Ashmore and Delboca (1979), a sex stereotype is usually considered to be cognitive, it is a set of beliefs, it deals with what men and are like, and it is shared by the members of a particular group.[10]

Stereotypes always teach the children to follow a fixed, conventional and generalized format of psychological training and when the training is modelled upon the gendered approach then

---

[8] *Webster's New World Dictionary*, 1998.
[9] Crespi, *Socialization and Gender Roles*.
[10] Das and Ghadially, "Parental Sex Role Orientation," in *Women in Indian Society*, 124.

is called as the gender stereotypes. In each society man and woman is expected to behave in different but distinct pattern. The way they will behave is first identified in mental plane and accordingly the cognition received by mind is adjusted with the physical world. So a man or woman is born but the masculine or feminine traits are culturally practised.

Stereotypes in schools may be formed through shaping of motivational and behavioural traits of boys and girls. The easy way to form such behaviour based on gender is to highlight the issue of masculinity or femininity and to encourage the students to internalize any one of them in conformity with the sex assigned at birth. Thus the cultural formation and moulding of masculinity or femininity are the direct result of the gender stereotypes. In order to highlight the traits related to masculinity, the boys are inspired to internalize the masculine messages sent through textbooks essays, features and tales. Textbooks on almost all subjects of arts ranging from social science to language emphasize the applauding of masculinity as one of the objectives of education. The textbooks and also the reference books writers live under the domain of patriarchy. So they put their patriarchal perception in the books in their subconscious mind and inspire the male students to be directed towards the achievement of masculinity. In the history of all the nations of the world, it is the male gender that has been represented properly and the role of female gender in the making of history and in doing something for society or humanity is seriously understated. History is popularly described as the portrayal of heroism and wars and it is also popularly believed that war is the masculine matter. Many a ruler ranging from the period of early history to the modern period shared this view that history of the countries is created by the male heroes mainly through war, aggression and expansion. In this way history has been the subject of 'his story', that is, the story of the male achievement and not the records of 'her story' or the records of female achievement. Likewise it appears that political science also suffers from 'MISOGYNY'. So the feminists have criticized the 'mainstream' political science as 'malestream' political science. Misogyny is the hatred or dislike of women or girls expressed culturally often through the sexual discrimination, marginalization of women, dehumanization and also objectification of women. The history of misogyny in Western political thought is as old as Aristotle who contended that women exist as natural deformities or imperfect males. Subsequently every thinker of Western philosophy belonging to political science has been accused of misogyny. 'In the late 20th century, second wave feminism theorists claim that misogyny is both a cause and result of patriarchal social structures'.[11] Thus it is seen that women in political thought are completely objectified, dehumanized and fragmented as a result of misogynist consequences.

> Actually these three consequences of misogyny—objectification, dehumanization and fragmentation—maintain a cause and effect relationship among them. Once objectified a woman is bound to face the rest. The process of treating woman as object or denial of her humanness or addressing her personality without totality and in a fragmented way always starts with the reasoning of identifying woman's personality and being with their body. When all the focus is given on women's biology or body or sexual potentiality, then in a way her head, brain, mind and personality are made non-important and she is to face all the harsh consequences one by one as a system.'[12]

Thus these three forms of misogynist consequences are encapsulated in a single point of viewing woman as a body 'since her body is separated from her person and is thought as representing the woman'.[13] So limiting womanhood, her nature, being and personality into 'body' causes fragmentation through which a woman is objectified and dehumanized too. This is what has been done in political philosophy through a so called format of logic and reasoning. So Political science can never deny the charges of endorsing and enforcing 'gender inequality' in society through its theoretical organization and ideological legitimization in a perpetual way. In this way many a disciplines of social science have been popularly considered to be either the pro-male or anti-women. Textbooks are prepared in such a manner that an indirect idea is developed among the

---

[11] Kate Millet, *Sexual Politics* (New York, NY: Doubleday, 1970), 86.

[12] Chattopadhyay, *Fighting Gender Inequality*, 129.

[13] Sandra Lee Bartky, *Femininity and Domination: Studies in the Phenomenology of Oppression* (New York, NY: Routledge, 1990), 130.

students that vast portion of knowledge is the creation of the male masters of thought. Female have a least contribution in the stock of knowledge irrespective of subjects. Teachers also directly teach the male students to be brave, loud, hard and aggressive. In contrast, teachers teach the girl students to be docile, caring, soft, submissive, hard-working and tolerant. Teachers also motivate the girls to opt for the social science as their course of study and they motivate the boys to opt for the science study. It is the age-old stereotypical myth which says that women do not have the ability to study science. The philosophers also nourished this notion through their writings. A passage from Kant endorses this statement. Kant states,

> A woman therefore will learn no geometry; of the principle of sufficient reason or the nomads she will know only so much as is needed to perceive the salt in a satire which the insipid guilts of our sex have censured. The fair leave Descartes his vortices to whirl for ever without troubling themselves about them....[14]

Thus the intellectual and philosophical assessment of the ability of the female completely from a negative viewpoint prompted the textbooks and academic curriculum of school education to preach and reinforce the negative gender stereotypes that will undermine the position of the female in society. As a result girls of tender age throughout the world have been the victims of 'math-phobia' and 'science-phobia'. 'At the secondary level, females tend to be invisible in most science and math textbooks, perpetuating the view that these are male subjects.'[15] Teachers' motivational roles are also responsible for the enforcement of gender stereotypes. Teachers, very often during interaction with the students, applaud the role of the girls in home-running, childcare and family management and thus they highlight the stereotypical representation of female role and femininity. In contrast, the teachers very consciously remind the boys for their breadwinning role and the masculine features associated with

---

[14] Immanuel Kant, *Observations on the Feelings of the Beautiful and Sublime*, trans. John J. Goldthwait (Berkeley, Los Angeles, and London: University of California Press, 1960), 79.

[15] Giddens, *Sociology*, 515.

the character of the boys. Thus schools create and reinforce gender stereotypes both through textbooks and through the teachers. Schools are characterized by gender segregation. When many peers are available, children tend to select same-sex playmates. Children's gender segregation, in turn, affects their play experiences, leading them to spend more time in stereotypic play. Furthermore, gender segregation predicts children's future conformity to gender stereotypes.

Differential Treatment

The importance of education in mitigating gender inequalities have been recognized in India in 1986, when the National Policy of Education stated, 'to neutralize the accumulated distortions of the past, there will be a well-conceived edge in favour of women'. Eliminating gender disparities by 2005 in primary education and by 2015 at all levels is the Millennium Development Goal which is facing a threat nowadays due to the historical legacy of the constrained sociocultural milieu of India. For nearly all psychological traits on which young boys and girls differ, the contribution of school cannot be ignored. Schools' affect gender differentiation through three primary sources: teachers, classmates and the textbooks. Teachers, classmates and the textbooks directly influence gender differentiation by providing boys and girls with differential treatment and different learning opportunities and feedback. Girls and boys today are receiving separate and unequal educations due to the differential gender socialization that takes place in our schools and due to the sexist hidden curriculum students are faced with every day and thus the system results in differential formation of gender identities of the students. The process of identity formation in schools emerges from the interplay of differential expectations (different roles that the students, i.e., boys and girls are supposed to play in the future), differential attitudes (different expressions of feelings from boys and girls), and differential behaviours (different practices for boys and girls in the classroom). A definition of gender identity establishes it as: 'A person's own feeling about their gender—whether they are male, female, both or neither'.[16] When this personal feeling about gender is formed as an expression of 'other' or as a different version of other sex, it is termed as differential formation and shaping of gender identity. Schools have been viewed as the common site of differential socialization and differential treatment as a result of which students especially the girl students face the familiar type of marginalization. When boys are taunted by the teachers for talking like a girl, or crying like a girl, then it implies that being a girl is worse than being a boy. According to the American Association of University Women Report, 'The clear message to both boys and girls is that girls are not worthy of respect and that appropriate behavior for boys includes exerting power over girls ... or over other, weaker boys.'[17] Unless teachers are made aware of the gender-role socialization and the biased messages they are unintentionally imparting to students every day, and until teachers are provided with the methods and resources necessary to eliminate gender bias in their classrooms, girls will continue to receive an inequitable education. 'Until educational sexism is eradicated, more than half our children will be shortchanged and their gifts lost to society.... Sitting in the same classroom, reading the same textbook, listening to the same teacher, boys and girls receive very different educations.'[18] 'However, the American Association of University Women published a report in 1992 indicating that females receive less attention from teachers and the attention that female students do receive is often more negative than attention received by boys.'[19] In fact, 'examination of the socialization of gender within schools and evidence of a gender-biased hidden curriculum demonstrates that girls are shortchanged in the classroom'.[20] The concept of hidden curriculum refers to the process of interactions of the teachers with the students by which the conventional gender perceptions are indirectly reinforced in the class. Hidden curriculum is

---

[16] C. Paechter, "Using Poststructuralist Ideas in Gender Theory and Research," in *Investigating Gender: Contemporary Perspectives in Education*, eds B. Francis and C. Skelton. (Buckingham: Open University Press, 2001), 47.

[17] Bailey, *How Schools Shortchange Girls*, 2.

[18] D. Sadker and M. Sadker, *Failing at Fairness: How Our Schools Cheat Girls* (Toronto, ON: Simon & Schuster, Inc., 1994), 284.

[19] Bailey, *How Schools Shortchange Girls*, 6.

[20] www.edchange.org/multicultural/papers/genderbias.html

actually the representation of the gender stereotypes by which gender differences are established in society.

Much is learnt in school which has nothing to do with the formal content of lessons. Schools tend to inculcate what Illich called *Passive Consumption*—an uncritical acceptance of the existing social order—by the nature of the discipline and regimentation they involve. These lessons are not consciously taught; they are implicit in school procedures and organization.[21]

The collection of these unofficial lessons forms the content of hidden curriculum which teaches the students that their role in life is 'to know their place and to sit still in it'[22] and the place for boys and girls is differently set based on gender. When the teachers teach the boys to be loud, participating and interactive, he is also teaching the boys leadership ability and male dominated roles which they are expected to play in future in society. In contrast, by teaching the girls to be soft, submissive and disciplined, the teacher is actually teaching them the sex role which is feminine and which they are expected to play in future in society. That means gender bias is also taught implicitly through the resources chosen for classroom use. Hidden curriculum acts only in a setting of negative curriculum devoted to the reinforcement of gender stereotypes and gender differences. Using texts that omit contributions of women, that tokenize the experiences of women, or that stereotype gender role, further compounds gender bias in schools' curriculum.

Researchers at a 1990 conference reported that even texts designed to fit within the current California guidelines on gender and race equity for textbook adoption showed subtle language bias, neglect of scholarship on women, omission of women as developers of history and initiators of events, and absence of women from accounts of technological developments.[23]

Unfortunately, teachers receive relatively little training in recognizing and combating gender stereotypes and prejudices— their own and others—and, as a consequence, teachers often model, expect, reinforce, and lay the foundation for gender

---

[21] Giddens, *Sociology*, 512.
[22] Ivan D. Illich, *Deschooling Society* (Harmondsworth: Penguin, 1973), 29.
[23] Bailey, *How Schools Shortchange Girls*, 5.

differentiation among their pupils. Thus, most schools create and maintain—rather than counteract—traditional gender stereotypes, biases, and differences.[24]

In many rural schools in developing countries, there are no books available, in which case the role of the teacher becomes extremely important. It is teachers through whom millions of rural boys and girls of the underdeveloped countries learn. Teachers send multiple gendered messages through the curriculum and organizational decisions. The teachers value the work of the boys and girls differently, they hold differential attitudes and expectations for the boys and girls and they treat the students of different sexes differently. As of ability, the teachers try to socialize the boys and girls differently. They often pass the remark that male students have the ability in the study of math, science, economics and political science. In contrast, the girls are able to study language, philosophy, history and psychology. Stream and subjects demanding innovative attitude belong to the boys, and stream and subjects demanding reading habit and memorizing ability belong to the girls. Such a compartmentalization of the ability of the boys and the girls certainly leads to the differential socialization as a result of which girls, on the one hand, lag in education and, on the other, the country becomes deprived of the innovative power of a vast stock of female students in the field of scientific and technological invention. As of rating the skill also, the teachers display differential treatment. If any male student does well in examination, his performance is rated on the basis of his talent and merit. But in contrast, when a female student does well in examination, her performance is considered to be result of luck or hardwork. 'These behaviors of the teachers may foster among the less favored students a sense of alienation and hinder personal, academic, and professional development'[25] in particular and among the students of female gender in general. Differential treatment and differential socialization introduce and reinforce gender inequalities based on sex assigned at birth, and as a result the girl students face

[24] Stromquist, *The Gender Socialization Process in Schools*, 12.
[25] B. Davis. *Diversity and Complexity in the Classroom: Considerations of Race, Ethnicity, and Gender* (San Francisco: Jossey-Bass, 1993), 39.

severe constraint in getting a forward movement in the field of education. In a sharply gender-divided society when education is costly then, in most cases, the expenditure is spent on the son, that is, the male child and the female child is sent to free government schools. Studies by Dreze and Sen have also con- firmed this observation.[26] Again, often the female child is sent to the nearest school or college chiefly for the safety reason so that they do not become the soft target of the perpetrators on their way from home to school and vice versa. In recent years a number of incidents have been reported and flashed where girls on their way to a faraway school or college have been molested, raped and even murdered. Such records are surely bound to arrest the graph of women's education.

Differential treatment often leads to gender violence in schools which in most cases affect the girl students both physically and mentally. Such cases of violence are not only perpetrated by the male students but what is more frustrating that the teachers also commit such crimes often in the name of tutoring, controlling and fondling the girl students. Such a news flashed in the newspapers may be cited here as a token.

> It is reported that two teachers of Rameshchandra Primary School in Ward no. 3 of Srirampore Municipality had committed immod- est behaviour with the girl students for quite a few months. The guardians raised and organized a protest against this incident and submitted a memorandum to the Headmistress. The guard- ians expressed a deep concern over the lasting implication of this incident which, on the one hand, will push the affected girls towards a trauma and, on the other hand, will arrest the motiva- tion of the girls as well as the parents for further development in education.[27]

The incidents of sexual assault are often reported in print and electronic media in school bus where the driver commits such crimes. Even in university setting such types of incidents are often reported. Thus the girls become the victims of sexual assault, harassment and even gender violence in the educational

---

[26] Jean Dreze and Amartya Sen, *India: Development and Participation* (New Delhi and Oxford: Oxford University Press, 2002), 232–35, 257–66.
[27] *Bartaman* (Bengali daily newspaper), 13.03.2015, 5.

setting during the days of schooling simply because of their gender. 'When schools ignore sexist, racist, homophobic, and violent interactions between students, they are giving tacit approval to such behaviors.'[28] A permissive attitude towards sexual harassment is another way in which schools reinforce the socialization of girls as inferior. While the entry barriers remain a concern, retention and regular attendance is another challenge so far as the incidents of sexual harassment in school or during schooling is reported. Lack of proper sanitation facilities at schools, expectations of doing domestic chores and early marriage are common impediments to education of women as a result of which access of the girls to education is not satisfactory in developing and in underdeveloped countries. If again the threat of violence and safely is added with the infrastructural, motivational and cultural constraint already in use, the girls' education is surely bound to be hampered. A survey commissioned by the Haryana education department revealed disturbing details of sexual harassment in schools, with more than 1,000 girls in a single district reporting some form of exploitation or abuse. In another study conducted by *Plan India*, 77 per cent of the girls reported sexual harassment. Infrastructural facilities, security, change in perceptions and strong institutional support is required to overcome this vicious cycle of discrimination.

'Like teachers, peers contribute to the socialization of gender difference via multiple pathways. Upon entering school, children encounter large numbers of peers, many of whom model traditional gender behaviour, producing and reinforcing the content of gender stereotypes'.[29] 'Peers also contribute to gender differentiation by teaching their classmates stereotypes (e.g., short hair is for boys not girls) and punishing them for failing to conform to stereotypes via. verbal harassment and physical aggression'.[30] Peers in schools motivate for the concept of gender segregation as a result of which same-sex friendship becomes more common in schools. Segregation based on gender is the breeding ground of differential treatment. Dress code for the girls

[28] Bailey, *How Schools Shortchange Girls*, 6.

[29] Retrieved 10 July 2017, from www.child-encyclopedia.com

[30] B. Thorne, *Gender Play: Girls and Boys in school* (New Brunswick, New Jersey: Rutgers University Press, 1993), 105.

often becomes over-restricted. In almost all the schools in India, girls are directed to come in the conventional dress which is more accepted in society especially during the celebration of either any national day or any cultural function. In contrast, the boys are not dictated to come in such conventional dresses. The attachment of national perception especially with the dress code of the girls surely bears the sign of differential treatment. The field of sports is another field of differential treatment. In a co-ed school and college, the sports are conducted with the participation of the boys and the girls separately. Most of the heavy outdoor games are open for the participation of the boys who are considered rough and tough. Some light outdoor games and mostly the indoor games are kept open for the participation of the girls. Even in the girls' schools the same format of segregation of events from the gender viewpoint is followed. In both types of schools and colleges the event of musical chair is reserved for the participation of the girl students only. Perhaps this is symbolic in view of the women's struggle for getting a space in society for the establishment of their identity in all the countries of the world. Thus differential treatment in schools based on gender arrest the spontaneous development of the students of both sexes although it seriously threatens the forward movement of the girls in education.

Gender Role

The schools in particular and the field of education in general come to participate in gender socialization through the distributions of gender roles. The school is very much concerned with the *gender role distribution* in society through which the agenda of gender socialization is implemented. Women in every society are socialized and indoctrinated toward a set of roles and since these roles are different for the men and women, they are termed as gender roles. Individual choice does not get any priority usually for the selection of gender roles. Gender (being a social and cultural construct) roles are always fixed by the society through family in conformity with the gender ideology of a given society. So gender role is the societal expectations of what the man or the woman should do or how should they behave in society in conformity with their sex at birth. Different societies have different sets of norms for activities of the men and women and according to the degree of the level of cultural achievement and style of thinking and also according to the economic and technological advancement of that society men and women are expected to perform their roles in conformity with the gender stereotypes of that society. Most often the men or women choose the roles which are in some way or another related to their genders and their performance of those roles are approved by the gender ideology of the given society. Gender stereotypes and gender roles have a cause and effect relationship meaning thereby that gender stereotypes stem from the empirical experiences of gender roles as distributed in the family and outer setting and gender roles are the practical outcome of the nurturance of gender stereotypes. So gender roles are always stereotypical 'insofar as the roles consist of definite and known patterns of behavior, they provide blueprints for anticipatory socialization. The individuals can prepare himself beforehand for an expected or hoped-for future role. Learning professional skills is one example of anticipatory socialization'.[31] Gender roles articulate the interaction of one gender with another and thereby members of two sexes, male and female, learn what is expected of them in comparison with other gender. Thus ultimately gender roles are complementary in nature with a view to organize and integrate the social action for the smooth running of the society. Thus gender role distribution is the functional necessity of any gendered society. According to this theory, all types of works, private or personal and public or political, work within the home or work outside the home, are necessary for the continuation of the society. Again neither all work pays uniformly nor are they possible for the members of both sexes, male and female. So there has been a segregation of works based on gender and men and women are encouraged to do differently, think differently and behave differently. Thus the differential distribution of works is the basic message of the functional theory through which a functional stratification based on gender is shaped in society where male and female

---

[31] Broom and Selznick, *Principles of Sociology*, 105.

are placed for performing different roles in society. School is the place where the children primarily learn about the functional difference of roles of male and female through the internalization of roles preached through curriculum, stories and features, peer members in the class and the teachers.

Internalizations of gender roles are very much dependent on the acquisition of values, norms, practices and cognitive development of identity. The textbooks in particular and the academic curriculum in general serve as the major source of gender values, norms and practices. Through the fables and the features under textbooks, through the subjects like history, geography and through the pronouns like he, she in the list of grammar, the boys and girls internalize the value of masculinity and femininity which prompt the boys to learn masculine traits and the girls to learn the feminine traits. The messages of *patibrata, heroism, righteousness, authority, motherliness,* etc., are serious values taught either by textbooks or by teachers. These values motivate the boys to be brave, aggressive, loud and authoritative (masculine traits) and teach the girls to be docile, submissive, soft, homely and tolerant (feminine traits). The teachers also praise the girls for their soft and submissive behaviour and thus guide them by a hidden curriculum to be prepared for their present and future roles as daughter, wife and mother. The package of gender role includes gender identity, gender values, gender traits, gender norms and practices. In the context of all these only can the gender role be successful. 'The relationships between sex role attitude and personality traits of individuals have been established. Men and women with traditional sex role attitude are more likely to be masculine and feminine respectively.'[32] If any man or woman is stripped of these elements of the package of gender role, he or she will not feel comfortable with the position in society. So through the instructions of social learning, the school comes to distribute the future gender roles of the boys and the girls.

'Studies have indicated a close association between personality traits (masculinity/femininity) and choice of jobs or

---

[32] Das and Ghadially, "Parental Sex Role Orientation," in *Women in Indian Society,* 134.

occupations.[33,34] The feminine jobs usually call for qualities like nurturance, helping others, interpersonal skill whereas occupations labeled as masculine require autonomy, competition, leadership etc.'[35] The teachers and the peers especially and the textbooks and the curriculum generally line up the future plan of the boys and the girls during the days of schooling. As a result, the boys prefer the occupations of engineer, technocrats, manager, scientist and doctor whereas the girls prefer the conventional occupations of teacher, nurse, data operator, stenographer and company secretary. Although recent changes in the perception of gender role of the female have occurred almost in all the countries of the world, it is still the traditional thinking of the teachers who very often consciously or unconsciously emphasize the domestic angle of the female gender role. Due to the growing graph of female education the conventional gender role perception has changed a lot and female participation in labour market has sharply increased. In the face of the reality of the emergence of female in working role what is surprising is that the curriculum and the teachers openly give the message that it is the pious duty of the female to manage the home and to rear the child somehow in adjustment with their corporate role in labour market or their working role in other areas. Through the textbooks, through the stories and through the illustrations presented by the teachers, the school comes to inspire the girl students to be good daughter (loyal, obedient), good wife (chaste) and good mother (tolerant). In contrast, boys are always inspired to be the breadwinner of the family and thus to be also the brave son, dominating husband and authoritative father.

Thus the school contributes in the process of gender socialization in a variety of ways. Of late, owing to the drastic changes in the rate of female education and female gender role, the role of school as well as the process of gender socialization has undergone a marginal transformation with the key-note remaining the same.

---

[33] R. A. Young, "Vocational Choice and Values in Adolescent Women," *Sex Roles* 7/8 (1984), 485–92.

[34] J. N. O'Neil, "Patterns of Gender Role Conflict and Strain," *Personnel and Guidance Journal* 60 (1981), 203–10.

[35] Das and Ghadially, "Parental Sex Role Orientation," in *Women in Indian Society,* 134.

In recent years, however, the debate over gender in schools has undergone a dramatic reversal.... Beginning in the early 1990s, girls began to consistently outperform boys in all areas and at all levels of the British educational system.... Similar findings have been reported from America.... As Britain's economic profile continues to change ... a large proportion—up to 70 per cent—of jobs ... are being filled by women.[36]

In India also situations are changing since 1986, the year when the National Education Policy was adopted and undertaken. Women are rapidly joining in the employment market and as a result, the perception of family and marriage, gender stereotypes, gender roles, gender typing, etc., all are at a stake and on the verge of rapid transformation. But since the basic structure of society of India, in particular, and of all the countries of the world, in general, is patriarchal, the freedom of women is more a marginal concept than total, more nominal than real, and more relative than absolute. In such a situation the fate of women, especially Indian women, hang in a balance between tradition and modernity. The advent of globalization, the rise of the concept of private and corporate school, the invention of e-teaching and learning and the worldwide States' resolution of eradicating illiteracy have made the gender socialization through school all the more compelling topic of discussion which needs separate attention for intellectual penetration with a view to open the possibility of further research in this newly developing area. School curriculum, educational curriculum in higher education, teachers' recruitment process, teachers' profile, students' perception all are changing and the changes are taking place in the family much before the students' access to formal education centre. Thus it has been a matter of wait and watch as to how far the patriarchy can succeed in keeping its base solid in the face of the imminent resistance developing out of these changes. So the nature of gender socialization through education in near future rests upon the degree and nature of transformation of patriarchy and its method and style of combating the resistances against patriarchy.

[36] Giddens, *Sociology*, 516–17.

7

Role of Media

Media plays an important role in the process of gender socialization. Other agents like family, school and peer group also
participated in the process of gender socialization but the role of
media is slightly different than those, both in nature and mode
of operation. Other agents of gender socialization were linked
in very many ways to personal perception of authority, such as
the authority of the father, teacher, or peer leader. But in case
of media, the authority, as such, is not present here and mostly
an impersonal set of views, opinions and ideas come to influence us. The distance between the 'command and the client' is
much closed in case of family, school and peer group. This means
that in family the physical distance between father (source of
command) and the child (client), in school the distance between
teacher (command) and the student (client) and in peer group the
distance between the peer-leader (source of command) and the
peer (client) is closed and the relation is direct so much so that
clients remain in position to interact with the source of command
if the situation so demands. But in case of media, the interaction
is not always instantly possible for the clients. Other agents of
gender socialization are mainly concerned with the systems of
physical influences through coercion and dictations, the violation
of which results in punishment. Thus they proceed from building
of physical behaviours to development of mental perception. But
the media, in all its forms, perhaps proceed from the building of
mental perception to the development of physical norms. Other
agents like family, school and peer group are always prone to
enforce the gender norms compulsorily and coercively, but the
media is keen on reinforcing the gender biases spontaneously
and through social method of the teaching-learning. Thus in a
number of ways, the role of media has been considered important
in the process of gender socialization. This role has especially
come in the centre of discussion in view of the advent of globalization which has changed the structure, content and the
implication of media in recent days and thereby has made the

topic much more compelling as well as interesting. Globalization also has liquidated the conventional differences among various forms of communication.

> If at one time ways of communicating such as print, television and film were relatively self-contained spheres, they have now become intertwined to a remarkable degree.... While newspapers and so forth remain central to our lives, the ways they are organized and deliver their services are changing. Newspapers can be read online, mobile telephone use is exploding and digital television and satellite broadcasting services allow an unprecedented diversity of choice for viewing audiences. It is the internet, however, that is at the heart of this communication revolution.[1]

Today one can use internet through mobile; mobile has been the most important friend of the newspapers and television reporters; newspapers and televisions use the internet as potential source of information and data. Cinema and its techniques have been completely computerized. It is through the internet that all forms of mass media and social media have come to form a compact notion of the media. Under such a situation where the 'cyberspace' has swallowed almost all of the forms of media resulting in a new outlook and form, it is quite natural that the influence of the media in respect of gender related issues will be rated as the most important and timely.

Media can be divided into two broad groups: mass media and social media. According to Free Online Dictionary, mass media is 'the means of communication that reach large number of people in a short time, such as television, newspapers, magazines and radio'. According to Wikipedia, 'Social media are computer-mediated tools that allow people to create, share or exchange information, ideas, picture/videos in virtual communities and networks'. In this section, I shall discuss the nature and mode of operation of the two categories of media and also how the uniqueness of these two categories become a part and parcel of the agenda of gender socialization. Mass media again can be divided into two sub-groups: print media and electronic media. Newspapers and magazines are included in the print media and

---

[1] Giddens, *Sociology,* 452.

television, cable, radio are included in the list of electronic media. Mass media, especially the print media, is the earliest form of mediums of public opinion although it has been established that in ancient day when printing had not emerged as a technological gift, people were used to form public opinion through gossips, discussions and interactions in the popular public places. In ancient Greece coffee shops were used for this purpose, and in ancient India *Chandimandap* or the public meeting places were used as the centre of discussion on public matters. However, after the invention of printing technology, print media started encompassing all the possible spaces of public opinion in view of which it has been termed as the fourth estate of democracy. Recently, the power of the electronic media has also been the point of discussion in respect of its role as safeguards of democracy. In view of its all-encompassing role, the mass media is often viewed as the most potential determinant of the policies and the activities of the government. In most of the cases, the mass media comes forward in the criticism of the government when the policies adopted by the government are proved harmful for the public. Thus the mass media can take a role both in favour of and in opposition to the government. The social media, which is considered as comparatively free and progressive, can also come in support of or in opposition to the status quo. But the role of social media in this regard is mostly directed on and along the ideological and intellectual lines. The differences between mass media and social media can be identified at different levels of *emotion, information, awareness and responsibility.*

Mass media and social media are closely associated with the *emotional level* of the consumers. Different stories flashed in the newspapers and magazines and in social media sites often influence the reader to form their opinion. As of the issue of gender, stories and news covered centring round the achievement and struggle of the women, different incidents of gender violence especially the incidents of violence against women inspire the reader to assume an emotional appearance on the question of gender. Relevantly it can be mentioned that the gang rape case of 'Nirbhaya' in a private bus at Delhi on 16 December 2012 aroused a great emotional sensation among the readers of print media. Resultantly Delhi as well as the country visited the first ever mass protest against such heinous crime against women. People, from all sections irrespective of creed, colour, race, community, educational and social level, rallied behind the one and only demand of severe punishment of the accused. After the expiry of 'Nirbhaya' at Singapore on 29 December 2012 people throughout India and abroad also expressed their deep sorrow over the death of 'Nirbhaya', the brave-heart. All social media sites also were engaged in forming and collecting opinions about the issue of 'Nirbhaya', the brave-heart in the same scale and intensity of emotions as were expressed in the mass media. The difference between the two types of media in respect of the emotion expressed on the issue of 'Nirbhaya' is not all the same so far as their target audiences, exhaustiveness and implications are concerned. The reactions of social media were more personal, organized, instant and integrated. In contrast, the reactions of mass media were somehow impersonal, scattered and slow whereby the emotional level was supposed to be tied in an apparently low scale. The role of emotion is much more relevant in case of electronic media than the print media. In radio and television programmes, perception of gender is mostly determined by the emotional dramas, serials, cinema and other family stories. So it can be said that emotion as a cause and effect of gender perception is distributed and transmitted in the electronic media through many a regular programmes whereas emotion is expressed in social media only on the basis of a specific incident and such emotion, as the basis of formation of gender perception, is no more a continued matter. The intensity of emotion ends with the focus of attention of the main incident being shifted in course of time but the links to the main incident remains discoverable through the search engines.

As of *information*, it can be said that both mass media and social media supply information based on which gender perception is formed and developed in a particular society. Mass media supply the incidental information about gender. In newspapers and magazines and in radio and television information of gender served is based mainly on different incidents that take place in society and mostly through the journalistic coverage of those incidents, the reporters bring the information in public notice. Sometimes through the panel discussion on gender issues (gender inequality, gender empowerment, gender violence and gender socialization, etc.) in television and radio (especially FM) various information are received by the consumers in respect of gender and gender-related issues. In the magazines, especially women-related magazines, much information is released almost all of which are directed to the formation and implementation of the gender messages modelled upon the gender ideology of a given society. The information about gender in mass media is basically released and controlled by the decision makers (CEO, Chief Editor, Concept Manager, etc.) of the different sections of the media and the audience and the listeners just consume what is released by the decision-makers. Practically the consumers enjoy least control over the matters, contents and also over the manner of presentation of the programmes. But in case of social media nature of information is slightly different than that of the mass media. Social media, being directly related with the internet, is considered as a rich storehouse of information which can be accessed by the users at any time they like. Thus the type of information, amount of information and their detailed history are within the closed fist of the consumers. So practically it is the consumer who is to determine what to learn and how much of it to learn and in what manner. Through internet it is possible for any user to access any information about gender identity, gender ideology and gender socialization. Thus regarding gender-related information in the social media, the consumer is comparatively free in respect of selection of items of information and the nature of their consumption than the mass media.

As of *awareness*, print media, that is, newspaper and magazine, especially newspaper plays a very vital role in creating awareness through the coverage of day to day reporting of incidents of gender violence such as bride-burning, acid attack, battering and rape. Incidents of gang-rape are often reported in the newspaper with a tone of protest against such crimes. Mass media had a very vital role in forming the protest movement against the gang-rape case of 'Nirbhaya' on 16 December 2012. It is through the mass media, especially newspapers that the record and statistics of the crime against women in different countries are flashed based on which the people determine their course of action in respect of gender. Magazines and journals also contribute a lot in creating awareness of gender. In the traditional societies like India where women are socially marginalized and culturally presented so as to undermine their position, magazines and journals continuously supply information with a view to alter this version of reality. It is very natural that as a system of capitalistic enterprise, the magazine and journals serve the interest of patriarchy through all possible means of cultural manipulation and gender socialization. But it is also the fact that as a system of intellectual activities, magazines and journals inherently carry with them a symptom of resistance against power. Like all power, gender power is also to be countered by a form of resistance which takes place in intellectual plane expressed through various writings and features of the writers and columnists. Thus magazines and journals maintain a balance between patriarchal values and the agenda for its transformation. In radio and television, gender message is sent through mainly the tele-play, serials and panel discussion on gender issues. Cinema also offers gender messages that are prone to implement the gender ideology of a given society. In all three mediums of gender opinion, awareness about the gender in all respect is formed, manipulated, shaped and reshaped through the process of gender socialization. People are encouraged to follow the spirit of the story presented in all these mediums whereby men come to learn masculinity and women come to learn femininity as the basic ideological pattern. So the elements of awareness received through the mass media are not always free of impurity and constraint. Since a large part of mass media is engaged in cultural activities and since culture carries with it both progressive and retrogressive features, the awareness is often mixed up with the prejudice and gender bias. In contrast, the level of awareness created through social media is more dynamic. Social media encourage the consumers to participate in two-way 'one-to-one' communication through social networking sites like Facebook, Twitter, etc. Since capitalistic perception is not so much strong in social media, the users may very often dare to cross the limits of gender norms set by patriarchy and thus social media becomes a free space of forming gender awareness. But the fact is that the retrogressive features encapsulate the culture of all kinds, global or local; the interactive culture of the social media is also negatively influenced by them. As for example, on 26 March 2015,

Bollywood's actress Anushka Sharma, who is currently dating Virat Kohli, faced a lot of criticism and bad comments from people all over the internet for Team India's defeat in the cricket World

Cup semifinals. A lot of tweets, Facebook trolls and jokes were made on the actress for something she did not do.[2]

This incident is the perfect reflection of the cyber bullying, sexism and misogyny in social media. Some posts full of harsh criticisms and negative comments against Anushka are retrieved from internet[3] and placed here as a mark of misogyny preached through social media.

1. What's true love? Anushka Sharma travelled all the way to Sydney to cheer VK dropping a catch and then score a run with bat! :P
2. I hate kohali ... who needs only anushka not India.
   3:53 PM - 26 Mar 2015
   Asah shah @AsahShah
3. Anushka was telling Kholi that come quickly in hotel room, no need to waste time to play a long innings, we will play together :p #AUSvIND
   3:50 PM - 26 Mar 2015 Lahore, Pakistan, پاکستان
   chandresh henia @ca_henia
4. @akashbanerjee @mohitraj dhoni ne kaha virat ko spend more time with sharma...he meant rohit...virat samjha anushka
   3:54 PM - 26 Mar 2015
   Rajan Sharma @rajan12rajan12
5. Anushka Sharma went all the way to Sydney to see Virat Kohli hit one run. why you came to sydney idiot!
   3:48 PM - 26 Mar 2015
   sarcasticsardar @Turbanator200
6. Never liked the ugly anushka sharma. Shes a sign of bad luck and her films should be boycotted #IndvsAus #AUSvIND
   4:24 PM - 26 Mar 2015

As of *responsibility*, there are differences in the level between the perception of responsibility of the mass media and that

---

[2] Taken from the news on the title, 'Anushka Sharma lashes back against cyber bullying' flashed in the business of cinema.com, 28 March 2015.
[3] Taken from the news on the title, 'Anushka Sharma lashes back against cyber bullying' flashed in the business of cinema.com, 26 March 2015.

of the social media. Mass media has to be more sensitive and responsible in respect of gender issues because of five distinct reasons. One, mass media is popularly believed as the agent of transmitting education and consciousness of the society. So the misogynist standpoint is very consciously contested in mass media. Two, mass media, in most of the cases, is capital-based industry and so it is to stand beside the women issue in order to boost up its sale when the practical reality is that women folk share about half of total population of any country. 'Moreover, the sponsors of their programmes and the advertisers regard women as the largest consumers.'[4] And the fact is that what Touchman said, 'Radio, television, newspapers and magazines all seek to deliver as many consumers as possible to advertisers'.[5] Three, mass media is the faithful agent of gender socialization that always preaches status quo which is only possible through the adoption of a balanced approach regarding gender. That is why mass media invites opinions and features for combating the gender bias in society. Four, mass media being a capital-based industry is to comply with the rules of the land which, in almost all the countries of the world, has been women-friendly and is devoted to the task of eradicating gender inequality, especially the inequality and discrimination exercised against women. Five, since mass media is a culture-based industry, it is by nature directed to the transformation of thoughts and practices of a given society and as such it becomes the harbinger of change, protest and resistance against all sorts of superstitions and prejudices of the society. That way gender prejudice is also challenged and combated in mass media with sufficient arguments and statistics from the desk of the editor. But since mass media, like all other agents of gender socialization, serve the interest of the patriarchy at the very basic level it cannot play an all-out progressive role in respect of gender. Social media, being relatively free from the control of capital, had the scope of playing a responsible role in respect of gender but it

[4] Jyoti Punwani, "Portrayal of Women on Television," in *Women in Indian Society,* ed. Rehana Ghadially (New Delhi: SAGE Publications, 1988), 231.

[5] G. Touchman, "Women's Depiction by the Mass Media," in *Feminist Frontiers: Rethinking Sex, Gender and Society*, eds L. Richardson and V. Taylor (London: Addison-Wesley Publishing Co., 1983), 528–42.

do not happen so all the time. Perhaps the retrogressive role of the social media in respect of gender results from the culture of the users who use the social media for the expression of their sexist attitudes. It was the sexist and misogynist attitude of the users that prompted them to pass and post negative comments against Anushka Sharma after the defeat of Team India in World Cup Semifinal against Australia on 25 March 2015. The makers of the tweets and posts did not stop only with the posting of comments against the actress and producer of NH10 but they also incited the audience for burning the posters and pictures of the heroine on the street of Sydney. Some of them also provoked for attacking the house of the actress so far as it is known from the posts. This is not new in social media. Women politicians are often attacked in social media simply for being women. In the live telecast of games played by women such as Sania Mirza, Saina Nehwal, Steffy Graff, Venus Williams, etc., the angle of camera is so adjusted that a question is bound to come in the mind of the open-minded person as to which is the priority of the telerights holder: to present the game in all details or to entertain the gendered (misogynist) viewers by capturing the exposed part of the body of the woman player in camera during the game? The mass media especially the print media is no exception in this regard. The pose (picture) in which Saina Nehwal had been presented in the newspapers after being the No. 1 in world badminton in March 2015 was surely the reflection of negative perception about the women. It is the usual technique of the patriarchy to present the woman in association with sex and erotic form since woman, in patriarchy, is viewed as the object of sexual pleasure and enjoyment for the male. Patriarchy has failed to discover the talent and efficiency of the women simply for its fragmented outlook of gender. Media, be it mass media or social media, in spite of its relatively high level of the power of cultural penetration is often seen to be engaged in the propagation of retrogressive cultures especially in respect of gender. Perhaps the responsibility of the media is constrained by the influence and dictates of patriarchy.

The difference between mass media and social media is presented briefly in the following table:

Mass Media	Social Media
1. Mass media is the oldest form of the expression of public opinion.	1. Social media is comparatively the newer form of the expression of public opinion.
2. Mass media is passive in nature in respect of consumer participation.	2. Social media is active in nature in respect of consumer participation.
3. Mass media, especially print media, is one-way communication directed in the manner of one-to-many communication.	3. Social media is based on two-way communication system, i.e., one-to-one communication.
4. Mass media is concerned with apparently isolated consumers.	4. Social media is concerned with the consumers who coordinate themselves with one-another through a system of generating conversations and comments.
5. Mass media has a limited reach and the costs of media expand with the increase of the covered area of consumers.	5. Social media has unlimited reach and the costs of media remain relatively constant even if the number of users increase.
6. Mass media is capita-intensive culture industry and thereby capital plays an important role in shaping the value system of the industry.	6. Social media is relatively free from the control of the capital and capitalism does not directly influence the opinion of the users.
7. Mass media is devoted to the task of enforcing gender norms very strictly and it is primarily modelled upon the dictates of gender ideology of a given society.	7. Social media is relatively free zone in respect of gender norms and practices and opinions in expression of the deviation to the gender norms are not always rebuked.
8. Mass media, especially the magazine and the electronic media, serves as the potent weapon of gender socialization through features, stories, gossips, columns and serials, panel discussions and cinema propagated in different channels of television and also through the dramas transmitted in radio.	8. Social media is not so organized a medium of gender socialization as it does not have so much of cultural sections like the mass media and it does not have the scope of influencing the users emotionally and through sensitive telenarratives of different types.

(continued)

(continued)

Mass Media	Social Media
9. Mass media serves as the source of second rate information of gender which comes mainly through reporting, covered news, features, columns and imagined narratives presented in television.	9. Social media serves as the source of first rate information of gender which are available through varieties of portal in internet and thereby social media gives enough of scope of developing views about gender norms, gender identity, gender inequality as well as gender equality strictly from a theoretical approach.
10. Mass media, especially the magazines and the electronic media, serves as the medium of the formation of gender stereotypes and gender role distribution.	10. Social media is not considered so potent a source of gender stereotypes and gender role distribution.

The successful operation of gender socialization (in patriarchal mode) depends upon three things: *gender stereotypes, messages about gender norms and practices and messages about gender role distribution.* Media, as such, is a very important medium of the implementation of these three determinants. It is also a fact that all parts of media do not participate for creating these determinants in the same scale and level of intensity. What the newspapers and magazines can do may not be done properly by television and radio. Again the contribution of social media obviously differs from that of the other media. But it is beyond any doubt that media, irrespective of its form, serves as the faithful agent of patriarchy in spite of its sporadic expressions of progressive features. It has been discussed earlier that due to the fact of being a capital-intensive industry and due to its basic cultural configuration modelled upon the patriarchal gender ideology, it is hardly possible for the media to be completely free from the constraint of the past and to be the champion of radical social transformation in respect of gender. So, like other agents, media also comes to play its role in gender socialization through some unique methods.

Gender stereotypes are fixed notions about the values, norms and attributes related to the gender and such stereotypes guide the male or female gender to the absorption of these notions in such a way that the persons belonging to the male or female gender can become representatives of the collective formulation of masculinity or femininity. Expressions of gender stereotypes are often the over generalizations of the traits and attributes of a group, such as male or female, based on gender as the stereotypes are not usually formed on accurate information of the group, rather based on biased information and prejudiced approach to the categories of gender. Resultantly, stereotypes may be negative also and it is these negative gender stereotypes that give birth to gender inequality and gender discrimination. Gender stereotypes are born out of the cultural legacy of a society, its style of thinking and habits and behaviours practised year after year. It is the common format of gender stereotypes that view male as strong, ambitious, leadership-oriented, brave, aggressive, and loud and breadwinner. In contrast, gender stereotypes view female as weak, submissive, home-oriented, timid, soft, righteous, chaste and childbearer and naturally fitted for childrearing. Coming of newspapers, the important part of print media, it can be said that gender stereotypes are born and brought up through it in a number of ways. Masculinity and femininity, being the super form of gender stereotypes come to be reinforced by the newspaper in the camouflage of journalistic style. Other sub-group of stereotypes either follows the masculine traits or the feminine traits. There are three important aspects of newspapers by which they come to shape or reshape the gender stereotypes, especially the traits of masculinity and femininity: *news, house-vision and advertisements.* Through news and reporting we get a number of images associated with masculinity or femininity. When a boy or a man perform any heroic jobs like the fighting with the robbers or rescuing some persons from fire, flood or any type of dangerous situation, these jobs are openly applauded as masculine. When a girl or any woman performs the same job, they are also applauded as 'masculine-like'. The news does not term the heroic jobs as feminine. This means that heroic jobs are always masculine and only a man can do them. In case any woman also does so, she will be reported as 'like man' or 'masculine-like'. Often the political leaders also give the messages of masculinity or femininity through their provocative speeches against rival political parties. They often resort to political violence which they boast of as the reflection of high degree of masculinity. The parliamentary democracy of India is especially constrained with the increasing numbers of the incidents of political violence. The chest-thumping, the politics of the muscleman (*Bahubali Rajneeti*), the violent politics are presented by the leaders in association with manliness and the opposite of these are often considered as feminine. Dress code debate often becomes the top news flashed in the newspaper. Women teachers are very often forbidden by the male guardians and the leaders of the locality to enter the school premises for wearing any dress of the woman's own choice and news covered in this regard indirectly comes to reinforce the traditional images of the women. Dress code of Indian women of every state is fixed by the tradition and any departure from it means challenging the tradition and femininity which again creates a public debate. House-vision means the very angle of presenting news through which the pre-fixed notion of gender of the newspaper house can be highlighted. House-vision is the viewpoint of the reporting sponsored by the house. It is unfortunate to notice that in most of the cases, house-vision is gender-biased. A report can be presented from many angles. The viewpoint of presentation is very important so far as the formation of gender stereotypes are concerned. Sometimes through news flashed in the newspaper, posters and pictures of the women are so presented as to arouse the undercurrent sexual sensation among the readers, especially the male readers. The photos of the female celebrities are often flashed in the newspaper from a sexual angle. Again the photos of the celebrity new married couples are presented with the inherent object of highlighting the value and importance of marriage which is seen to be the ultimate destiny of women. Advertisement in the newspapers is the most important medium of creating and enforcing gender stereotypes. Through advertisement women are often presented either as objects of sexual pleasure, or as representatives of some stereotypes related to home, kitchen, beauty or childcare. It is often noticed to project the male in the advertisements of car, bikes, tyres, hard drinks, men's shaving cream, etc., and the female in the advertisement of toys, kitchen utensils, cooking items and body spray. Thus through these ads the newspapers come to create a type of gender perception among the readers which ultimately guide them to form gender stereotypes which play the vital role in the process of gender socialization of the readers. The newspapers also play a very vital role in sending gender messages so that processes of gender norms and gender role distribution are reinforced in conformity with the dictates of patriarchy. Very often the political leaders and the celebrities of different sectors pass such comments so as to undermine the position of women, on the one hand, and on the other, harden the tie of patriarchy in order to arrest their free development. When the Reservation Bill for Women was first introduced in 1996 in the Lower House (Lok Sabha), Sharad Yadav, the President of Janata Dal (U), at that time raised the question as to 'if so many women come in parliament who will prepare chapattis for the male?'[6] This remark is obviously suggestive of a misogynist approach although media's role, in flashing this comment from a pro-woman angle, can be viewed as an example of progressiveness. It is known from a report of *The Times of India* that

> Union minister of state Giriraj Singh has courted fresh controversy with his sexist remarks aimed at Congress president Sonia Gandhi wondering if Congress would have accepted Sonia Gandhi's leadership if she was not white-skinned.... In the video he is seen saying that If Rajiv Gandhi would have married a Nigerian lady instead of white-skinned girl, would Congress party have accepted her leadership?.... The Congress dubbed Singh's remarks as being reflective of their 'mindset'.... Various women leaders also attacked Singh, who is minister of state for micro, small and medium enterprises, saying that it reflected his racial mindset and attitude towards women.[7]

Giriraj Singh made this remark in a meeting of Vaishali on 31 March 2015. Such comments passed by political leaders obviously hit the women in general and give a biased gender message. But here also media, by flashing and criticizing this misogynist attitude, played a progressive role. Sakshi Maharaj, an MP of the Bharatiya Janata Party (BJP), remarked that each Hindu woman should give birth to at least four children and thus should come to increase the Hindu population of India. Putting the BJP into a more embarrassing situation, another

[6] Kalyani Bandopadhyay, *Rajniti O Narishakti* (in Bengali) (Howrah: Manuscript India, 2002), 179–95.
[7] *The Times of India*, New Delhi, 1 April 2015.

party leader from West Bengal said on Tuesday that every Hindu woman should produce at least five children.[8] All these were covered as top press headline news in almost all the national and international newspapers and through such comment the position of women in general and the position of Hindu women in particular has been sufficiently undermined. Thus biased gender messages coming from the leaders of the society are flashed regularly in newspapers and accordingly mass media causes negative gender socialization in society.

Magazines and journals have a huge potentiality in forming gender stereotypes. There are several women's magazines in almost all languages. There are also some magazines for teenage boys and girls. In all the countries of the world film magazines and journals are very popular among readers of all age groups. Magazines and journals come to form gender stereotypes through the discussion on fashion and beauty, childrearing, cooking and instructions for ideal woman. Fashion and beauty pages are devoted to the creation of the idea that women are basically meant for satisfying the sexual urge of the male partner and so for being sexually attractive and appealing women are to be fashion and beauty conscious since their teenage. The advertisements under this section are always prone to present women as beautiful. Skin whitening creams, hair oils, facial kits, breast massage oil, women's deodorants and sex-stimulating creams are the usual beauty related advertisements seen in most of the magazines. Magazines come to teach girls for adopting the fashion and style statement in a stereotypical way so that femininity as a trait is highlighted, and accordingly all the feminine qualities are developed in tune with the gender ideology of a given society. So the magazines teach the girls to reflect their femininity through their dresses, accessories, wristwatch, shoe and spectacle. Childrearing is a very popular section of the magazines where women are taught about the does and don'ts in respect of childrearing. Often it is preached that marriage is the ultimate destiny of the women and the motherhood the completion of marriage. So any woman, in order to be the perfect representative of femininity, must embrace the institution of marriage and must fulfill the jobs of mothering. Also in order

---

[8] Retrieved 13 January 2015, from www.newindianexpress.com

to supplement the role of mother, women must have to adopt the qualities of perfect woman and perfect mother. They must be tolerant, caring, homemaker, self-effacing, beautiful, attractive and pleasing. Either through the advertisement or through the feature writing, the magazines and journals always project this ideal feminine type, the primary job of which is childbearing and childrearing. In the advertisement of child-related products, several tips are supplied for the women so that they can perform the jobs of childrearing very efficiently. Cooking and kitchen materials section is the next important one for the formation of gender stereotypes for the female through magazines and journals. Usually female models play the main roles in the advertisements under this section. Under the column story or under the advertisement, it is always presented that the job of cooking and the supervision and management of kitchen is the job of the women. Through this job women can perform the role of homemaking, caring and serving and so in order to achieve these qualities, women must accommodate the stereotypical traits in conformity with their sex. Marriage, family and home should get top priority during the practical application of femininity and womanliness, and in conformity with these institutions women must develop and acquire the faculty of gender stereotypes as suited to the female sex.

Radio and television play perhaps the strongest role in forming gender stereotypes, sending the gender messages and distributing the gender roles among the sexes. Radio, through dramas and different programmes on women, teach the women about the gender norms, stereotypes and gender roles. First, it is through a number of programmes in different channels that the television create two types of stereotypes—one for man and another for woman. There are usually several types of serials transmitting the gender ethos through televisions. One, some serials are seen to be transmitting the traditional feminine qualities through the family. As of March 2015, a serial named *Ganga* was seen to be telecast on &TV where a child widow named Ganga is seen to be struggling against the superstitions and prejudices exercised against the widow in the Indian society. This serial is also suggestive of the presence of the curse of child marriage in society. The serials that reinforce the traditional stereotypes for the female perform this job by teaching those feminine qualities such as tolerance, muteness, softness, serving attitude, righteousness, chastity and motherliness. It is within this area of stereotypes that a woman is allowed to express herself in public. Thus, messages about the duty of the women are the basic subject matters of these serials that also teach the women about their gender roles in society. An ideal woman must perform the role of daughter, sister, wife and mother perfectly in conformity with the sex assigned at birth. So televisions serials also include the teaching of gender role distribution. *Punar Vivah* (remarriage) is a serial telecast on Zee TV where a woman is denied the right to marriage for the second time. The general tendency of the society towards the divorcee and the widow is depicted in these types of serials. Two, there have been some serials full of patriarchal values such as *Saubhagyavati Bhava* (may you be fortunate) telecast on Life OK where a woman named Jhanvi is seen to be facing a lot of trials and tribulation in the form of domestic violence. In these serials, strictness of patriarchal norms is presented with a view to bring the women under control and to curb the freedom of women. These serials are engaged in portraying the fragmentation and dehumanization of women. So miniaturization of women's traits and talents is the object of such serials based on patriarchal values. Such a serial is *Begusarai* presented on &TV where the moribund features of patriarchy have been projected and the heroine is seen to be struggling for coming out of the patriarchal values and control. A serial named *Geet* was presented on Sony channel where the heroine was seen to be dominated by a family run under patriarchal values and the heroine was forced to be married against her consent. Consequently, the heroine Geet became the victim of physical and social exploitation. Three, there are some serials where the girl child is denied the right to education at her choice in spite of her possessing enough of talent. In a serial *Sadda Haq* presented on Channel V the heroine is seen to be struggling for her right to education by implementing it through her admission in mechanical engineering. The heroine's father, a traditional patriarchal family head, is of the opinion that engineering is not for the girls; it is a male subject of study. Additionally, the traditional family head also thinks that girls should not be allowed to go far away from home even for study. Thus the heroine's struggle against the patriarchal values of gender restriction is depicted here. Four, there are many programmes based on the crimes against women presented on many channels. On Sony channel *Crime Patrol* is telecast; on Life OK *Savdhaan India* and on Colors TV *Code Red* is telecast every night. These programmes depict true incidents in most of the cases through the artificially reproduced version of the original incident. All these serials are mostly concerned with the task of exploring the possible source of gender violence through the projection of prevalent ideas so that women can be alert and save themselves from such dangers. Five, there are many panel discussions on women's issues held in different channels in television and through these discussions gender messages are very nicely sent to the viewers. It is not the case that this type of discussion held is always retrogressive and go against the women as such. The fact is that there may be different layers of discussion of which some are progressive and some retrogressive in some cases. Many a time such panel discussion is presented through live telecast as a result of which the scope for a public debate is created. But the fact is that due to the inherent contradiction between culture and capital, it becomes hardly possible for the television to cross the limit of patriarchy entirely. So what happens ultimately is that television becomes a faithful agent of gender socialization. Thus television programmes not only entertain the viewers but also influence them directly in imitating the stereotypes, gender messages and gender roles preached in television and come to reinforce the patriarchal viewpoint of gender in society. It is known from the reports covered by various television channels that in 2012 Chiranjeet Chakraborty, one MLA and leader of TMC contented that short dresses worn by the women were one of the reasons for the increase of the incidents of sexual violence and harassment in his Barasat constituency in the district of North 24 Parganas, West Bengal. He is seen to be saying,

> Eve-teasing is a very old thing. It has been going on for ages. One of the reasons behind the increase of the incidents of eve-teasing is short dresses and short skirts worn by women. This in turn instigates young men.... We need to see one thing that there can be no Ramayana without a Ravana.[9]

[9] www.hindustantimes.com, 28 July 2012.

Thus it is seen that incidents of sexual violence against the women are going to be justified by the political leaders of almost all parties. By citing the example of the *Ramayana*, Dipak Chakraborty (alias Chiranjeet) has liquidated the real gravity of the situation of sexual harassment and violence against the women. Again

> in a brazen, ludicrous and insensitive statement, Trinamool Congress MP Tapas Pal has been caught on camera openly threatening to send his boys and get women of opposition party raped. He is actually seen to be saying that if anyone from the Opposition dares to touch any woman then I will send my boys and get women of CPI(M) raped. Tapas Pal told this in a gathering reportedly in his constituency Krishnanagar.[10]

All television channels covered this news in prime time slot and many comments from all over the world stormed all panel discussions on television. Such negative comments against the women by political leaders certainly add fuel to the system of negative gender socialization.

Television also plays a role in positive gender socialization that applauds the woman who fights back and constantly struggles for a better world for the women. On DD National channel one such programme named *Stri Shakti* is telecast where the struggling women all over the country are presented before the viewers for the exchange of opinion. Another programme on Lok Sabha channel is telecast by the name of *Hum Vi To Hai* where different issues related to the struggle against gender inequality and gender discrimination are discussed with the help of experts of the gender matter. This is also an awareness programme. *Emotional Atyachaar* is also a programme where women are given instructions and warnings so that they do not suffer in future due to their gender and so that the present mistakes are repeated. *Code Red* is a very gender-sensitive programme presented on Colors TV where problems of women are taken and discussed sympathetically in order to create awareness among women. Thus in this way television is working with a view to create an alternative version of gender message and gender ideology in the society. Since by the grace of technology

---

[10] Zeenews.india.com, 1 July 2014.

television has reached the most humble person of the society, it has come to penetrate the rural area of all societies where actually the new messages of gender will be a real necessity. At the governmental level also the necessity of positive gender messages was recognized much before today. The P. C. Joshi Committee (1985) had recommended ways in which women should be portrayed. It has said,

> The government must at the earliest formulate clear-cut guidelines regarding positive portrayal of women on television.... Both men and women should be portrayed in ways that encourage mutual respect and a spirit of give and take between the sexes.... In order to promote a positive ideology that is sensitive to women's needs ... and also to have a coordinated, consistent policy it would be necessary for all Doordarshan policy-makers, programming and production staff to have regular orientation courses that sensitize them to women's issues.[11]

Social media is such a powerful medium that both makes and unmakes the gender. The dynamic role of social media is best understood through its technological uniqueness and the culture of its users. So far as the technology is concerned, it is considered to be the most advanced platform of public opinion. But technology cannot change the man from within overnight. It is ultimately the man who determines the directions of technology—good or bad. Man uses technology more than technology uses man. So far as man and his culture is concerned, social media is seen to be reflecting the retrogressive cultures of the people who use it. Personal prejudices and superstitions are posted on social media sites in the name of so-called free opinions in respect of gender. With the advent of globalization and with the rise of internet and information technology, social media has also been popularized throughout the world. Sometimes social media is presented as the global media, that is, the media associated with the concept of globalization. From some quarters, it is highlighted that global culture is the top most level of cultural manifestation. But there is no denying the fact that globalization or the culture coming out of it is not fully free from the constraints of capitalism, colonialism

---

[11] Punwani, "Portrayal of Women on Television," in *Women in Indian Society*, 231.

and imperialism, all of which are expressed at the domestic level through patriarchy. So just like the local culture, global culture is also very much gender-biased and suggestive of retrogressive features. Social media, in terms of being connected with the World Wide Web (WWW), represents the global culture on the one hand, and on the other, the retrogressive features coming out of the contradiction inherent in globalization. Thus social media serves the messages of gender inequality, gender discrimination and gender violence along with the other progressive messages as are suggestive of globalization.

Social media is mainly engaged in making gender by millions of posts and comments, both positive and negative, through twitter, face book and also through videos uploaded on YouTube and internet. Sometimes through the documentary uploaded in internet gender messages are largely transmitted among the viewers. As for example, the documentary named *India's Daughter* by Leslee Udwin may be mentioned. The documentary is based on the interview of the criminals involved in the gang-rape case of *Nirbhaya* committed in a bus of New Delhi at night of 16 December 2012. One accused named Mukesh blamed the girls for being raped as, for him, girls should not go out of home at night. Girls moving at night are cheap and equal to prostitutes and so there is nothing wrong in raping them. In his words, 'A girl is far more responsible for rape than a boy.... A decent girl won't roam around at nine o'clock at night.... Housework and housekeeping is for girls, not roaming in discos and bars at night doing wrong things, wearing wrong clothes.'[12] Second, the accused criminals facing straight the camera said that since the girl was accompanied by her boyfriend at night, she was summarily made a soft target of rape. Third, Mukesh told that if the girl ('Nirbhaya') did not resist and oppose to rape at the material time, they (the criminals) perhaps would not have murdered her. He said in the interview, 'When being raped, she shouldn't fight back. She should just be silent and allow the rape. Then they'd have dropped her off after 'doing her', and only hit the boy.'[13] A. P. Singh, a defence lawyer in the case, was shown saying,

---

[12] *India's Daughter*, en.wikipedia.org
[13] Ibid.

If my daughter or sister engaged in pre-marital activities and disgraced herself and allowed herself to lose face and character by doing such things, I would most certainly take this sort of sister or daughter to my farmhouse, and in front of my entire family, I would put petrol on her and set her alight.[14]

Asked later if he stood by those comments, he insisted that he did. The lawyer defending the Delhi attackers compared women at various points in the interview to a precious flower and a diamond, saying, 'If you put the diamond on the street, certainly the dog will take it out, you can't stop it'. 'This implication, that the urge to act upon sexual desires in a violent manner is natural and therefore socially acceptable, is prevalent elsewhere.'[15] Women are often placed within a hierarchy of value, depending on their social status, sexuality, caste, religion or behaviour, used to justify how certain 'types' of women 'deserve' to be treated. Thus by stereotyping the women through a set of norms, traits and behaviours based on patriarchal values, the criminal actually serves as the representative of patriarchy. In an almost unwatchable clip, one of Jyoti's attackers says unblinkingly, 'You can't clap with one hand; it takes two hands to clap. A decent girl won't roam around at 9 o'clock at night'. *India's Daughter* has stormed the social media not because of any breaking news but because of the negative comments it contains and the retrogressive outlook in its presentation. The objective of Leslee Udwin is not clear enough from the film. If she was directed to the task of exposing the gender-biased attitudes and degraded gender values of India that resulted in the rape and murder of 'Nirbhaya', two questions are bound to be raised subsequently. One, if she was dedicated to the task of addressing the causes and consequences of rape as such, why the film is titled *India's Daughter*? Rape is always a rape and it is equally painful for all, be she Indian or Englishman. However when the statistics of rape in England are sufficiently alarming, then why such an effort has been made indirectly to malign India's culture by branding rape as just Indian. The title 'India's Daughter' does not match with the broader objective, if any, of the film. Two,

[14] Ibid.

[15] www.newstatesman.com

the negative comments and criticisms that have been made in the film by Mukesh Singh, one of the six attackers, and his lawyer A. P. Singh have spoiled all objectives of fighting rape as a social crime. In every line of their interview, both of them appeared as the feudal representatives of the patriarchy. They talked of traditional gender roles, traditional stereotypes for the women and traditional gender codes such as dress, behaviour, norms, movement time, etc., and thus they tried to send out some messages for confining the women within the closed circuits of patriarchy. What is unfortunate is that this film *India's Daughter* has given the criminals a chance for bringing these retrogressive views in public through social media which has a tremendous influence over the users especially the common mass users who are modern so far as the technological use is concerned, but traditional in thinking so far as their perception is concerned. The negative effects of the documentary *India's Daughter* may be mentioned as follows:

1. Gender stereotypes especially negative stereotypes have been grossly reinforced in the film through the comments of Mukesh and his lawyer. As of traits, what they pointed out that women should be silent, soft, tolerant, mute, confined within home and sexually attractive for the male.
2. They also represented the views against women's freedom. It is common for the patriarchy to limit the space of women by restricting their movement in terms of place, time and dress. Women's safe place is home for the patriarchy and the temple, kitchen and the house well is considered as their exclusive areas of free movement. Safe time for the movement of women is considered as 6 AM to 6 PM and beyond this time their safety and security may not be ensured. As of dress, they must wear in such a fashion that the undercurrent sexual desire of the male is not aroused. It is not the male, but the female who should be blamed for being victimized for any departure from these points of women code. The comments of Mukesh and his lawyer match with the dictates of patriarchy in full. What a coincidence! Udwin cannot shake off the responsibility in this regard.
3. Udwin also presented the age-old version of gender roles as preached by patriarchy in the narration of the rapist

and his lawyer. Patriarchy is prone to view women as loyal sister, faithful daughter, caring wife and tolerant mother. All roles of women should revolve round the sacred institutions of marriage, family and housekeeping. Women must be punished for any deviation from this role and thus acts of violence against women get a license from patriarchy. In the film, the lawyer of Mukesh Singh has clearly stated that in such a situation of deviation to gender norms and roles, he is in favour of honour killing by burning even his sister or daughter, the so-called culprit, by putting petrol on them openly in broad daylight.

4. A considerable part of the documentary is engaged in detecting the family conditions of the rape criminals. The way the poverty and wretched condition of the locality and the dwelling house of the rapists have been presented in the film is suggestive of a grossly rape-insensitive outlook. Indirectly an attempt has been made to state that it is only the miserable material condition of the perpetrators that is responsible for the rape. The aggressive attitudes and the anti-social profile of the criminals have been kept in hiding very cleverly. Thus this documentary is, in no way, a step for seeking justice for 'Nirbhaya'; it has been an excuse and safeguard for the rapists. That is why the friend of 'Nirbhaya' who was also injured for resisting the rapists during the gang rape of 'Nirbhaya', stated that this documentary is far from the truth. It is very much astonishing that Udwin did not interview this friend for unknown reasons.

Thus by the presentation of some fictitious, imposed and imaginative data and statement, the documentary *India's Daughter* by Leslee Udwin has failed to go into the root cause of rape and other forms of gender violence. Charges from many quarters are forwarded that Mukesh and his family has been paid for making such statements before the camera. If the charge is true, it is a matter of question as to how the producers and Udwin could do that! Rape is a crime and all of us must come open against this curse. The way the attempt has been made for detecting the root of the rape is sufficiently vague and erroneous. All basic information of the documentary has come either from

Mukesh and his family or his lawyer. It is quite surprising as to how can a criminal's views be so authentic in collecting and exposing the data which are basically directed to ensuring a system of justice against rape! Mukesh and his lawyer, after all, are not the representatives of India. Basically, rape is the disease coming out of patriarchy which is not the matter of any country in particular. So the documentary has tried to shift the focus of attention from patriarchy to the values of India in particular. The documentary has stormed the social media with thousands of posts and comments—some of which are in favour of Udwin and some are against Udwin. It is unfortunate to have such negative comments as to provide support to rape. There are many negative posts that are prone to malign both India and her culture and the women as a class of gender. So ultimately the publicity of the *India's Daughter* through social media has resulted in negative gender socialization of the viewers.

Another example of the role of social media in fostering gender socialization is a video named *My Choice* where Deepika Padukone has challenged the basic format of patriarchy through the implementation of the women's right of taking decision according to their will. *My Choice*, directed by Homi Adajania, calls for a change in the mindset of men about women and asks them to stop judging women for their choices of clothes, profession and life. Through the voice of Deepika, the message of the dominating appearance of the women in all sectors of their choice and the resultant empowerment of the women is sent with confidence. In patriarchal society, women are to undergo through various norms and practices that are settled and imposed by patriarchy and as such they are verily denied of the right to live in their own terms and interests. The space of women has been repeatedly determined by the male; women have to shape and reshape themselves in the way that is dictated and opted by the patriarchy. The video *My Choice* is the angry alternative version of this patriarchal paradigm of confining the women. *My Choice* has already drawn the attention of the viewers in a large number. Many positive posts have appeared on the sites. Although it is also the fact that some celebrities such as Shilpa Shetty, Sonam Kapoor, etc. have opposed *My Choice*. However *My Choice* has succeeded in creating a sensation among the viewers and sent a different gender message for the women so that they can rescue themselves from the conventional format of the patriarchy.

> The *My Choice* video is shouting out loud that a woman also has the choice to have an affair, to have sex in marriage or outside marriage, to not have sex and I would go one step more, and say that women also have the choice to drink alcohol and to smoke cigarettes. There is nothing like a man can do it and a woman cannot do it. Yes, the consequences of this choice also affect both equally. Patriarchal masculinity needs to wake up and realize that women also have these choices and will dare to make them.[16]

Priya Tanna, Editor, *Vogue India*, said,

> For me, *My Choice* holds a mirror to what women feel, think and want to express. In its approach and voice it is fundamentally an anthem for women who want to live life on their own terms, and pursue their own sun. It is both touching and thought provoking.[17]

After the release of the video's two and a half minutes clip, thousands of posts have stormed the social media. Many persons, not being feminists as such, posted comments for and against the message of the video. But there is no doubt that the video has been successful in hitting the traditional concept of gender and the patriarchal set-up for its inculcation. The very first line 'my body, my mind, my choice' is suggestive of the women's infinite right to access to her-self. The explosive content of the video has been clear by two statements of the clip—'having sex outside the marriage' and 'I can love a man, a woman or both' is also my choice. The first statement is hitting the very foundation of the institutions of family, marriage and motherhood all of which are considered as the basic structures of patriarchy. Many a post in social media expressed agony over the choice of extramarital sex by a woman. But the question here is that when a man is doing so in a regular manner in our society and when millions of men of almost every society are engaged in extramarital sexual relationship just because of being male, then where was the agony? Why the agony was not expressed in favour of women? In fact

---

[16] www.womensweb.in/2015/04/deepika-my-choice-video/
[17] www.campaignlive.com

it is the patriarchy that is guiding us (both male and female) to pass reaction on gender issues. So in case of man we remain mute and in case of woman we come to protest. This is not a fair and neutral approach to gender. Patriarchy has taught us to be stereotypical in expression of our masculinity or femininity. The video *My Choice* has hit the conventional pattern of gender stereotypes and traditional concept of gender role distribution. 'To have baby or not—is my choice' is a statement hitting the myth of gender role that woman are born to be loyal sister, faithful daughter, caring wife and tolerant mother. By the demand of establishing mating relationship with a man, or a woman or both, *My Choice* has broken the traditional gender norms and practices and thus has been successful in hitting and hating patriarchy. This paper is not directed to the objective of passing any instructions in respect of gender norms, issues and gender ideology, or gender socialization. But this paper is interested in gauging the role of social media and millions of posts and comments on the issues related to gender. From that angle, it may be said that the video *My Choice* preached and publicized through social media has been 100 per cent successful in creating gender sensitization among the viewers and the users of social media.

Napkin movement in different universities can be cited as the example that stormed the social media. The movement is primarily aimed at redefining gender and reviewing the traditional methods of gender construction and recreating the gender sensitization process of the university campus in particular and the society in general. Sanitary napkin movement, popularly called as pad against patriarchy movement, is a unique method of raising the protest against molestation and rape of the female student through the slogans against patriarchy written on sanitary napkins and their display. According to *The Times of India*, 'Jamia Milia Islamia's unique protest against sexism and patriarchy with slogans written on sanitary napkins found an echo on the Jadavpur University campus days after Jamia authorities showcaused four students for the act. A section of JU students, who have formed a new group called Periods, took the same route on Friday, spreading feminist messages written on sanitary napkins all over the campus. The message says, 'Girls are raped not because they are girls but because we live in a patriarchal society.'

The protest came days after a postgraduate student lodged a molestation complaint with the JU authorities and police. 'We adopted this movement to raise gender sensitization on the campus and stop the girl who was molested from being blamed,' said Arumita Mitra, a student of JU.[18] The vice chancellor of the university remarked against the form of protest simply on aesthetic ground. He opined that students should be aware of what is socially acceptable or unacceptable. But the students of the napkin movement argue that it is the patriarchy that wants to confine women within the narrow limits of sexual beauty (aesthetic). 'Behind the rhetoric of aesthetic is the politics of gender construction, which dictates how women should behave, how they should dress, what they should wear, what words they should use.'[19] The students also argue that patriarchy presents a double-standard in respect of women's beauty. For the patriarchy in general and for the preachers of socially acceptable forms of violence in particular, sanitary napkins are ugly and unacceptable items taken as forms of protest, whereas women who wear these napkins are taken as soft target of sexual violence even during menstruation!

Sanitary napkin movement has surely hit the conventional paradigm of gender stereotypes, gender norms and practices and the very process of gender construction and gender socialization. Thousands of posts in social media for and against the napkin movement have obviously opened a new route and new form of protest against patriarchy. It is the patriarchal values that have caused women to be ashamed of own body organ and its functions. Patriarchy, in order to fix the paternity, created the institution of marriage and family and confined the women within the four walls of 'home'. Thus the process of controlling the female sexuality began in course of which the women were taught to take the private part of their body as secret and a matter of shame. The social and cultural construction of gender has also taught the women to bear the idea that having vagina is the sign of physical weakness which provokes the woman to surrender to the male under all situations. Guided by this

---

[18] *The Times of India*, Kolkata, 29 March 2015.
[19] Kindlemag.in/decorum-purity/- comment of Prof. Soma Marik in the column of Srishti Datta Chaudhury.

patriarchal viewpoint, women of all countries and across all cultures have considered menstruation not as an anatomical feature of the female body but as a taboo and as stigma of a discreet social category, named woman. Thus women have been alienated from their own body in course of social and cultural construction of gender in conformity with the dictates of patriarchy, on the one hand, and on the other, have taken all attacks on their body in the form of rape or molestation as their natural fate. So by choosing sanitary napkin as the form of protest this conspiracy of patriarchy has been exposed. Napkin movement is surely to influence thousands of viewers and users of social media and is an addition to the forms of protest against patriarchy.

Thus media as such plays the role in gender socialization and gender construction which mostly becomes possible through reports, features, advertisements, tele-presentation of the narratives, and panel discussion and visualization of the gender codes and messages through cinema. From the role of media in sending gender messages to society, one question is bound to be raised as to which one is most important: reality or culture. A gendered society perceives gender in reality through social and cultural construction of every process involved with gender. Culture uses us much more than we use culture. Since culture, in some way or another, is a part of our feeling and perception, we cannot avoid the effects of culture in respect of gender. It is the fact that in the modern globalized society the experiences what we earn from reality are drawn not from any interaction with the reality but majorly through different sources of culture. So reality constructed through culture is a type of *pseudo-reality* what we superimpose on our perception and come to influence the society on the basis of it.

> After the Second World War when human suffering was out in the open for all to see, there were talks *redemption of physical reality* by which it was meant that cinema has the capacity to *mirror* reality without intervention.... Hence the reality that is presented is actually a reality modified, pruned and altered to suit one's world view.... Attempts to look at representations of women on the screen, must hence not be on the basis of whether the facts are true or not, but on the basis of how in the total

cinematic process the images appear in spite of being rooted in *truth*.[20]

Modern society is thus reflecting a culture-reality dichotomy as a result of which culture becomes real and real is taken as the effect of culture. Culture, being so powerful in modern society, is considered as the most reliable medium of gender socialization. Since mass media and social media are basically the cultural platform where people and users participate in cultural inter-action, share and post comments on various issues related to gender and assimilate the gender messages sent through audio-visualization of the narratives in cinema and television people come to shape the reality through their cultural perception. So ultimately culture shapes the reality of gender and media shapes the culture of gender. Since culture plays an important role in the manufacturing of the mental and spiritual package of the personality and perception of human being, the influence of culture becomes lasting and dominating on the one hand and on the other hand becomes smooth and spontaneous. Thus it is the magic of culture that creates a hallucination among the viewers and users and prompts them to decode the culture and to implement the gender messages and the gender ideology in their life as well as in the society. It is the magic world where 'the public sphere' as mentioned by Jürgen Habermas is fast disappearing and leaving its space to what Noam Chomsky termed as 'mass society'. It is the magic world where 'in effect, a new reality—hyperreality—is created, composed of the inter-mingling of people's behavior and media images ... and hence have no grounding in an *external reality*'.[21] So culture here comes as a product through a package of emotional human feelings that are also manufactured for sale only, and the irony is that these superimpositions of reality ultimately come to be taken as reality of life and society.

Sometimes culture also plays its role moving in the opposite direction of the conventional format of gender socialization and tries to alter the concept of gender with a view to have a better

---

[20] C. S. Lakshmi, "Feminism and the Cinema of Realism," in *Women in Indian Society,* 219–20.

[21] Giddens, *Sociology,* 463.

society both for male and female. There is no denying the fact that gender ideology, gender construction and gender socialization in particular and patriarchy in general results in the creation of gender inequality and gender discrimination in society since gender socialization is grounded on the notion of unequal socialization between the sexes. Various features and other forms of media culture portrayed in newspaper, magazine, television, radio, cinema and social media have been teaching gender roles differently for men and women in compliance with the social norms and expectations corresponding to their sexes. 'Sociologists today share the view that gender inequalities result because men and women are socialized into different roles.'[22] So gender socialization is aimed at reinforcing and consolidating the male power in society. However, like all power, gender power is also to be countered by some sorts of resistance that basically comes through the culture portrayed and preached in media. Alternative versions of gender socialization and gender messages are being constantly sent to the people through media. Many programmes in television are being launched regularly in order to change the gendered society and especially to change the outlook of gender. Cinema has been a major medium of projecting the alternative version of gender ideology and gender approach. Throughout the world many films are being released almost every week with a view to fight back the patriarchal view and construction of gender based solely on masculinity and femininity. Social media have been a regular field of public debate by which views of gender are constantly going to be shaped and reshaped with a view to have a better world both for men and women. So media is working, on the one hand, for the reinforcement of patriarchal values and again on the other hand it is constantly creating a resistance to patriarchy through the formation of a different gender culture and rational gender approach. With the advent of globalization in general and with the rise of internet in particular, the role of media in gender socialization has been a much more compelling topic of discussion. So new gender outlook emerging out of globalized web world is imminent and is going to be an interesting area of further research on gender and its future.

---

[22] Chattopadhyay, *Gender Inequality*, 20.

8

Role of Religion: Norms and Practices

Gender socialization, being an ongoing process, continuously shapes and reshapes the gender perception of boys and girls of every society by the use of so many social and cultural norms and practices of that given society. When the socialization process aims at exploring the gendered nature of these norms and practices and accordingly inspires the men and women to shape and reshape their behaviour in accordance with the perception of gender of a given society, then it is called gender socialization. Historical evidences prove that in almost all societies and across all cultures religion works as the chief source of all the norms of a society—be it social, political or cultural. 'Most cultures are largely shaped by their dominant religions and vice versa'.[1] So judged from the viewpoint of social and cultural construction of gender, it is very much necessary to explore the role of religion as an agent of gender socialization. The history of religion may corroborate the idea that religion influences culture and vice versa. It may also convince individuals that Christianity, Islam and Judaism are social constructs deeply rooted in history. Perhaps every one of them, at the time of their conception, was constructed with specific social interests. Tomoko Masuzawa, a US Professor and author of Inventions of World Religions, focuses her research on the historical development of the 19th and early 20th century search for the origin of religion. In terms of the relationship between religion and culture, she makes a pertinent suggestion that may help to support the fact religion and culture often influence each other; 'Religion is not an abstraction. It has vital significance only as it is deeply rooted in the moving process of folk life'.[2] Careful observation of cultures may suffice in confirming the fact that humans have, since their existence, been trying to shape social customs in order to establish a common good.

---

[1] Malory Nye, *Religion: The Basics* (New York, NY: Routledge, 2003), 14.
[2] Tomoko Masuzawa, *The Invention of World Religions* (Chicago: The University of Chicago Press, 2005), 39.

This section offers an exploration of the theological practices containing sufficient materials of authoritativeness as a result of which the system of exerting control over the women has been easy and the process of gender socialization has been linked to the supreme command of the God. 'Theology is a system of doctrines developed on the basis of a definite historic religion—say, Brahmanism or Islam or Christianity.'[3] Religious authority and control never works through logic and argument but rather they are popularly preached and believed as the dictates of God which in no case should be challenged by anybody and in case of its violation such a challenge would be a sin which must have to be punished by the same dictate of the God. Thus either by the threat of punishment or by direct control exerted in the name of God theological practices always mould the individual personality and social organization in its terms. Since the theological norms, instructions and practices are not based on logic, they are seen to be working smoothly in a society without education or with less education. Thereby it is experienced that the first fertile soil of theological hegemony in human history is the tribal society.

The tribe, as a form of social organization, has some unique features of its own which have made the establishment of gender inequality easier in tribal society. The members of tribal society lived together as a small group with the social bond of blood relation and all these made the tribe a very compact social organization. The compactness, again, has contributed in the achievement of social solidarity and unity which were considered very important for combating surrounding tribes regarded as potential enemies. One tribe was used to fight another tribe and an atmosphere of constant war continued to exist. Thus search for food through hunting, fishing, etc., or self-defence against the natural constraints and victory against another tribe in war were the marked features of their struggle for existence which also shaped their 'religious customs as well as other customs connected with food-getting, marriage, birth, sickness, death, initiation, war, protection from beasts and from the weather'.[4]

---

[3] D. Miall Edwards, *The Philosophy of Religion* (Indian edition) (Calcutta: Progressive Publishers, 1975), 25.

[4] Ibid, 96.

Thus tribal religion was conditioned by their material interests and since primitive people did not have a higher material development their religion also developed on the same low plane. This produced in their wake further domination of women in tribal society. So women's freedom was an odd question out of this situation. Women were considered as collective asset as women's fertility, that is, their reproductive power was the only viable tool of increasing population ensuring the collective strength to which women of the primitive society had to surrender unconditionally. In primitive society control over women was the first marked symbol of unity, force and victory against all other rival oppositions, natural or human. Religion came forward to legitimize this course of actions and necessary norms and practices were framed in this regard.

Subsequent societies, in spite of being materially, culturally and technically advanced, retained the basic features and approaches of the tribal society in respect of power, solidarity of the community, management of conflicts, exertion of control and religion. The way the tribal society ensured social order and control through the manipulation of theological practices and the use of religion was also followed by all the subsequent societies of the world. Thus the theological norms and practices became the basis of all social rules and norms as a result of which theological and religious approach to gender came to pervade all subsequent societies and the resultant gender inequality appeared on the scene. Judged from this point of logic it can be said that the first growth of patriarchy in human history was marked in tribal society. The matter of social control, especially the control of women through the use of religion is probably the most important discovery of the tribal society and subsequently it was also accepted and followed by the societies of the later age. The element of domination, supremacy, authoritativeness and illusion made the religion very much acceptable to the managers of power and the preachers of patriarchy. Religion never leaves any space for free opinion. By preaching the theory of birth and rebirth, by the threat of punishment in the world beyond death, by initiating the theory of consequences of deeds in previous birth and also in this mortal life, by preaching the value of toleration and by highlighting the value of surrender and self-effacement, religion came to suppress the free development of personality, especially of the women, on the one hand, and on the other, worked as a tool for controlling the society in its term at large. Following the dictates of religion blindly people make them dependent on a so-called supernatural force and lose their power of resistance totally. As a result they become the slaves of supernatural power in course of time. Thus social change becomes almost impossible in a society dominated by religion. Religion, through its false promises, threat of punishment and lower birth and also by emphasizing the matter of toleration, creates inertia among the common people. That is why Karl Marx described religion as the opium of the people. So against this background of morphologic features of religion, it is clearly understood that religion carries with it enough material for the suppression of women. Gender has historically been a concept devised by men because religion and culture are closely associated. This is confirmed by the fact that even the study of religion is soaked in the pervasiveness of androcentricism. Nye suggests, 'the ideology of a male god is what paved the way for the subordination of women in many societies'.[5] Because androcentricism is pervasive in the study of religion, God is literally explained as a male person. Christianity, Judaism and Islam teach that Adam was created first and Eve afterwards. This belief is interpreted by some cultures to mean that women are inferior to men in principle. Now we can proceed to see as to how this suppression of the women has been reflected in different types of religions.

Christianity

It has considered women as the representative and successor of Eve and has given woman an inferior status as compared to man. With reference to Genesis, we may quote the gospel of the Lord on the perspective of eating the prohibited fruit by Eve and of tempting Adam, 'I will greatly multiply thy sorrow and thy conception, in sorrow thou shall bring forth children, and thy desire shall be to thy husband, and he shall rule over thee.' In

[5] Malory Nye, *Religion*, 82.

Europe, the Catholic Church has taken frequent role to control the reproductive power of women and passed its option about birth control and abortion in accordance with the dictates of patriarchy. It was preached that woman is the emblem of erotic sexual desire and is the cause of sexual deviation of man and so she is also the emblem of sin. From the 7th to the 12th century, women of Europe were deprived of the right to education since the Church did not approve it. According to the Christian Church, child production and home management are the specific functions allotted to women. Even the Church did not allow the women to read the Bible, the sacred scripture of the Christians. It was a popular propaganda that women are normally less intelligent than men and since they are treated as the emblem of sin due to their occupation of the dangerous sexual power, they should not be directly allowed to read the Bible. For their religious consciousness through Bible, they should proceed through the father or husband. Even the great reformer Martin Luther King and John Kelvin preached that women, by nature, are subordinate to men and women can liberate themselves from the sin of Eve only by surrendering to men, especially to their husbands. However, the Renaissance and Reformation movements subsequently questioned the logic of women subordination and challenged the teachings and preaching of the Church in this regard. But ultimately supremacy of the male was re-established and women challenging this system of male domination were declared as 'witch' and were convicted to death by the protector of the religion.

People may perceive gender as a social category but careful observation of the priesthood in Catholicism maintains, 'the category of gender is in use among us only to benefit some members of the group'.[6]

Islam

Known generally for its concept of equality, Islam has grossly supported gender inequality. A predominant perception about

---

[6] Ian Hacking, The Social *Construction of What?* (Cambridge, MA: Harvard University Press, 1999), 8.

Islam is that it is a misogynistic religion. Though all major world religions have scriptures that establish the superiority of men over women, male superiority is attributed to Islam more so than other major world religions.[7,8] Some scholars argue that Koran has taken a conservative functional approach to the differences between male and female sex. It is argued that since men have greater physical and mental qualities and since men have the abilities to protect the women who are gentler and weaker than men, it is justified to locate the men above women in the social arrangements. Thus Qur'an endorses a traditional masculine ideology based on patriarchy. Sometimes the reformist scholars argue that in Qur'an men and women have been given the same parental rights and thereby an equal status.[9,10] But the fact is that in lieu of providing details about the so called equality between the sexes, the Qur'an acknowledges and emphasizes the biological role of the women in childbearing and childrearing. The supporters of the conservative approach to the Qur'an argue that the women's pursuit of education should not violate conservative Islamic values or prevent them from meeting their domestic obligations a wives and mothers.[11] In Islam, the social interaction between unmarried men and women at all social events where non-family members are present is strictly prohibited. This viewpoint of Islam has wider implications for opposite sex interactions in other settings such as employment or education. 'By licensing polygamy, concubinage, and easy divorce for men, originally allowed under different circumstances in a different society, Islam lent itself to being interpreted as endorsing and giving religious sanction to a deeply negative and debased conception of women'.[12]

---

[7] V. Harrison, "Modern Women, Traditional Abrahamic Religions and Interpreting Sacred Texts," *Feminist Theology*, 15 (2007), 145–59.

[8] M. Hasan, "Feminism as Islamophobia: A Review of Misogyny Charges Against Islam," *Intellectual Discourse* 20 (2012), 55–78.

[9] A. Barlas, *"Believing Women" in Islam: Un-reading Patriarchal Interpretations of the Qur'an* (Austin: Texas University Press, 2002), 137.

[10] Faizur Rahman, *Major Themes of the Qur'an*, 2nd edition (Chicago, IL: University of Chicago Press, 2009), 31.

[11] J. Badawi, *The Status of Women in Islam* (Plainfield: MSA of US and Canada, 1980), 18.

[12] Lahoucine Ouzgane. "Women and Islam," *Postmodern Culture 3.3* (1993), Project MUSE. Retrieved 15 November 2012, from http://muse.jhu.edu/

Hinduism

Hinduism has presented women as degraded and downtrodden through its very many textual references and religious rites. 'The concept of female in Hinduism presents an important duality: on the one hand, the woman is fertile, benevolent—the bearer, on the other, she is aggressive, malevolent—the destroyer.'[13] Women are the source of both good and bad power. Since women are treated as a potential source of dangerously bad power, they must be controlled by men who are treated as part of the Spirit, that is, *Purusha*'. So this study of men's control over women has shaped the image of Hindu women both in religious texts and in practices. The basic rules for women's behaviour were fixed by the laws of Manu who dictated that woman must be subject to her father in her infancy, to her husband in her youth and to her son in her old age. Manu also advised women to constantly worship their husband as God and a faithful wife will never violate her duty to her husband and she will never act independently breaking the bonds of control imposed by her husband. The inner significance of such control is not difficult to understand. Men's control over women was exercised mainly to ensure the identification of paternity and the notion of Hindu women has emerged out of this control. Accordingly, Hindu scriptures and practices have built an image of women who are necessarily dutiful, righteous, virtuous, passive, chaste, self-effacing and loyal and everything what are needed to be good daughter, good wife and good mother. Sita in the Ramayana and Draupadi in the Mahabharata have been constantly a victim of gender inequality and their ideals formatted in the line of male supremacy have been the source of lifestyle of the Indian women for centuries. The ideological layer of history is formed under the influence of religious scriptures and practices in all societies. India is no exception in this regard. Accordingly, the concept of male supremacy and gender inequality has emerged as a mega pattern supported by many social practices such as casteism, marriage and family system. 'The Vedas, the sacred scripture of

---

[13] Susan Wadley, "Women and the Hindu Tradition," in *Women in Indian Society*, 24.

the Hindus, has described women as more poisonous than snake, vulture, razor and poison it.' Hinduism has officially sponsored the custom of 'sati', that is, the burning of wife with the dead husband, male polygamy, child marriage of female and so many inhuman practices for women. The reason behind the stand of Hinduism against women lies in the concept of femaleness portrayed in Hindu ideology. According to Hinduism, woman embodies *Shakti*, that is, the original energy of the universe which again is expressed through female body.

> Women are active religious practitioners but they have little religious authority. Official religious power has been vested with men. So far as the culture is concerned women are chiefly entrusted with the responsibility of observing rites and vows for the welfare of the male members of the family. Women's ritual and cultural practices reinforces the view of women as obedient daughter, dutiful wife and affectionate mother. Institutions like marriage, family and patriarchy are always aimed at indoctrinating gender socialization in such a manner that male supremacy over these institutions comes to be established very easily and these are done completely with the religious and Hindu textual sanctioning. Thus Hinduism has taken such a religious approach as has contributed to the development of gender inequality as a pervasive feature of society.[14]

Thus the religious approach has served as a major source of gender inequality in all societies and across all cultures. The religious approach is probably the oldest concept of gender inequality and it is perhaps also the strongest source of the problem. Since all religions are concerned with cosmological theory locating women in a very degraded position as compared to men and since in all religions cosmos is given a graphical set-up at the mercy and will of God the problem of gender inequality has appeared very naturally. It is not also very difficult to understand the source of the potential strength of the problem of gender inequality subsequently throughout history as much as the religious approach is concerned.

[14] Chattopadhyay, *Gender Inequality,* 26.

All the dominating religions of the world participate in the process of gender socialization and accordingly play a central role in the social and cultural construction of gender. Particularly since all the gods of nearly all the religions are male gods and since nearly all the religions admit the relative superiority of the male gender, the resultant position of the women has been lower than the men. All the religions of the world—be it Christianity, Islam or Hinduism—carry sufficient attributes that undermine the position of the women. Thus religious teachings always work for justifying the basic postulates of the theology that the women are inferior to men. In this way religion causes differential socialization for men and women.

The first thing of religions that causes differential social-ization is their notion of gender roles of men and women. Religions preach different roles for different genders. For the male gender, all the religions more or less share some common attributes in respect of gender role distribution in society. Like Christianity and Islam, Hinduism also believes that men, that is, male gender is modelled by God as leader of the society as well as the family. As the chief of the family, man is viewed as the breadwinner and caretaker of the women of the family, especially wives. They are naturally powerful husbands and are, thus, allowed to exert any sort of control over the female members of the family. Especially the control of female sexual-ity is the bounden duty of the male members of the family. It is recognized important for ensuring the paternity of the baby. The person who cannot control his wife is often criticized as henpecked. Men are viewed by all the religions from the angle of power. Public affairs are to be dealt exclusively by men. So the jobs ranging from political affairs to business and from hunting to hardworking are the main areas of male activity. For all the religions, traditional approach to gender roles has been perpetuated. The myths about the notion of gender roles for men are twofold: one, women are more religious than men and two, men have greater propensity of risky behaviour as a result of which men indulge in irreligious attitudes on the one hand, and on the other, get interest in material activities or pursuits. In spite of diverse arguments, there is complete agreement among scholars that the reason behind the dif-ferences in the religiousness of the women are differential gender socialization and the reason for the propensity of risky behaviour of men is the differential attitude of religion itself towards gender roles for men and women.

In contrast to the gender role of the men, religions of the world have come to reinforce a traditional approach to gender role for the women. Almost all the religions have viewed the women as wives or mothers. As wife, a woman is to carry out all the orders of her husband and she is to take care of all the comforts of her husband. It is also the bounden duty of the wife to satisfy the sexual urge of her husband as and when necessary. She should be not only loyal but also dutiful. Religions are commonly interested to view the women in procreating role. So role of mother is the most important role of the women in the society. Thus childbearing and childrearing is the exclusive role of the women. Since childrearing is a long process intertwined with a lot of complicated activities such as the nursing, education, nutrition, health and safety of the child a mother in particular and a woman in general will have to spend their life inside the closed corridor of the home. So restricting her movement in the private area of home is the precondition of the women's gender role performance. Again world religions are very much interested to view the women spiritually during the performance of their roles as mothers or wives since the role of mother is believed to subsume religiousness as teaching the children morality and caring for the physical and spiritual well-being of the other family members.[15,16] All religions of the world try to view gender role from the viewpoint of 'natural order'. This means religions have a great influence in reinforcing the idea of differential gender role for men and women. Natural viewpoint of gender role emphasizes on the point of domestic role for women and the breadwinning role for men. This clearly means that religions, on the one hand, are prone to see women to be dependent on men, whilst on the other, men are expected to play dominant role in supplying basic necessities to the household. Churches play an important role in defining family norms and regulating

---

[15] Charles Glock, Ringer Benjamin, and Babbie Earl, *To Comfort and to Challenge* (Berkeley: University of California Press, 1967), 199.

[16] Tony Walter and Grace Davie, "The Religiosity of Women in the Modern West," *British Journal of Sociology* 49(4) (1998), 640–69.

behaviours around gender and sexuality. Therefore main religions of the world contain certain ideas about the appropriate roles for men and women in society, and traditionally, this has placed women in the home and men in the 'outside' world. Religions may differ to some extent in this regard, but similar normative claims about men's and women's roles are present across all denominations of religions in the world.

The conservative perspective of Islam's approach to gender argues that a woman's primary role should be as a wife and mother. If any woman needs to work then her job should be gender-appropriate and must not violate Islamic norms and practices and must not interfere with her domestic responsibilities. For the conservative scholars, if women participate in labour force equal to men, the health of family will suffer.[17,18] So any woman opting for practicing a free choice of gender role must have to attain a rarest ability of making a balance among gender, family and Islam. Islam is particularly concerned with imposing restrictions over women in respect of opposite sex interactions in order to prevent premarital sex, extramarital sex, dating and all other Western mode of practicing free sex. Interpretations of Islam also include prohibition on any form of physical contact such as shaking hands and hugging. Sexual modesty for the women in particular is also a deep concern of Islam. The Qur'an's concern for the sexual modesty of the women

> receives the most attention and is one of the most debated gender related issues within Islam. The debate is centred on whether or not the hijab, a form of dress that requires women to cover their entire body except for their hands and face, is a requirement in Islam. Conservative scholars argue that the Qur'an is clear about the restrictions on women's dress and the hijab is a requirement ... the hijab ... prevents women from being viewed as objects of lust by men.[19]

---

[17] M. Abdul-Rauf, *Islamic View of Women and Family* (Cairo: The Supreme Council for Islamic Affairs, 1993), 13.

[18] J. Badawi, *The Status of Women in Islam* (Plainfield: MSA of US and Canada, 1980), 20.

[19] Elham Bagheri, *A Qualitative Investigation of Religion, Gender Role Beliefs and Culture in the Lives of a Select Group of Muslim Men*, PhD Thesis, University of Iowa, 2012, 30. Retrieved 7 July 2017, from http: //ir.uiowa.edu/etd/3561

Dominating religions of the world more or less converge on the same plane in respect of their dictates and teachings for the construction of gender, assimilation of gender norms and practices and compliance of the gender ideology of the given society. Gender socialization has a great role in the making of gender, and religion in particular plays an important role in the process of gender socialization. On the basis of the materials received in nearly all the religions of the world it can be remarked that the structure and content of the world religions is misogynist. The material of gender inequality especially the anti-woman stand is perhaps present in the religions since inception. So gender socialization through religion is illustrated in sociology as a detailed picture of differential socialization for men and women. Although it is also the fact that the theoretical writings and literatures on the role of religion in gender socialization is scanty and superficial. However, gender socialization, being necessarily differential socialization for men and women, first, operates through the reinforcement of the ideas of differential gender roles for men and women. Second, the process of gender socialization operates through the construction of gender stereotypes that are also different for male and female. The stereotypes for men and women have been designed in accordance to their respective gender roles. Gender stereotypes for men are necessarily different than the gender stereotypes for the women because of the differences in their gender roles. All religions—Christianity, Islam and Hinduism—have inspired men to be brave, ambitious, hardworking, tough, dominating, loud, breadwinner, aggressive and strong. All these qualities ultimately are exercised against the women and all the religions of the world provide a tacit support in this regard. So the philosophy of stereotypes is based on male experiences and aimed at fulfilling the patriarchal intention of undermining the position of the women. As a result such stereotypical concepts have created many an 'opposite pairs' resulting in a gross gender inequality. Such 'pairs' are as follows:

Male—central: female—marginal; male—subject: female—object; male—reason: female—emotion; male—active: female—passive; male—public: female—private, etc.

In compliance with these set of 'opposite pairs model' women are always inspired to internalize the gender stereotypes which are opposite to the men. In this way the women are encouraged to be silent, submissive, weak, soft, caring, righteous, honest, chaste, dutiful, loyal, domesticated and self-effacing. It is argued that these women stereotypes are necessary for discharging their duties within home as wife and mother. Since women are conceived as exclusively homemaker and childbearer by all religions, these stereotypes will help them to ensure peace and well-being of the family. Thus these feminine stereotypes as taught by the religions may be termed as the ideological tools of the process of making of the gender in general and the femininity in particular. So far as the culture of feminine stereotypes is concerned women are chiefly entrusted with the responsibility of observing different stereotypical norms, practices, rites and vows for the welfare of the male members of the family. Women's normative, ritual and cultural practices reinforces the view of women as obedient daughter, dutiful wife and affectionate mother. Institutions like marriage, family and patriarchy are always aimed at creating gender stereotypes for indoctrinating gender socialization in such a manner that male supremacy over these institutions comes to be established very easily and these are done completely with the religious textual sanctioning in all countries and across all cultures.

There has been little effort in the theoretical level for justifying the relation between gender socialization and religion. Even the substantial reviews of literature on any topic related to gender inequality say very little about the relation between gender roles and gender stereotypes and gender socialization. The question is also very pertinent as to why and how do the women respond to the differential system of gender role distribution and gender stereotypes formation. Traditionally, it is argued that women are naturally born as nurturing, submissive, soft, honest and righteous and these qualities inspire them to accept the domination of religion very easily. Traditional religious institutions are seen to legitimize these stereotypes through differential socialization in order to locate the male in the centre of power and management of the society. But traditional logic does not hold water because no genuine explanation is available here by which the reason of social and cultural intervention including especially the intervention of the religion in the field of the making of gender can be detected per se. Based on the reality of such social and cultural intervention in making of gender Simone de Beauvoir remarked, 'One is not born, but rather becomes, a woman. No biological, psychological or economic fate determines the figure that the human female presents in society; it is civilization as a whole that produces this creature, intermediate between male and eunuch, which is described as feminine. Only the intervention of someone else can establish an individual as an *Other*'.[20] Among many other interventionist agencies religion also work as a potent agent of gender socialization. In this section we will try to search out different theories and models by which grounds of gender socialization can be understood.

The relation among gender socialization, religiousness and gender role and gender stereotypes is often explored by three major feminine stereotypes—*inferiority, subservience and domesticity*. The above-mentioned gender role distribution and stereotypes formation approach encouraged by religions results in serious undermining of the position of the women and thus gives birth to gender inequality which often expresses itself through three major conventional forms of stereotypes— inferiority, subservience and domesticity. Inferiority as a weapon of creating gender inequality is based on the very common myth of the superior male intellect, that is, the idea that men are better species than women.[21] It is very clear that on the basis of the biological difference between men and women these three forms of gender inequality have emerged. The notion of inferiority includes two points which are biologically concerned and indirectly related to the anatomical characteristics of women. One, inferiority points out at the physical weakness of women. Biological approach, along with some sociologists, argue that it is due to the physical weakness of women that women were never engaged in hunting and subsequently they were confined at 'home' and were occupied primarily with the job of 'mothering' and home management along with some agricultural jobs. So due to their physical weakness women are exterminated from a vast variety of work. Two, since physical weakness becomes a constraint to their access in the broader working world, women's

---

[20]   de Beauvoir, *The Second Sex* (London: Vintage, 1953), 295.
[21]   Joanna Liddle and Roma Joshi, *Daughters of Independence: Gender, Caste and Class in India* (London: Zed Books Ltd, 1986), 177–80.

interaction with the outside world becomes very limited and accordingly this alienation results in erosion of intelligence which again makes them dull-witted, passive, mute and self-effacing. So in that sense, the term 'interiority' has a tremendous implication in undermining the position of women. The notion of subservience claims that women, due to their inferiority as compared to men, should remain under strict control of male.

> As soon as women refuse to pretend to be submissive and dependent, thereby exposing the myth, they lose the benefits of femininity. The women are punished for refusing men's protection, for female assertiveness represents a challenge to male authority and control and any woman, who shows assertive qualities, is defined as an abnormal female.[22]

The term 'abnormal female' has a biological implication in the sense that such women are not of the usual types, and they lack the essential qualities of femininity as biologically fit for women. The notion of domesticity suggests that

> marriage is the proper state for a woman. It is because of possessiveness by men that married women are treated safe for the continuation of the male control. It is also true that man's desire of property rights over women has pushed them in the stereotype of domesticity. Any woman, resisting the domestic stereotype of women as private sexual property, is defined instead as sexually available to anyone. The domestic stereotype defines woman as sexual object and male property. Thus the stereotypes about women's inferior abilities, subservient qualities and domestic needs form part of a gender ideology which makes sharp distinction between the social constructs of masculinity and femininity.[23]

The notion of domesticity has located women in an exclusive biological category which has a serious implication in justifying the fact of differential gender role distribution and gender stereotypes and resultant gender inequality. The inferiority, subservience and domesticity model can be termed as socio-psychological model of gender socialization.

The *social power approach* to the relation among gender socialization, religion and gender role and gender stereotypes

---

[22] Ibid, 183–84.
[23] Ibid.

argues that the relative lack of social power experienced by the women in society is primarily responsible for the reinforcement of differential gender roles and the construction of the feminine stereotypes in particular and for the smooth operation of gender socialization through religion in general.[24] First, differential gender socialization results in lack of social power that leads to a sense of helplessness or submissiveness that again compels the women to resort to a supernatural power as popularized by some religions. Second, 'a lack of social power is associated with lower workforce participation, which has been seen as related to greater female religious participation'.[25] Third, 'women's subordinate social role could lead to greater religiosity as a means of comfort to compensate for blocked aspirations and mistreatments'.[26] But empirical support in favour of these arguments is lacking. Studies, for example, have shown that career-oriented women are as religious as housewives, and both are far more religious than their male counterparts.[27,28] Thompson using a *masculinity–femininity scale* found a strong relationship between religiousness and feminine personality traits.[29] To him, persons with higher feminine characteristics will tend to be more religious regardless of their sex. Similarly persons with higher masculine characteristics will tend to be more irreligious. But Thompson's study fails to explore the origin of differential socialization and the construction of stereotypes. The masculinity–femininity model itself being a social and cultural construction cannot be treated appropriate for assessment of the reason of another social and cultural construction, that is, gender role and gender stereotypes. Masculinity—femininity is also the result of differential

---

[24] Bryan S. Turner, *Religion and Social Theory*, 2nd ed. (London: SAGE Publications, 1991), 110.

[25] Allan S. Miller and Rodney Stark, "Gender and Religiousness: Can Socialization Explanations Be Saved?" *American Journal of Sociology* 107(6) (May 2002), 1399–1423.

[26] Ibid.

[27] Marie Cornwall, "The Influence of Three Agents of Religious Socialization: Family, Church, and Peers." In *The Religion and Family Connection: Social Science Perspectives*, ed. Darwin L. Thomas (Provo, UT: Religious Studies Center, Brigham Young University, 1988), 207–31.

[28] Rodney Stark, *Doing Sociology* (Belmont, CA: Wadsworth, 1992), 77.

[29] E. H. Thompson, "Beneath the Status Characteristics: Gender Variations in Religiousness," *Journal for the Scientific Study of Religion* 30 (1991), 381–94.

gender socialization and thus it is logically impossible to explore the relation among gender socialization, religion and gender role distribution and gender stereotypes by this masculinity–femininity model. Again some studies following *biological approach* view the difference between man and woman as the difference between oestrogen and androgen, and accordingly, with the help of these studies, the biological approach argues that it is due to the influence of oestrogen hormone that women are identified with femininity and again accordingly they are placed in the unequal position of gender hierarchy. Thus in compliance with their placement in unequal gender role and with their identification with femininity the women come to internalize the feminine gender stereotypes more and more as a result of which gender socialization operates as a process of differential socialization. But the biological approach fails to explore the role of society and culture in the operation of gender socialization and very carefully conceals the part played by patriarchal intervention through social and cultural manipulation in the field of gender. As per biological approach, women's unequal placement in gender role and their assimilation of feminine stereotypes are supposed to be the result of their free choice due to their experiences of constraint in biology. But the fact is that women are never free in role acquisition or in stereotypical manifestation. For Beauvoir, 'every female human being is not necessarily a woman; to be so considered she must share in that mysterious and threatened reality known as femininity'.[30] This reality is not the creation of the women; it is a social and cultural construction modelled upon the patriarchal gender ideology. And at every stage of this construction process religion plays a very active role with a view to give it an ideological support.

Gender socialization is the process of internalizing society's values in order to adapt to the system of teaching–learning as to how people should behave as males and females in society. The social learning process that encourages people to imbibe and understand the various aspects of gender norms and practices initiates the process of gender socialization. Gender socialization encompasses the process of learning society's gender roles and

[30] de Beauvoir, *The Second Sex*, 13.

their advantages and limitations. The analysis of gender and culture has drawn on literary theory with the deconstructionism of Derrida and also on the discourse analysis of Michel Foucault. The emphasis has shifted from the individual's learning experience to the creation of the texts or representations that construct our cultural and ideological notions of gender. In the Indian context, woman is defined as an ambivalent person. Woman is located in myth and popular culture as both goddess and *Shakti* and as virtuous and evil at the same time. Women were not only revered and worshipped but also controlled through a direct regulation of her sexuality since it is believed in the orthodox religious sense as dangerous. The theoretical position in this regard can be clear through the understanding of the value structure in Indian society where the dual concept of the female in Hindu philosophy is seen. On the one hand, woman is fertile, benevolent, bestower of prosperity and, on the other, she is considered aggressive, malevolent and destructive. This dual character manifests in the goddesses also. The value structure by presenting the dual character of women seems to have been successful in creating a misogynist cultural system. Thus in all countries religion is a powerful social institution that shapes gender perception and identity of the persons in society. In order to exercise the strong control over the women and their sexuality religion in all societies and across all cultures have created sacred spaces where only men are allowed to enter and not women. There are norms by which only men can perform certain duties or obligations pertaining to religious activities. Religion has allowed the access of the women so long the access does not collide with the process of their internalization of feminine qualities and of enforcing the stereotypical views of inferiority, subservience and domesticity. As a result there have been many sacred texts which relegate women's place to lower or secondary rank to man. Such texts are frequently quoted as the spiritual basis for the legitimization of women's low status through the ages. They are the sacred authority that teaches that woman's status has to be low and unequal to that of man. In this way religion, in all societies and across all cultures, plays a strong role in the formation and continuation of gender inequality.

9

Role of Religious Myths and Concepts

Religion in all countries and across all cultures acts as an agent of patriarchy and thereby plays an important role in differential gender socialization. Religion, through its various dogmas, myths, concepts and beliefs, comes to shape the gender perception and orientation of women in a manner so that they accept very smoothly the ideals of femininity and thus become a part of the gender ideology modelled upon patriarchy. Different myths preached by religion ultimately work upon the women in particular with an objective of reinforcing the notion of inferiority, subservience and domesticity so that they cannot become a challenge to the male authority. Religious teachings indirectly give a sanction to the patriarchal design of gender inequality, gender discrimination and gender socialization. In order to assess the relation between differential gender socialization and gender differences in religiousness and in order to assess the role of religion in this regard, an exploration in the textual teachings of the religions is needed. Some mythical teachings are very common to all religions of the world. They are

1. The existence of previous life, afterlife and rebirth
2. Concept of hell and paradise
3. Concept of atonement
4. Belief in supernatural

Nearly all religions preach the existence of *previous life, after-life and rebirth.* In China, India and all other underdeveloped States of Asia, Middle East and Africa, especially in rural areas of the countries, the traditional cultural values and norms have put women at a very disadvantageous position. When a family dispute or crisis such as an extramarital affair occurs, or when any critical situation is faced by the family such as drought, flood, death especially unnatural death and problems in smooth reproduction, the woman is always to blame. It is often told that malevolent characteristics of the woman are responsible for the distress of the family and near relatives. The traditional religious attitudes have always put women to acid test of purity, righteousness and blessedness every now and then. The misfortune of the women in traditional societies starts with the very birth of the women. In many societies, it is firmly believed that the birth of the female child is the result of certain misdeeds of the parents and the descent. First, it is argued that the misdeeds of the parents in previous life have resulted in the birth of the female child in present life and, second, it is argued that it is the misdeeds of the female child herself that she is born as daughter, not as son. In India, there are many proverbs which openly declare the birth of daughter as the sin of previous life. In contrast, the birth of a son is celebrated as the instances of virtue. Thus, the religious support in endorsing this pattern of thinking always puts women in marginalized situation in society and culture. Accordingly, the gender socialization of the women in particular is very much influenced by the concept of previous life. Previous life theory exerts a tremendous pressure on their socialization process and, thus, the resultant gender inequality becomes ideologically legitimized. Previous life's connection with the present inferior status of the women is a very strong plea for Christianity. Christianity has considered women as the representative and successor of Eve and has given woman an inferior status as compared to man. With reference to Genesis, we may quote the gospel of the Lord on the perspective of eating the prohibited fruit by Eve and of tempting Adam, 'I will greatly multiply thy sorrow and thy conception, in sorrow thou shalt bring forth children, and thy desire shall be to thy husband, and he shall rule over thee'. Thus, it has been argued in Christianity that women's present life is determined by the wishes of the Lord and thus what is happening in the present life of the women is previously determined. Even the great reformer Martin Luther King and John Kelvin preached that women, by nature, are subordinate to men and women can liberate themselves from the sin of Eve only by surrendering to men, especially to their husbands. St. Thomas Aquinas contends that procreation was God's sole purpose to create the female species. For Aquinas, 'it is necessary for women to be made, as the scripture says, as a helper to man; not, indeed, as a helpmate in other works, as some say, since man can be more efficiently helped by another man in other works;

but as a helper in the work of generation...'.[1] So it is seen that previous life theory of Christianity plays a strong role in chalking out the pattern of gender socialization of the women. According to Hinduism, women embodies *Shakti*, that is, the original energy of the universe which again is expressed through the female body. The common metaphor of this view is that woman is the field or earth where man puts his seed and brings reproduction into reality. Another important facet of femaleness in Hinduism is that woman is also considered as *Prakriti* or uncultured nature. As nature, woman must carry forward the task of reproduction according to the command of *Purusha* or male master. The union of *Prakriti* and *Purusha* makes the creation of the universe possible. Since woman is the source of energy the nature of which is to contribute constantly to the process of reproduction, woman and her sexuality is to be controlled very tightly by man and by transferring the right of controlling the sexual power to man, woman can be truly liberated in the real sense of the term and then only woman can be declared as benevolent. Thus the basic nature of the conception of femaleness under Hinduism has not only manipulated the male–female relation but also restricted the spheres of women's movement in all fields such as religion, culture and institution. The view of Hinduism about the women's duties and nature has linked the present life with the previous life which is again presented as God's wish and desire. In the Hindu religious texts and culture, the birth of daughter is viewed as the sin of the previous life of the parents. In contrast, the birth of a son is applauded as the virtue of the previous and present life of the parents. It is seen in proverbs that the frustrated life of the woman starts with her birth. Whereas, the male child releases his father from the fear of going to the '*Punnam* hell', the birth of a female child does not get a warm reception. Parents are, in no way, benefited by a female child in this birth or in next birth, because as a result of being guided by false ideological conceptions and cultural superstitions parents treat the birth of daughter as a debt of father, sin of mother and a burden of society. The birth of a son has been termed by proverb as the 'virtuous appearance' meaning thereby that there is no connection of virtue of a father

---

[1] Majumdar, *A Short Introduction to Feminist Theory*, 5.

with the birth of a daughter. Rather it is due to the sin of anybody else that the daughter is born. The proverb is—

The son appears
Due to the virtue of father.

In this way, the previous life theory has made the differential gender socialization an inevitable consequence in a patriarchal traditional society.

Afterlife theory also has made the position of women very miserable in all societies and across all cultures. The philosophy of rebirth has been serving as the opium of the people in the sense that just being based on imagination of rebirth and afterlife, people especially the women tolerate all mistreatments of present life on the one hand, and on the other, aspire to surpass the limits of femininity by being born as male gender in their next birth. It has been noticed that in lieu of demonstrating resistance movements against all discriminations in present life, the women build castles in the air based on the belief of rebirth and thus surpass the trials and tribulations of this birth. If it is confidentially asked any woman of traditional society as to what she wished to become (a man or a woman) if she was given a rebirth, that is, second life after this one, the greatest possible answer of approximately the major percentage of the women will be in favour of being man. There are plenty of case studies that prove that behind the incidence of suicides of the women, the notion of rebirth works as promotional force. It is clear that, given a chance of rebirth, most women would leave their lower status or disadvantaged position in the society and would start afresh as man. In a folk rhyme, the picture has been depicted very faithfully. Sometimes it happens that women themselves start thinking that they are worthless. They become a prototype of the desires and passions of male. Subsequently, it turns into a dual male system. This system has been fully reflected in a vow rhyme. 'In the women vows ... we get an impression of the mind and thinking of a nation ... vows are the form of inner mental desire of the women.[2]

The matter of cursing the fate of previous and present life and of getting a better status in afterlife is reflected in many rhymes

---

[2] Abanindranath Tagore, *Banglar Broto* (Biswavidyalaya Sangrah) (Kolkata: India Publishing House, 1919), 6.

such as rhymes of *Dasputuli* vow which is a part of the cultural mosaic of Bengal. The rhymes of *Dasputuli* vow read as follows:

1. This time, after death, I shall be a human being and I shall get a husband like Rama.
2. This time, after death, I shall be a human being and I shall be a chaste wife like Sita.
3. This time, after death, I shall be a human being and I shall get a brother-in-law like Laxmana.
4. This time, after death, I shall be a human being and I shall get a father-in-law like Dasharatha.
5. This time, after death, I shall be a human being and I shall get a mother-in-law like Kaushalla.
6. This time, after death, I shall be a human being and I shall be like Kunti having sons.
7. This time, after death, I shall be a human being and I shall be Cook like Draupadi.
8. This time, after death, I shall be a human being and I shall be loving like Durga.
9. This time, after death, I shall be a human being and I shall undertake burden like Earth.
10. This time, after death, I shall be a human being and I shall be productive like Shastthi.[3]

The above-mentioned rhyme is a collection of ten mantras (hymns) uttered by the unmarried girls towards 10 dolls made of thin paste of ray rice. Each mantra has two sections. The first section of all mantras is the same, that is, 'This time, after death, I shall be a human being'. The painful experience which is engraved innately within this desire is that the female is no human being. After the end of present woman-life, they want to be human—not woman—because the honour, glory and identity of a human being is not present in woman-life in a folk society. If they would have said, 'again, after death, I shall be a human being' then that would have carried a different meaning. But the desire, that is, 'This time, after death, I shall be a human being' has been reflecting a dormant and silent censure towards

---

[3] Swami Nirmalananda, *Baromase Teroparban* (Kolkata: Pronob Math, 1978), 12–13.

the present woman-life. Thus the concept of rebirth has been a means of getting permanent relief from the miseries of woman-life of this birth. So when the present birth of the woman is marked by so much of discrimination, deprivation and denial, how can it be enlightened with proper chances of gender socialization? The marginalized situation is the result of differential socialization and again the differential gender socialization is also the cause of the marginalization of the women. Thus the two, that is, the marginalization of the women and the process of gender socialization is tied with a cause and effect relationship.

The concept of hell and paradise in all the religions has also played a potent role in sponsoring differential gender socialization for the women. In many mythological, folklore and religious traditions, *hell* is a place of torment and punishment in an afterlife. Punishment in hell typically corresponds to sins committed during this life. The Roman Catholic Church defines hell as 'a state of definitive self-exclusion from communion with God and the blessed'. The holy book of Islam, the Qur'an, gives many literal descriptions of the condemned in a fiery hell, contrasting them with the garden-like paradise (*jannah*) enjoyed by righteous believers. Suffering in hell is both physical and spiritual, and varies according to the sins of the condemned. In Hindu literature, especially the law books and Puranas, a realm is mentioned similar to hell, called *naraka*. In the law books (*Smooks* and *Dharma-sūtras*, like the *Manusmnuk*), *naraka* is a place of punishment for sins. It is a lower spiritual plane (called *naraka-loka*) where the spirit is judged and the partial fruits of karma affect the next life. It is believed that people who commit sins go to hell and have to go through punishments in accordance with the sins they committed. The god Yamaraja, who is also the god of death, presides over hell. Detailed accounts of all the sins committed by an individual are kept by Chitragupta, who is the record keeper in Yama's court. Chitragupta reads out the sins committed and Yama orders appropriate punishments to be given to individuals. These punishments include dipping in boiling oil, burning in fire, torture using various weapons, etc., in various hells. Individuals who finish their quota of the punishments are reborn in accordance with their balance of karma.

The *Agni Purana* mentions only 4 hells, The *Manusmṛti* mentions 21 hells: Tamisra, Andhatamisra, Maharaurava, Raurava, Kalasutra, Mahanaraka, Samjivana, Mahavichi, Tapana, Sampratapana, Samhata, Sakakola, Kudmala, Putimrittika, Lohasanku, Rijisha, Pathana, Vaitarani, Salmali, Asipatravana and Lohadaraka. The *Bhagavata Purana* enumerates the following 28: Tamisra, Andhatamisra, Raurava, Maharaurava, Kumbhipaka, Kalasutra, Asipatravana, Sukaramukha, Andhakupa, Krimibhojana, Samdamsa, Taptasurmi, Vajrakantaka-salmali, Vaitarani, Puyoda, Pranarodha, Visasana, Lalabhaksa, Sarameyadana, Avichi, Ayahpana, Ksharakardama, Raksogana-bhojana, Sulaprota, Dandasuka, Avata-nirodhana, Paryavartana and Suchimukha.[4]

These lists present varieties of hells in which a person is thrown after rebirth as punishment for the ordinary and heinous crimes (*Paataka* and *Mahapaataka*) of the current life. The exhaustiveness of the list of Hells under Hinduism is the proof of the pressure exerted over the individuals, male or female. However, suffice to say that women become the worst victims of the concept of hellish punishment in present and afterlife.

An opposite social facet to these hellish rebirths is the precise way in which a person can redeem oneself from a particular crime through a series of vows (such as fasting, water purification rituals, chanting, and even sacrifices). These vows must take place during the same life cycle that the crimes were committed in. These religious lessons assist the societal structure by defining approved and unapproved social behaviour.[5]

The concept of paradise is also a very popular belief in nearly all the religions of the world. In contrast to the concept of hell, the paradise exists for rewarding the persons who have done their duties as per the instructions of the religious texts. As the notion of hell creates fear among the people, oppositely the concept of paradise creates happiness and pleasure among them. In Christianity, Islam and Hinduism, the concept of paradise is used as an inspiring mechanism for performing duties as per religious instructions. In Hinduism, the concept of paradise has

---

4 https:// en.wikipedia.org/wiki/Naraka_(Hinduism)#cite_note-10
5 Ibid.

been presented through the concept of heaven which is just the opposite of hell. It is preached in all the religions that those who perform all their duties as per norms and those who respect God and higher authorities of the religion deserve a space in heaven in their afterlife. Both the concepts, that is, the concept of hell and heaven have different implications for shaping the behaviour of man and woman and thus exert a tremendous influence on the process of gender socialization.

The concept of hell is used as a tool for exerting pressure on the women so that they do not deviate from the patriarchal standard of rules and norms and so that they accept very smoothly all the stereotypical feminine traits of inferiority, subservience and domesticity. Based on a sort of divine origin theory of gender, it is argued that stereotypical traits of the women are modelled and created by God and nature, and thereby it is the bounden duty of the women to comply with them rigorously. Since the feminine traits are created by the dictates of supernatural power, any deviation from femininity would certainly mean challenging that power and for that offence the deviating woman must have to be punished. As a mark of that punishment, the woman will have to go to hell in her next birth. Like all religions, Hinduism also applies hell and heaven theory for judging the cause and effect of women's negative and positive works done in the current life. For Hinduism, women are the apostle of both hell and heaven. But this viewpoint has clearly a biased gender perspective. So far as the women behave in compliance with the patriarchal standards, they are judged by heaven theory and so far as they deviate from that patriarchal standard, they are branded as the door of hell. 'The concept of the female in Hinduism presents an important duality: on the one hand, the woman is fertile, benevolent—the bestower; on the other, she is aggressive, malevolent—the destroyer.'[6] In Hinduism, a female who is properly married, follows and serves her husband in life and death and loses control of sexuality by transferring it to her husband is portrayed as consistently benevolent. In contrast, a woman who controls her own sexuality, who is not chaste and violates her duties towards her husband and who is barren and

---

[6] Susan Wadley, "Women and the Hindu Tradition," in *Women in Indian Society*, 24.

accordingly cannot contribute to the expansion of the lineage is often treated as malevolent. The basic rules for women's behaviour are expressed in the following passages from the laws of Manu, the ancient law-giver of India:

> By a young girl, by a young woman, or even by an aged one, nothing must be done independently, even in her own house.
>
> In childhood a female must be subject to her father, in youth to her husband, when her lord is dead, to her sons; a woman must never be independent...
>
> Though destitute of virtue, or seeking pleasure (elsewhere), or devoid of good qualities, (yet) a husband must be constantly worshipped as a god by a faithful wife...
>
> By violating her duty towards her husband, a wife is disgraced in this world; (after death) she enters the womb of a jackal and is tormented by diseases (the punishment) of her sin.
>
> She who controlling her thoughts, words and deeds, never slights her lord, resides (after death) with her husband (in heaven) and is called a virtuous (wife).[7]

The concept of heaven is also highlighted for the manipulation of femininity towards the functional and structural consolidation of the patriarchal values. Based on the philosophy of historical materialism, Marx called heaven as the carrot used by the wealthy to keep the labourers working hard for little money. By using the techniques of Marx, a gender angle of the heaven theory can be presented. Like the categories of 'bourgeois' and 'proletariat', the categories of man and woman can be regarded as adequate techniques in gender study, and accordingly the heaven theory can also be judged from that viewpoint. Most Marxists regard heaven as a tool employed by patriarchal authorities to bribe the women into a certain way of life by promising a reward after death. The anarchist Emma Goldman expressed this view when she wrote, 'consciously or unconsciously, most atheists see in gods and devils, heaven and hell; reward and punishment, a whip to lash the people into obedience, meekness and contentment'.[8] For the critique heaven is always presented as

---

[7] G. Buhler, trans. *The Laws of Manu*, in *Sacred Books of the East*, xxv, ed. M. Muller (New Delhi: Motilal Banarsidas,1964). Quoted from Susan Wadley in *Women in Indian Society*, 1988.

[8] https: // en.wikipedia.org/wiki/Heaven#cite_note 38

a bribe to the persons for the regulation of their behaviour and for implementation of the patriarchal agenda. Especially, this is true for the women. Many people consider George Orwell's use of 'Sugar Candy Mountain' in his novel *Animal Farm* to be a literary expression of this view. In the book, the animals are told that after their miserable lives were over they would go to a place in which 'it was Sunday seven days a week, clover was in season all the year round, and lump sugar and linseed cake grew on the hedges'.[9] Thus, the concept of heaven is used as a tool for motivating the women for internalizing and implementing the stereotypical traits which are branded as feminine. It is argued that the traits such as righteousness, chastity, purity, simplicity, sacrifice, virtuousness, submissiveness, softness, dutifulness and kindness are the positive heavenly qualities of the women. So in order to book the confirmed ticket to the heaven, the women must have to be aligned with these qualities and thus would come to reinforce the linkage between religion and morality on the one hand and on the other between morality and the patriarchy. The reason that is forwarded for the internalization of stereotypes by the women is that the Creator, that is, God wants them to do it and will reward for doing it or will punish them otherwise. Since God will love them for internalizing the stereotypical qualities which are branded as feminine and will open the door of heaven for them, the women surrender to the view without questioning the implicit agenda. Thus ultimately in the name of appeasing God, the women practically appease their male authorities who are considered demigod in a traditional patriarchal set-up and thus contribute to the creation of a heavenly system for the males in their present life being guided by the imagination of a heaven in the afterlife.

The concept of hell and heaven works as punishment for deviation and reward for conformity for all the persons especially the women. Women become the soft target of hell and heaven theory due to several reasons. First, it is due to the biological differences in hormonal system that men are more prone to risk-taking behaviour than women. So inclination to crimes and taking risk for any action or misdeed is comparatively more common in men than women. Thus ignoring the prospect of punishment

---

[9] Ibid, note 39, 40.

of hell and the reward of heaven becomes easier for a man in a patriarchal society. There are texts available in every society where it is declared that the punishment and torment of the hell are especially meant for the deviating women. So there must be some concessional system for the hellish crimes of the men. Second, it is due to the social system and set-up, hell and heaven theory come to influence the women more easily. The women of the traditional patriarchal society are ousted from the working sector and also from all possible sources of power. They are completely confined in the private area of the home and have more free time to pursue religious interests. Furthermore, it has been argued, 'the development of gender-based division of labour, which feminizes family duties for women and masculinizes workplace duties for men, produces higher levels of female religiousness since religion falls under the general sphere of family matter'.[10] Third, the pattern of differential socialization followed for men and women results in development of more religious attitude in women than men. Gender socialization reinforces stereotypes in men and women differently. Men in patriarchal society are expected and encouraged to be adventurous, aggressive and ambitious, whereas women are encouraged to be passive, submissive and righteous. So men in patriarchal order grow to be risk-taking and women grow as risk-averse. As a result of such differences in psychological orientation of men and women, hell and heaven theory acts as more useful for the women than men. Fourth, the gender role pattern of patriarchal society is also responsible for the development of more religiousness in women and accordingly for more assimilation of the theory of hell and heaven. Traditional argument is that women are by nature designed as loyal daughter, righteous sister, dutiful wife and tolerant mother. In each of these roles, the very domain of religion is the most potent source of their power. As wife a woman is expected to be submissive, self-effacing and chaste and these qualities direct her to the acceptance of religiosity more easily. In the role of mother, women are expected to subsume religiousness since mother role involves

[10] Ann Douglas, *The Feminization of American Culture* (New York, NY: Knopf, 1977), 1403. Cited in Miller and Stark, "Gender and Religiousness: Can Socialization Explanations Be Saved?", 1399–1423.

such activities as teaching the children morality and caring for the physical and spiritual well-being of other family members (Glock, Ringer and Babbie 1967; Walter and Davie 1998). So it is due to the uniqueness of gender role of the women, hell and heaven theory works upon them more easily. Thus, social placement of the women and their vulnerability to religion and the concept of hell and heaven preached by it results in a different process of making of the gender of the women. Hell and heaven theory in particular exerts a strong influence on the physical, mental and social upbringing of the women as a result of which differential gender socialization appears on the scene.

The concept of atonement is a very much useful and popular tool of keeping the people in right track of the religion. 'In western *Christian* theology atonement describes how human beings can be reconciled to God. Atonement refers to the forgiving or pardoning of sin in general and original sin in particular through the death and resurrection of divine Jesus'[11] enabling the reconciliation between God and his creation. There exist four major theories in Christianity: (a) ransom theory, (b) satisfaction theory, (c) moral influence theory and (d) penal substitution theory. Today, an increasing number of Christian theologians argue that none of the existing theories is enough for having a clear conception of atonement. The concept of atonement in Hinduism is very old, and it is proportionately linked with the sin of past life and also present life. The method, duration and amount of atonement depends on the nature and gravity of the sin of an individual. The concept of atonement in Hinduism aims at satisfying the God through various rituals and through various forms of self-punishment. *Hinduism* has a ritual of sacrifice, called *yajna* and more commonly practiced during Vedic times. It is performed to please the *devas* (gods), or sometimes, the authorized representative of the Supreme Spirit, that is, Brahman. Satisfying God and attracting God's attention through *yajna*, that is, rites of sacrifice works by sacrificing a number of sacred items in sacrificial fire. It is believed that everything that is offered in the divine *Agni*, that is, sacrificial fire is believed to reach the gods and to satisfy them. 'Having a more explicit purpose of atonement than *yajna*

---

[11] https: // en.wikipedia.org/wiki/Atonement_ in_ Christianity #cite_note-1

is the practice of *prayaschitta* (penance). When people commit sins, violating the dharma—a value system that teaches religious and ceremonial duties in front of the gods and ethical codes on their relationships to their fellow human beings —they practise *prayaschitta,* involving fasting, chanting of *mantras* (religious syllables), charity, pilgrimage, etc., in order to atone with the gods and also with their fellow humans. This penance is also understood to help them toward their liberation from the karma, which causes their sins'.[12] *The Islamic Law* specifies the expiration of any particular sin for atonement.

> Depending on the sin, it can range from repentance and compensation of the sin if possible, feeding the poor, freeing slaves to even stoning to death or cutting hands. Some of the major sins are held to be legally punishable in an Islamic state (for example, murder, theft, adultery, and, in some views, apostasy). The Qur'an also encourages atonement between believers. Acknowledging one's wrongdoing, apologizing, and repenting in front of the wronged person and in front of God can make possible forgiveness from the wronged person and also from God. Muslims are encouraged to forgive because God is the most forgiving.[13]

There are five pillars of Islam as formal practices considered to be the framework of Muslim life:

> The five pillars are (1) Iman or faith (belief in one God), (2) Prayer five times daily (salat), (3) Giving of charity, (4) fasting from sunrise to sunset for thirty days during the month of Ramadan (the month that the Qur'an was revealed to Prophet Mohammad and (5) taking a lifetime pilgrimage to Mecca.[14]

Beyond these five pillars, there are also some other practices as forms of self-punishment and they are refraining from pork, alcohol, gambling and leaving other personal hobbies and means of gratification for satisfying Allah.

If the system of atonement is studied by the lens of gender study, it is seen that in all the religions of the world the

---

[12] www.newworldencyclopedia.org/entry/Atonement
[13] Ibid.
[14] Elham Bagheri, "A Qualitative Investigation of Religion, Gender Role Beliefs and Culture in the Lives of a Select Group of Muslim Men"), 8.

women folk is the worst sufferer of this system and they are to pay heavily towards atonement just due to the fact of being women. Religion uses the social system as much as the social system uses religion. There must be a much closed interlinkage between the two. So if the society is patriarchal in nature, then it must manipulate the religion of the concerned society from the male-biased angle with a view to protect the interest of the male authority. Accordingly, all the religious arrangements work with a double standard—one standard for male and another for female. This is out and out true in case of the system of atonement which is more concessional for the men than the women. It is experienced throughout the history that for all sorts of deviation (especially physical, mental and moral) men are all the time excused as naturally inclined to crime and riskful behaviour whereas the women are kept under continuous and thorough scrutiny and they, nearly for every offence committed by them, are tormented by atonement of different forms. These forms are sometimes executed socially and sometimes spiritually. There is clear distinction between social punishment and religious punishment. But when the system of atonement works from a misogynist angle, then the apparent distinction between society and religion is deleted and a mutual though unholy alliance is formed temporarily. Thus, it is seen that when the question is all about punishing the women and keeping them under strict control of the male authority through the exercise of the system of atonement, then both society and religion have appeared on the scene with a mutual support to each other.

Women in all the countries and across all cultures had to pay heavily as a cost of such unholy alliances between society and religion. As of Christianity, it has considered woman as the representative and successor of Eve and has given her an inferior status as compared to man. It was preached that woman is the emblem of erotic sexual desire and is the cause of sexual deviation of man and so she is also the emblem of sin, and thus they should not be directly allowed to read the Bible. They were not also allowed to participate in the public area like the men. Women who, like the Joan of Arc, have tried to break this format imposed by Church and have challenged the patriarchy have been declared as witches and burnt to death.

It has been roughly estimated that at least 100,000 women have been punished to death by the Church in Europe due to their effort of overstepping the limits of femininity chalked out by theological framework. Between the years 1561–1670 total 3,200 people were murdered in South Germany due to theological deviation of which 82% were women. In Loren of France between the years 1581–1591 total 2000 women came under trial of which 90% were convicted to death by the religious authority. Statistical evidences abound in Europe where such occurrences of religious killing of women were supported and sponsored by the Church.[15]

Thus, it is seen that the system of atonement expressed through social punishment exercised against the women got extreme support from the religious authority of Christianity.

Accordingly, in Hinduism also there are ample examples of mistreatment of women in the name of atonement. Hindu scriptures and practices have built an image of women who are necessarily dutiful, righteous, virtuous, passive, chaste, self-effacing and loyal and everything that are needed to be good daughter, good wife and good mother. Any deviation from these stereotypes is regarded as sin and accordingly needs atonement. Even when no such deviations happen on the part of the women individually, they may be forced to atone for the unforeseen challenges such as famine, war, flood, epidemic and other natural calamities faced by the community at large. It is expected in Hinduism that the women not only refrain themselves from expressing the malevolent attitudes but also will apply their benevolent power for the development of the community and the family. Thereby Sita in the Ramayana and Draupadi in the Mahabharata, in spite of being the ideal type of Hindu women, have been constantly a victim of gender inequality and the system of atonement. In the open royal court Draupadi was sexually harassed by Kauravas and especially Duryodhana when Pandavas lost the diceplay. Draupadi had to suffer atonement for a number of times for her failure to save the Pandava community from possible dangers through the application of her benevolent force. Sita was forced to enter in the fire as atonement for her sin of being kidnapped by Ravana although she was not at all responsible for what

---

[15] Ghosh, *Towards Equality*, 35.

happened to her after being kidnapped. The ideals of Sita and Draupadi formatted in line with male supremacy have been the source of the prescribed lifestyle for the Indian women for centuries. The ideological layer of history is formed under the influence of religious scriptures and practices in all societies. India is no exception in this regard. Accordingly, the concept of male supremacy and gender inequality has emerged as a mega pattern supported by many social practices such as casteism, marriage and family system, and especially the system of atonement. The Vedas, the sacred scripture of the Hindus, has described women as 'more poisonous than snake, vulture and razor'. Hinduism has officially sponsored the customs of sati, that is, the burning of wife with the dead husband, male polygamy, child marriage of female, custom of devdasi and so many inhuman practices for women. The reason behind the stand of Hinduism against women lies in the concept of femaleness portrayed in Hindu ideology. According to Hinduism, woman embodies *Shakti*, that is, the original energy of the universe which again is expressed through the female body. In Hinduism there are two types of atonement. One, atonement dictated by the religious texts and authority. Two, atonement effected through self-punishment. Atonement through religious punishment is always imposed and coercive and the atonement through self-punishment is voluntary and spontaneous. Rules of atonement dictated by religion include social segregation, social boycott and social expulsion due to fall from religious belief and failure to comply with the purity of caste as designed in Hinduism. In the name of serving God a form of atonement was in vogue in Hinduism for centuries. But it is seen that the women who are dictated to serve the God and thus to atone for any deviation are being mostly exploited sexually by the religious authority who claim and present themselves as the sole representatives of God. In this way, the custom of devdasi (the maid of God) developed in India and the well-known fact is that the devdasis were nothing but the prostitutes under religion, that is, Hinduism. Atonement through self-punishment include fasting, different method of worship, leaving bodily beauty such as shaving the head and wearing ordinary dress, offering sacrifices and observing different vows such as *shivachaturdasi, punnipukur, dasputul and senjuti* vow. The compulsory rules of atonement are executed to punish for the malevolent attitudes of the female. But the system of atonement through self-punishment is internalized by the women to highlight their benevolent attitudes. The implicit message of such atonement policy is that only the women with benevolent qualities deserve a honourable place in patriarchal society and erosion of these qualities can throw the women in a marginalized situation at any time.

In *Islam*, there are many a socio-religious systems of atonement beyond the prescribed systems of atonement of the Qur'an. In Pakistan, Afghanistan and Middle East countries women are often socially ostracized for the offence of non-conformity to the popular male line laws often falsely presented as Islamic laws. It is reported often due to the offence of playing cricket, football or any game in the public or due to the offence of moving without borka and for the offence of smiling in the public Muslim women of those countries is to undergo severe punishment as forms of atonement. Such punishment include stone-throwing, beating severely, whipping in the public and even measure like death sentence. In Islam all the religious arrangements have a misogynist viewpoint. A general discussion of the discriminating systems enumerated in Islam can justify the reason as to why the concept of atonement is excessively strict for the women. Islam, known generally for its concept of equality, has grossly supported gender inequality. The religion of Islam has approved polygamy for male and again has allowed male to come out of marital relationship by granting an easy divorce through *talak*. The Koran has approved up to four marriages for male.[16] The polygamy of the Muslim men is supported by the personal law of the respective country. According to the 'Personal Law, 1961' of Bangladesh, a Muslim male is entitled to four marriages subject to the consent of previous wives. This law is protecting the interest of the husband. About 90 per cent married women are forced to give consent for such marriages. Those who protest are tortured and ultimately murdered. In fact the system of marriage in Islam is not at all women-friendly.[17] So women are the worst victims during marriage and divorce. Islam does not also admit

---

[16] *Koran*, 4:3 (Sura An-Nisa).
[17] Maleka Begum, "Bipanna Nari: Satidaha Theke Kanyabhrun Hatya," in *Naribiswa*, 80.

of the right to witness for women in the matter of settling legal disputes. The notion of gender inequality is very clearly expressed through the custom of 'purdah' which is imposed over women only. It has been advised in the Koran as 'ask the believer women to restrain their look and to protect their secret limb'[18] The veil or 'Borka' is the symbolic shelter of the women in the religion on the one hand and on the other hand it is a system of de-recognition of the individual identity of the women.[19] The system of 'Purdah' is not only a symbolic obstruction but in the practical world also it is against the convenient atmosphere of receiving education and developing social relation of women with other people. Through the system of 'Purdah' or 'Borka'(veil) the message what is sent to the people is that women are the personal property of the male. That tendency has been reflected also in the system of the marriage between cousin brothers and sisters which is supported primarily to keep the women and their property under control of a particular lineage. Where women are to face severe marginalization, discrimination and mistreatment officially by the support of Islam, there it is very natural that the women under Islam will have to atone for any and every possible deviation.

Thus, it is seen that nearly all the dominating religions of the world have a misogynist approach to the concept of atonement. The general mega pattern of gender inequality and discrimination against women has been consolidated in all the countries and across all cultures through multiple social arrangements. But the patriarchal system does not think it prudent to depend on the social arrangements exclusively in respect of controlling, undermining and mistreating the women of the respective religion and society. Accordingly, the religious arrangements and textual instructions also have been modelled, designed and executed in favour of the patriarchy. As a result, the concept of atonement, like all other systems of religion, has come to reinforce the gender messages and gender ideology of a given society the kernel of which is to present the male as a subject, the centre of life and society and to present the women

---

[18] Girish Chandra Sen Maulavi Bhai, *The Holy Koran* (Bengali Translation) (Kolkata: Haraf Prakashani, 2011), 25.

[19] Saiad Nasrin Tanveer, "Musalman, Bangali O Nari: Samakalin Paschimbanga," in *Naribiswa*, 315.

as the other. Simone de Beauvoir stated the general position of the women in a male-biased society. The biased assessment of the women by the men in patriarchy has been presented in the following words by Beauvoir,

> And she is simply what man decrees; thus she is called 'the sex', by which is meant that she appears essentially to the male as a sexual being. For him she is sex—absolute sex, no less. She is defined and differentiated with reference to man and not he with reference to her; she is the incidental, the inessential as opposed to the essential. He is the Subject, he is the Absolute—she is the Other.[20]

Religions of the world have just come to justify this position of patriarchy. Thereby the gender messages sent by the religion have resulted in a sort of differential socialization of man and woman. The differential gender socialization, also reinforced through the concept of atonement, is ultimately aimed at justifying the arrangements of gender inequality, discrimination and mistreatment of the women in all societies and across all cultures.

Belief in supernatural is also another important point found and practised in different religions and this has also presented the role of religion as an agent of gender socialization. It has been established by different studies that women express more belief in supernatural than men. The primary reason behind this fact is that men in a patriarchal society are expected to be developed both physically and mentally by the assimilation of some stereotypes different than women. Men are expected to be aggressive, ambitious, loud, strong, tough, daring, adventurous, breadwinner, dominating and risk-loving. In contrast to these stereotypes of the men, women in patriarchal society are expected to be submissive, loyal, chaste, righteous, dutiful, soft, weak, childbearer, homemaker, self-effacing and risk-averse. The differences in stereotypical traits of men and women result in the growth of risk-prone attitudes among men as a result of which men, as compared to women, become relatively irreligious and accordingly manifest low amount of belief in supernatural. Oppositely, the stereotypical traits of the women are directly

---

[20] de Beauvoir, *The Second Sex* (London: Vintage, 1997), 16.

or indirectly related to emotion, morality and religiousness. Belief in supernatural on the part of the women is the result of such stereotypical profile. From the functional and sociological standpoint it is argued that women's belief in supernatural is the result of the process of ousting women from all possible sources of power, public engagements and income generation and confining them in the private area of family and home. The detachment of women with the power, labour market and public life have resulted in the development of a risk-averse attitude among them and has made their mental profile more aligned to religiousness. On the other hand, the process of confining the women in the private area of family and home has resulted in a religious attitude and belief in supernatural. First, it is argued that in order to beget and foster the belief in supernatural, the private sphere of the family and home is ideal as an atmosphere because religion is regarded as their general subject matter. Second, it is argued that since in and around the home, women are entrusted with the responsibility of rearing and caring of the children and spiritual well-being of the family members and since these activities involve moral teaching, health management and saving the children from all possible threats affecting their life and health, women have come to internalize belief in supernatural. A different argument is forwarded from the standpoint of gender inequality in order to clarify the reason of women's belief in supernatural. The discrimination against women and mistreatment emerging out of it lead the women to a state of helplessness, subordination and submissiveness and as a result the women resort to the belief in supernatural as a means to compensate their blocked aspirations and mistreatments and to come out of their marginalization and victimization by a different mode of channelization through devotion to God and miracle.

If the point of belief in supernatural is examined by the lens of gender study, then the role of this point in gender socialization will be clearly understood. In Hinduism, belief in supernatural means devotion and unconditional surrender to God, the supreme entity and the creator of the world. Hinduism believes that God is one and all. But he is worshipped in many forms—both male and female. This ritualistic position does not match with the practical situation. In practice, the women are undermined and underrated in all the ways even through the functional rites of the religion. Women are not generally allowed to act as priest in the worship of these different male and female gods, although the ritual arrangement and necessary functions for the worship are done and performed by the female. In Hinduism, women are viewed as both benevolent and malevolent. But ritual arrangements have been designed so that women can come out as benevolent in all spheres of life and thus can serve the interest of patriarchy. Benevolent attitudes include the ideal feminine stereotypical traits such as simplicity, chastity, virtuousness, righteousness, honesty, tolerance, sacrifice, kindness, dutifulness, softness and philoprogenitiveness. Benevolent role of the women also emphasizes their gender role stereotypes such as stereotypical role of daughter, sister, wife and mother. With a view to encouraging the women to internalize the benevolent spirit they are asked to perform different rites, vows and religious duties the relation of which with the belief in supernatural is one of cause and effect relationship. It is believed that the performance of these rites such as vows, fasting, sacrificing different means of enjoyment and different types of offerings to God will help in building a contact with the supernatural which again will increase the positive magical power of the women through the application of which they can save the family and the society from all possible threats of dangers and thus can come out as benevolent. So the belief in supernatural on the part of the women serves dual purpose: one, women's affiliation to supernatural theory helps them to develop their internal magical power to be applied for benevolent purpose; two, craving for supernatural and associated rites serves also as the controller of female sexuality. Thus ultimately belief in supernatural limits the scope of freedom for the women and guides them to internalize the concept of femininity as designed by the patriarchy. In this way, belief in supernatural becomes ultimately the belief in patriarchy.

Christianity has also taken anti-women attitude in respect of religiosity of women. Christian religion, for ages, has been famous for its patriarchal anthropological position in the West. Beyond the Christian religious texts some Christian social and political thinkers are also responsible for such misogynist perception of Christian religion. For example, St. Augustine was the preacher of Christianity as well as the preacher of anti-women attitude in Western political thought. For many scholars, St. Augustine has been a standard target for criticism for his introduction of sexist philosophical thinking. Elaine Pagels has blamed Augustine for 1000 years of sexism in Catholic Church.[21] Reuther pronounced Augustine the source of Western Christian patriarchal anthropology.[22] He clearly supported the supremacy of patriarchal society. The religion of a woman is to obey the male authority of the family and to play her role of childbearing and childrearing. In his *City of God*, Augustine has considered male as whole and female as part. He also argued that women's nature is the reflection of 'emotion' and male nature is of 'reason'. In his two worlds, women lived in the world of sin. By declaring women as weak, subordinate and submissive, Augustine attempted to fix the bounds of sexual relationship and behaviour for women. In this purpose, Augustine took marriage as a safe institution although he has given the license to men for going out of the marital bond. In his eyes, marriage gives a type of justification to the innate negative qualities which make women untrustworthy and deceitful. For him, marriage also helps concealing woman's role as a source of sexuality and accordingly sin. By referring to the myth of eating apple by Adam and Eve, he intended to argue that it is the magical fascination of marriage that directed Adam to the wrong decision of taking the apple from Eve. But, in general, Augustine considered marriage as a means of procreation, the guarantee of chastity and the bond of union.[23] Thus, Augustine ultimately presented a traditional viewpoint about women. Augustine viewed women as submissive, obedient and weak. His clear declaration that woman is made for man opened the door of Christian patriarchal anthropology in West. Augustine fixed family life as the field and limit of movement for women. Other contemporary Christian thought did not have any different liberal view of women. Almost all the thinkers of that age did not forward any straight way opinion in favour

---

[21] Elaine Pagels, *Adam, Eve and the Serpent* (New York, NY: Random House, 1988), 27.
[22] Rosemary Radford Reuther, *Sexism and God-Talk: Towards a Feminist Theology* (Boston: Beacon Press, 1983), 14.
[23] Chattopadhyay, *Fighting Gender Inequality*, 115.

of female education. All of them placed women in a position below men. Aquinas was very much influenced by St. Paul and his teachings of scripture. St. Paul says in 1 Corinthians 11:10, 'man was not created for the sake of woman, but woman was created for the sake of man'. This passage echoes Genesis 2:18, 19 as "It is not good that man should be alone. I will give him a helpmate". St. Paul again in 1 Corinthians 11:3 says, 'man is the head of woman' and in Ephesians 5:22 says, 'a husband is the head of his wife'. As an instance of surrender, St. Paul highlights woman's role of childbearing which can save her from annihilation. Aquinas argues in the line of St. Paul that there is no other purpose to femininity except childbearing for which only woman exclusively exists. Thus Aquinas, following Aristotle, has concluded that motherhood is the extent of female's role and the masculine sex playing the active part in the act of generation is superior to feminine sex. That apart Aquinas has remarked that production of male is the ultimate objective of generation and the production of female indicate an accident or defect in the process of generation. As Aristotle described woman as 'infertile male' Aquinas also has described the female as 'defective' or 'misbegotten male'. Earlier fathers of Christianity preached the female sex as the consequence of sin. For them, woman is a mistake and she arrived only after sin caused nature to be defective. The curse is brought on woman by Eve's sin. By the influence of the then Christian ethical and philosophical tradition Aquinas also shares the view that the chief objective of generation is to produce the male only. So the production of female must arise because of some gaps and defects in generation. Hence birth of female is the result of sin. Like the previous philosophers, Aquinas also believes that woman's birth is accidental as they are generated against the natural tendency of nature to produce male. In order to remove the curse of female birth, the only duty of woman is to help male in generation. Woman is made for man and man is not only her principle but her end. In his treatment of first human sin, Aquinas revealed that Adam tempted Eve first because she was weaker and more vulnerable to be easily seduced. Thus it is also a further evidence of the inferiority of female sex as viewed by St. Thomas Aquinas and other Christian thinkers. In the light of these misogynist positions of the Christianity and Christian thinkers, it is very much clear that female religiosity is treated as being suggestive of their risk-averse attitude and stereotypical formation of their mental profile. Christianity has solely taken the female sex as homemaker, childbearer and fit for childrearing activities. Since the religion and its practice is the general subject matter of the family and home, woman is considered more suitable for it. Like all other dominating religions, Christianity also believes that affiliation to supernatural will make the women more benevolent and dutiful to the family, community and society which actually serve the interest of the patriarchy. Thus belief in supernatural in Christianity is always associated with the concept of ideal femininity and accordingly plays a strong role in the formation of gender and in gender socialization.

In Islam, the belief in supernatural is the result of the basic teachings of the Qur'an. 'A key component in Islam is the belief in six core tenets. These tenets are belief in 1) one God, 2) Angels, 3) the Prophets 4) the Scriptures, 5) the Day of Judgment and 6) the supremacy of God's will.'[24] It is clear from these tenets of Islam that belief in supernatural is part and parcel of the religion of Muslim men and women. Due to the differences of gender of male and female created and constructed by the society in general and patriarchy in particular, the stereotypical traits assigned to masculinity and femininity become sharply different. This difference also influences the level and intensity of religiosity of male and female genders. Assimilation of masculine traits makes the men somewhat risk-prone in most of their attitudes, and accordingly low level of religiosity and expression of irreligious attitudes become more common among the men than the women. In contrast, internalization of feminine traits makes the women risk-averse in the expressions of their behaviour, and thus they come to reinforce the religious attitudes as part of their natural duty. In this way, it is seen that gender division, gender construction and gender traits have a much close relation with the issue of religiosity. Thereby, it has been more natural for the Muslim women to grasp the teachings of Islam in respect of its basic tenets than the Muslim men. Thus, like all other religions Islam also is held responsible for the fact by which belief in supernatural is going to be used for the

---

[24] Elham Bagheri, "A Qualitative Investigation of Religion, Gender Role Beliefs and Culture in the Lives of a Select Group of Muslim Men," 7.

making of gender, gender inequality and differential gender socialization in the society.

From the above-mentioned analysis and presentation of arguments it is discernible enough that all the dominating religions of the world irrespective of their history of cultures act as agent of patriarchy and influences the process of making of gender. Through all its theories, beliefs and practices, religion, throughout the world, ultimately come to shape the gender orientation of women in a manner different than that of the men. Concept of previous birth and rebirth, concept of hell and paradise, concept of atonement and belief in supernatural serve manifold necessities of patriarchy. First, all these concepts create fear in the minds of women so that they remain under psychological compulsion to obey the patriarchal authority of the given society and to comply with the rules and norms of that society. The women, being socialized for internalizing the feminine stereotypical traits, always succumb to such fear and use the religious teachings in developing their gender perceptions which often tend to be breeding ground of the subsequent gender inequality of the society. Second, religious theories and teachings are always considered to be benevolent, beneficial and positive for all. Challenging these religious concepts naturally means going against the collective welfare of the society. When such challenges come from a man then this behaviour is assigned to the adventurous and aggressive nature of masculinity and this is treated as a simple case of deviation. But when challenge against the religious concepts come from any woman then it is seriously taken as a threat to society (read patriarchy). Challenge against established norms and a myth of religion on the part of the women is considered as deviation and departure from femininity.

> As soon as women refuse to pretend to be submissive and dependent, thereby exposing the myth, they lose the benefits of femininity. The women are punished for refusing men's protection, for female assertiveness represents a challenge to male authority and control and any woman, who shows assertive qualities, is defined as an abnormal female.[25]

---

[25] Joanna Liddle and Roma Joshi, *Daughters of Independence—Gender, Caste and Class in India.* (London: Zed Books Ltd, 1986), 183–84.

The term 'abnormal female' has a biological implication in the sense that such female are not of usual types and they lack the essential qualities of femininity as biologically fit for women. Thus affiliation to the religious concepts, theories, myths and beliefs are often treated as equivalent or supplementary to femininity and accordingly religion directs the women to the differential gender socialization prescribed by the patriarchy. Third, religion is taken as a potent weapon of controlling the female sexuality which, almost in all the religions of the world, is considered as the most dangerous element in its nature and function. It is the uncultured nature of female sexuality that has created doubt, confusion and fear in the minds of the male for ages in all countries and across all cultures. So in order to control the sexuality of the women patriarchy has confined them in the family and home on the one hand, and on the other, it has encouraged them to internalize the religious attitudes. Religious norms and practices and sacrifices, pains and sufferings related to them minimize their physical thrust which again results in the minimization of their sex drives. At the same time, affiliation to religion makes the women mentally aligned to stereotypical feminine traits and femininity and thus encourage them to internalize the codes of differential gender socialization.

Conclusion

The field of gender study today is the most popular to the scholars of sociology and feminism. Since Mary Wollstonecraft's path-breaking analysis in *A Vindication of the Rights of Woman*, gender studies especially women's studies has drawn considerable attention of the intellectuals and reformers. Subsequently Simone de Beauvoir's epoch-making book *The Second Sex* has brought the gender interpretation in the centre of all feminist discussions. The renowned statement made by Beauvoir, 'One is not born, but rather becomes, a woman' supplied the basic clue to the formation of gender especially feminine gender. Beauvoir remarked, 'it is civilization as a whole that produces this creature, intermediate between male and eunuch, which is described as feminine....'[1] This is probably the first logically argued viewpoint of the gender formation by which the difference between the sex and gender was highlighted on the one hand, and on the other, the tradition of viewing gender as social and cultural construct was made popular and was applied to social sciences in course of time by the sociologists and the feminists. With the advent of feminism as a separate discipline and with its growing popularity among the researchers and the reformers, gender studies has emerged as an autonomous subject with thought provoking viewpoints incorporating women in the centre of discussion for the analysis of the women's issues. But locating gender in the socialization process and presenting gender socialization as the potent social, cultural, psychological and ideological technique of legitimizing and inculcating the patriarchal values is the most unique feature of the book, *Gender Socialization and the Making of Gender in the Indian Context*.

Human society is the result of historical evolution of the institutions, ideas and practices. It is generally argued that man and woman, being the central characters of this society, had

---

[1] de Beauvoir, *The Second Sex*, 295.

influenced the evolution process on the one hand, and on the other, they themselves were influenced by the evolution process of the society. But due to specific social, economic and historical situations the power of influencing the evolution of norms, ideas and practices was deposited and vested in the hands of male gender that protected the gender interest of the male folk by manipulating the evolutionary processes against the interests of the female gender. In course of this process the women were ousted from the economic sector especially agriculture, in particular and all possible sources of power in society, in general. This incident has been described by Engels as 'the historic defeat of the female sex'. Thus judged from the gender angle it can be said that the subsequent lopsided development of women was the result of male effort of making the course of evolution gender biased and of taking a misogynist approach in order to reap all the benefits of evolution exclusively for the male gender. But the fact is that the matter of ousting the women from power and seizing the power by male gender was never spontaneous and natural. It was the result of a deliberate operation of male-centric authority system which is popularly termed as 'patriarchy'.

Patriarchy makes this operation possible through very many social institutions and religious and cultural norms and practices which will undermine the position of the women on the one hand, and on the other, will strengthen the command of the male authority. In order to reinforce these norms and practices in favour of male, various institutions and organizations (which are presented as agents of gender socialization in this book) were used for providing ideological support to this process. So unfolding the proper role of these institutions and organizations is very important for understanding the process of gender inequality and gender discrimination in general and gender socialization in particular. Perhaps the objective and the unique role of these institutions and organizations is aimed at convincing women that the discriminatory gender treatment they are getting is perfectly natural as far as their biological and psychological nature is concerned. Agents such as family, peer group, school, media and religion have also come to justify gender inequality by forwarding the necessity of functionalist stratification. 'Functionalism is the doctrine that social institutions and practices can be understood in terms of the functions they carry out in sustaining the larger social system.'[2] This theory is presented by Kingsley Davis and Wilbert Moore (1945) as the theory of functional stratification. To them, stratification is always a functional necessity in any society and importance of any individual or group must be proportionate to the roles they perform. Subsequently this theory was also applied to the field of gender-based stratification. It is argued that there are differences between male and female in respect of their biological and psychological traits and it is such difference based on which the social role of each gender is determined. Thus, it is seen, 'The regulation of social system, from the functional point of view, has resulted in strengthening the domination of man over woman in all societies and across all culture'.[3] Talcott Parsons (1902–79) was a renowned preceptor of functionalist theory. To him, family directly works on the basis of sexual division of labour where women perform their role of childbearing, childrearing and providing mental and spiritual support to their words. Another functionalist perspective of childrearing has been presented by John Bowlby who argued, 'The mother is crucial to the primary socialization of the children'.[4] In fact, sexual division of labour is different from the general view of division of labour. It is argued, 'Sexual Division of Labour is a division of work not between equals but between superiors and inferiors (and) A relation which is imposed on women by social pressure'.[5] In this way, biological and physiological differences create a difference in social role acquisition of male and female, highlight the gender role and resultantly gender inequality emerges as the retrogressive feature of the society. The intervention of different agents in the field of making of gender through gender socialization make the entire operation of all these agenda of patriarchy very easy and smooth. In this way, different agents, that is, these social and cultural institutions, organizations, religious norms and practices continuously provide an ideological support to the gender ideology

---

[2] Andrew Heywood, *Key Concepts in Politics* (Chennai, India: Palgrave, 2005), 89.

[3] Chattopadhyay, *Gender Inequality,* 32.

[4] Giddens, *Sociology,* 114.

[5] Nirmala Banerjee, "Sexual Division of Labour," in *Indian Women: Myth and Reality,* ed. Jasodhara Bagchi (Hyderabad: Sangam Books, 1997), 75–76. (bracket mine)

modelled upon patriarchy through gender socialization and accordingly legitimize their functions.

The problem with regard to the study of the agents of gender socialization is that these agents are not static. Rather they are very much dynamic so far as the impact of technological inventions and globalization are concerned. The structure of family and its functions have widely changed. Family, in the age of globalization, is not exclusively run by rule and authority. With the increasing entry of the women in labour market and with the access of many entertainment gadgets, the family has been a multilayered unit within a single primary structure. So the nature of gender socialization is also bound to be changed within the family. The peer groups are not all the same as before. With the increasing education and the dismantling of the earlier structure of the family, the nature and influence of peer groups has also changed. This change must have an implication in respect of gender socialization. With the rise of free and compulsory education as an agenda of almost all the governments of the world, the social environment of the school has undergone a wide change. The school curriculum is continuously updated; the teachers are more oriented and the students are more focused than what was 50 years ago. So it is quite natural that the role of school in gender socialization will also be different. The biggest invention of the century probably lies in cyber media. The use of internet and mobile phone has drastically changed not only the outer relationship but also the mental configuration of the people. Cyber space has been a medium of free opinions and exchange of views and thereby the gender restrictions have liquidated to a considerable extent. The system of cyber chatting through many social networking sites has minimized the conventional gender distance between male and female. The so-called social and cultural norms of patriarchy are not fully workable here in the cyber media. So the nature of gender socialization in the age of internet is to be evaluated and analysed with a new outlook. With the rise of internet and mobile phones, the role of conventional print and electronic media has also changed. It is noticeable that whereas the role of internet in gender socialization has been viewed as more liberal and progressive, the role of print and electronic media have been more conservative and perhaps misogynist. Internet based social media participates in forming public opinion on different issues, especially on gender-related issues, in an open manner. Of course, some opinions are misogynist but most of the opinions, regarding gender, tend to be rational. The reason of progressiveness of internet and social media perhaps lies in the relative autonomy of social media. On the contrary, the chief reason of the growing misogynist role of the mass media is that it is primarily dependent on the revenues of the advertisements which are aimed at manipulating the physical beauty of the women and exposing it through advertisements in order to attract the clients (both male and female) towards the use of the products of the advertisements. That apart the media houses are led by the capitalist entrepreneurs, and in general, capitalism favours patriarchy in the sense that it does not take the risk of going against the patriarchal arrangement of the social setting because that means challenging the status quo and a major alteration of the social relationships and social and financial arrangements which will surely disturb the interest of the capitalism at least temporarily. Above all, in a rural society traditional portrayal of women, gender stereotypes and the gender role distribution in the traditional sense have a strong appeal to the common folk. So when the chief motto is to earn revenue then it is considered prudent and safe by the media houses to depict women in traditional sense and to allow the print and the electronic media to play the role of gender socialization along the line of gender ideology modelled upon the patriarchy. The role of religion in gender socialization also analyses the dynamic relation between social reality and religion by which it is argued that religion always encourages the existing social structure to be protected. In fact, after assimilating the codes of religion through various norms and practices, women, since their early childhood, come to possess a reconstruction of ideas on the one hand and on the other, they come to internalize the reconstruction of gender. But in the postmodern age, the nature of religiousness, the religiosity and the attitudes towards religion have also undergone changes as a result of globalization, industrialization and modernization. Plenty of literatures are being regularly published in all corners of the world challenging the dictates of religious texts and gospels of the preceptors as well. Due to the formidability of 'information boom', it has been possible for all to access any data questioning the logic of these religious texts, myths and gospels. The influence of democratization preaching openness, transparency and rule of law in general all over the world and also the impact of secularism in particular have changed the mindset on the one hand and on the other, encouraged people of all sections to question the authority of religion and its relevance in modern period. Especially the marginalized women, who are the direct victims of superstitions and dogmas of religion throughout the world, have started raising their voices against religious texts and myths. According to Foucault, 'Where there is power, there is resistance'.[6] Resultantly, the authority of religion is going to be liquidated day by day. So, with all such changes in the nature and functions of different social institutions and religious norms and practices, gender socialization and its appeal must be changed a lot. However, all these complications and changes in the role of these agents such as the family, peer group, school, media, religion and ritual myths, not being the subject matter of the book, have not been addressed and analysed in detail although the hints of these changes may be received in the book. All of them may be the matters of further research.

In spite of the existence of the two sexes—man and woman—there is no denying the fact that there are other genders that are going to be equally dominating and meaningful today throughout the world. They are homosexuals, lesbians, eunuchs, cross dressers, transgender, and gender queers. Their numbers are growing faster. A day may come when they will outnumber the people living under the myth of two sexes. So it is very much pertinent to question as to how and in what way they will go through the process of gender socialization which is modelled upon the myth of two sexes. The persons, living out of the myth of two sexes (male and female), do not have the same experiences of family, peer group, school and the media as are conventionally received by the so called normal children within the category of male and female. So the questions as to what type of socialization they need, how their gender identity will be developed and in what way they will come to interact with the formal agents of gender socialization are also matters of further research.

---

[6] Michel Foucault, *The History of Sexuality*, Vol. 1 (New York, NY: Vintage, 1980), 5.

At the end of the discussion contained in this book, it is found that in all countries and across all cultures gender socialization results in undermining the position of women by inculcating many stereotypical traits that come roughly under three chief stereotypically determined and specific indicators—inferiority, subservience and domesticity. 'Inferiority ... is based on the very common myth of the superior male intellect, that is, the idea that men are better species than women.'[7] Inferiority points out the physical weakness of woman and argues that it is due to their physical weakness that women could not participate in hunting in prehistoric age. Subsequent confinement of women at home and their engagement with motherhood and home management are the result of their physical weakness mainly due to which they were ousted from the broader world of public works. Accordingly, the interaction of women with outer world has been restricted and such alienation of women with the outer world has resulted in a gross erosion of intelligence as a result of which women have been un-smart, passive, mute and self-effacing. Differential gender socialization has played a significant role in preaching and inculcating this concept of inferiority among women through different agents such as family, peer group, school, media, religion and ritual myths. The concept of subservience claims that it is due to the inferiority of women in comparison to men that women should remain under strict control of men.

> As soon as women refuse to pretend to be submissive and dependent, ... they lose the benefits of femininity. The women are punished for refusing men's protection, for female assertiveness represents a challenge to male authority and control and any woman, who shows assertive qualities, is defined as abnormal female.[8]

The notion of abnormal female has a biological implication in the sense that such women are beyond the conventional format and they do not possess the biologically appropriate feminine qualities. If they are to be included in the socially approved format of 'femininity', they will have to go through the procedure of gender socialization implemented by various agents such as family, peer

---

[7] Liddle and Joshi, *Daughters of Independence*, 177–80.
[8] Ibid, 183–84.

group, etc., and the objective of such gender socialization is to present a domesticated model of feminine gender. The notion of domesticity argues, 'Marriage is the proper state for a woman.... It is also true that man's desire of property rights over women has pushed them in stereotype of domesticity.... The domestic stereotype defines women as sexual object and male property....'[9] The concept of domesticity has placed women in a 'separate biological category' which is very much significant in legitimizing gender inequality. 'Thus the stereotypes about women's inferior abilities, subservient qualities and domestic needs form part of a gender ideology which makes sharp distinction between the social constructs of masculinity and femininity.'[10] Thus, the social construction of male and female gender, the initiation of maleness and femaleness and encouraging the persons of both sexes to adopt the gender specific social role are the agenda of gender socialization mediated and implemented by different agents like family, peer group, school, media, religion and ritual myths. The gender inequality that we experience in our day to day life is actually the product of the process of gender socialization and the seed is transplanted in the nature and function of very many primary and secondary groups, social and mass media and institutions and rituals. Charity begins at home. So, if we are to combat gender inequality in a systematic manner we must start our war against gender inequality from within the most known and popular groups, organizations and institutions.

In this way, this book is the documentation of the processes of gender socialization of the boys and the girls through a number of formal agents such as family, peer group, school and media. This book also documents role of religion and different mythical concepts related to it through which people of the rural background especially the girls and the women come to be socialized in respect of gender stereotypes, gender roles and gender norms and practices. The book argues that if the ideological techniques of gender socialization are not properly understood, the struggle against gender inequality is bound to be futile. It is also argued that if the complex domain of gender socialization can be changed with a more moderate and

[9] Ibid.
[10] Ibid.

progressive approach, then it is possible to create and seek a better world for women. If the traditional social, cultural and religious arrangements are restructured with a view to achieve gender equity then it is possible to allow the development of women in a more free and voluntary manner. Very often it is seen that most of the books on gender studies and cultural sociology do not give due emphasis on the issue of gender socialization as the most important source of enforcing gender inequality, gender stereotypes and gender role distribution in all societies and across all cultures. This book is a much-needed effort to fill the gap. By taking the gender socialization as a total subject, this book actually focuses on the exhaustiveness and complexities of the system of operation of the ideology of patriarchy and thus gives a clue also to the ways of coming out of this situation. It is argued here that if the social and cultural institutions, organizations and religious practices are restructured with a gender-free outlook then perhaps we will not have to lament as Beauvoir remarked, 'one is not born, but rather becomes, a woman...'. This book is a step forward towards the formation of a new concept about gender and gender-related norms and practices.

Glossary

Adam	Imagined as the first male in Christianity.
Agni Purana	One of the Puranas.
Bahubali Rajneeti	The politics of the muscleman.
Begusarai	A district town of Bihar and a T.V. serial by this name.
Bhagbata Purana	One of the Puranas.
Bikash Society	N.G.O. working in the District of Bankura, West Bengal.
Borka	The same as Purdah or the veil hiding the whole body of the Muslim women.
Brahma	The supreme entity in Hinduism.
Chandimandap	The place of public meeting in villages of ancient India.
Chitragupta	Record keeper in Yama's court.
Dasaratha	Father of Rama, the hero in the epic Ramayana.
Dasputuli	A vow composed of 10 sacred hymns, observed in Bengal.
Devdasi	A custom of getting a girl married with God in Ancient India, especially operative in South India.
Dharma	Religion.
Dharma-sūtras	Ancient law books of Hinduism.
Doordarshan	Indian Television.
Draupadi	The wife of Panchapandava, i.e., five hero brothers in the epic Mahabharata.
Durga	The goddess of India celebrated for heroic act of killing Mahisasura, the symbol of destruction.
Hijab	A form of dress in Islam that covers the entire body of Muslim women.
Iman	Means honour in Islam.
Itu	Imagined as goddess and worshipped by married and unmarried women on each Sunday of Agrahayan, i.e., November–December.

Iv	Imagined as first female in Christianity.
Kalna	A town in the District of Burdwan, West Bengal.
Kaushalya	Mother of Rama.
Koran	The scripture of Islam.
Krishnanagar	A district town of West Bengal.
Kunti	Wife of Pandu and mother of 'Panchapandava'.
Laxmana	Brother of Rama.
Laxmi	The goddess of wealth.
Mahabharata	Epic of India.
Mangalchandi	Imagined as the popular goddess of the folk society of Bengal. They worship on each Tuesday of May–June (Jaistha) and chant rhymes.
Mantras	Sacred hymns.
Manu	The ancient sage and law-giver of India.
Manusmrti	Ancient law book depicted by Manu.
Naraka	Concept of hell in Hinduism.
Pati Param Guru	Husband is the absolute Lord.
Patibrata	The woman who is loyal to her husband.
Prakriti	The feminine form of the supreme God, i.e., Brahma.
Prayaschitta	Atonement.
Punnam	A type of hell in Hinduism.
Punyipukur	A vow observed by the unmarried girls of Bengal. They dig about one square feet pond in their courtyard and fill it with water and plant a basil and worship that pond and tree for gaining virtue. The vow is observed in April–May of each year.
Puranas	Sacred scriptures of India in post-Vedic period.
Purdah	A black gown by which Muslim women hide their face in public.
Purusha	The masculine form of supreme God.
Ramayana	The epic of India.
Ravana	King of ancient 'Lanka', who kidnapped Sita.
Sabitri	A mythological lady who made her husband alive just by the virtue of chastity.

Sati	Means chaste; but a Hindu wife burnt in the funeral pyre of her husband was also termed as Sati. The custom was abolished by law in 1829 by struggling effort of Rammohan Roy, the pioneer of Indian Renaissance.
Satyaban	The husband of Sabitri, the chaste woman.
Senjuti	A kind of female vow.
Shakti	The original force of creation in Hinduism.
Shastthi	The goddess of reproduction in Hinduism.
Sibabrata	A vow offered to the Lord Shiva, the Hindu god.
Sita	The wife of Rama, the hero of the epic Ramayana.
Smrtis	Ancient law books of Hinduism.
Talak	The form of personal law about divorce in Islam.
Tush-tushuli	The goddess of crop and worshiped by the women of Bengal during December–January.
Vaishali	A town of Uttar Pradesh in India.
Veda	The sacred scripture of the Hindus.
Yajna	The rites of sacred fire.
Yamaraja	The god of death under Hinduism.

Bibliography

Abdul-Rauf, M. *Islamic View of Women and Family*. Cairo: The Supreme Council for Islamic Affairs, 1993.

Agarwal, Bina. "Gender and Command Over Property: A Critical Gap in Economic Analysis and Policy in South Asia." *World Development* 22(10) (1994).

Agresti, Alan. *Categorical Data Analysis*. New York, NY: John Wiley, 1990.

Ahmed, L. *Women and Gender in Islam*. New Haven, CT: Yale University Press, 1992.

Altekar, A. S. *The Position of Women in Hindu Civilization*. New Delhi: Motilal Banarsidas, 1962.

Andersen, M. L. *Thinking about Women: Sociological Perspectives on Sex and Gender*. New York, NY: Macmillan, 1993.

Anderson, R. T., and W. W. Sharrock, eds. *Applied Sociological Perspectives*. New Delhi: Heritage Publishers, 1984.

Argyle, M., and Benjamin Beit-Hallahmi. *The Social Psychology of Religion*. London: Routledge & Kegan Paul, 1975.

Arliss, L. P. *Gender Communication*. Englewood Cliffs, NJ: Prentice-Hall, 1991.

Ashmore, Richard D., and Frances K. Del Boca. "Sex Stereotypes and Implicit Personality Theory: Toward a Cognitive Social Psychological Conceptualization." *Sex Roles* 5(2) (April 1979), 219–48.

Aulette, J. R. *Changing Families*. Belmont, CA: Wadsworth Publishing Company, 1994.

Badawi, J. *The Status of Women in Islam*. Plainfield: MSA of US and Canada, 1980.

Bagheri, Elham. *A Qualitative Investigation of Religion, Gender Role Beliefs and Culture in the Lives of a Select Group of Muslim Men*, PhD Thesis, University of Iowa, 2012, 30. Retrieved 7 July 2017, from http: //ir.uiowa.edu/etd/3561

Baig, T. A. *India's Woman Power*. New Delhi: S. Chand Publishing, 1976.

Bailey, S. *How Schools Shortchange Girls: The AAUW Report*. New York, NY: Marlowe & Company, 1992.

Bandura, Albert. *Social Learning and Personality Development*. New York, NY: Holt, Rinehart and Winston, 1963.

Bandopadhyay, Kalyani. *Rajniti O Narishakti* (in Bengali). Howrah: Manuscript India, 2002.

Banerjee, Nirmala. "Sexual Division of Labour." In *Indian Women: Myth and Reality*, edited by Jasodhara Bagchi. Hyderabad: Sangam Books, 1997.

Bannon, I., and M. C. Correia, eds. *The Other Half of Gender: Men's Issues in Development*. Washington, D.C.: The World Bank, 2006.

Barlas, A. *"Believing Women" in Islam: Un-reading Patriarchal Interpretations of the Qur'an*. Austin: Texas University Press, 2002.

Basow, Susan A. *Gender Stereotypes and Roles.* Pacific Grove, CA: Brooks/Cole, 1992.

———. *Sex-Role Stereotypes: Traditions and Alternatives.* Monterey, CA: Brooks/Cole Publishing Company, 1980.

———. *Gender: Stereotypes and Roles.* Pacific Grove, CA: Brooks/Cole Publishing, 1992.

Beal, C. *Boys and Girls: The Development of Gender Roles.* New York, NY: McGraw-Hill, 1994.

Bean, Frank D., and Marta Tienda. *The Hispanic Population of the United States.* New York, NY: Russell Sage, 1987.

Beck, U. *Risk Society: Towards a New Modernity.* London: SAGE Publications, 1992.

Becker, Gary S. *A Treatise on the Family* (expanded ed.). Cambridge, MA: Harvard University Press, 1991.

Begum, Maleka. "Bipanna Nari: Satidaha Theke Kanyabhrun Hatya." In *Naribiswa,* edited by Pulak Chanda. Kolkata: Gangchil, 2008.

Bem, S. L. "Gender Schema Theory: A Cognitive Account of Sex Typing." *Psychological Review* 88 (1981), 354–64.

———. *The Lenses of Gender: Transforming the Debate on Sexual Inequality.* New Haven, CT: Yale University Press, 1993.

Benbenishty, R., and R. Astor. *School Violence in Context. Culture, Neighborhoods, Family, School, and Gender.* New York, NY: Oxford University Press, 2005.

Berk, Sarah Fenstermaker. *The Gender Factory.* New York, NY: Plenum Press, 1985.

Bernard, J. *American Family Behaviour.* New York, NY: Harper & Row, 1942.

Berryman-Fink, C., D. Ballard-Reisch, and L. H. Newman. *Communication and Sex Role Socialization.* New York, NY: Garland Publishing, 1993.

Blakemore, J.E.O., S. A. Berenbaum, and L. S. Liben. *Gender Development.* New York, NY: Taylor & Francis, 2009.

Bhattacharyya, D. C. *Sociology* (new 7th ed.). Kolkata: Vijoya Publishing House, 2002.

Blau, Peter M., and Joseph E. Schwartz. *Crosscutting Social Circles: Testing a Macrostructural Theory of Intergroup Relations.* Orlando, FL: Academic Press, 1984.

Blumberg, R. *Gender Bias in Textbooks: A Hidden Obstacle on the Road to Gender Equality in Education.* Charlottesville, VA: University of Virginia, 2007.

———. *A General Theory of Gender Stratification.* San Francisco, CA: Jossey Bros, 1984.

Borgatta, Edgar F., and Karen S. Cook, eds. *The Future of Sociology.* Newbury Park, CA: SAGE Publications, 1988.

Bourdieu, P. *Reproduction in Education, Society and Culture.* London: SAGE Publications, 1977.

———. 1979. *Distinction: A Social Critique of the Judgment of Taste.* Translated by Richard Nice. Cambridge, MA: Harvard University Press, 1984.

Brehm, S. S., S. M. Kassin, and S. Fein. *Social Psychology.* Boston, MA: Houghton Mifflin Company, 1999.

Broom, Leonard, and Philip Selznick. *Principles of Sociology*, 4th ed. New York, NY: Harper and Row, 1970.

Buckley, Kerry Wayne. *Mechanical Man: John Broadus Watson and the Beginnings of Behaviorism*. New York, NY: Guilford Press, 1989.

Burn, S. M. *The Social Psychology of Gender*. New York, NY: McGraw-Hill, 1996.

Carlson, Neil R., and C. Donald Heth, eds. *Psychology: The Science of Behaviour*. Toronto: Pearson, 2010. Adopted from Wikipedia, the free encyclopedia.

Chafetz, J. S. *The Handbook of the Sociology of Gender*. New York, NY: Plenum Publishers, 1999.

Chakraborty, Barun Kumar. *Bangla Lok Sahitya Charchar Itihas*. Calicut: Sahityasri, 1977.

Channa, Karana, ed. *Socialization, Education and Women: Explorations in Gender Identity*. New Delhi: Orient Longman, 1988.

Chaodorow, Nancy. *The Reproduction of Mothering*. Berkeley, CA: University of California Press, 1978.

Chapman, Karen. *The Sociology of Schools*. London: Tavistock, 1986.Chatterjee, Bandana. "Women and Politics in India." In *Politics India: State Society Interface*, edited by Rakhahari Chatterjee, 2nd ed. New Delhi: South Asian Publishers, 2009.

Chattopadhyay, Sujit Kumar. *Fighting Gender Inequality: A Tribute to Nirbhaya*. Kolkata: K P Bagchi & Company, 2015.

Chitnis, Suma. "Feminism: Indian Ethos and Indian Convictions." In *Women in Indian* Society, edited by Rehana Ghadially. New Delhi: SAGE Publications, 1988.

Clifford, Cassandra. *Are Girls Still Marginalized? Discrimination and Gender Inequality Today*. Retrieved from https://foreignpolicyblogs.com/2007/05/29/are-girls-still-marginalized-discrimination-and-gender-inequality-in-today's-society/

Clogg, Clifford C., and Edward S. Shihadeh. *Statistical Models for Ordinal Variables*. Thousand Oaks, CA: SAGE Publications, 1994.

Closson, L. M. "Status and Gender Differences in Early Adolescents' Descriptions of Popularity." *Social Development* 18 (2009), 412–26.

Collins, Randall. *Four Sociological Traditions*. New York, NY: Oxford University Press, 1994.

Coltrane, Scott. *Family Man: Fatherhood, Housework and Gender Equity*. New York, NY: Oxford University Press, 1996.

Coltrane, Scott. *Gender and Families*. London: Pine Forge Press, 1998.

Connell, R. W. *Masculinities*. Cambridge, MA: Polity Press, 1995.

Cooley, Charles Horton. *Social Organization*. New York, NY: Scribner's, 1909.

Cornwall, Marie. "The Influence of Three Agents of Religious Socialization: Family, Church, and Peers." In *The Religion and Family Connection: Social Science Perspectives*, edited by Darwin L. Thomas. Provo, UT: Religious Studies Center, Brigham Young University, 1988.

Craig, S. *Men, Masculinity and the Media*. Thousand Oaks, CA: SAGE Publications, 1997.

Crespi, Isabella. *Socialization and Gender Roles Within the Family: A Study on Adolescents and their Parents in Great Britain*. Retrieved 10 July 2017, from www.mariecurie.org/annals/volume3/crespi.pdf

Damon, W., ed. *Handbook of Child Psychology*, Vol. III. New York, NY: Wiley, 2006.

Davis, B. *Diversity and Complexity in the Classroom: Considerations of Race, Ethnicity, and Gender*. San Francisco, CA: Jossey-Bass, 1993.

Davis, Kingsley. "Intermarriage in Caste Societies." *American Anthropologist* 43 (1941), 376–95.

de Beauvoir, Simone. *The Second Sex*. Translated and edited by H. M. Parshley. London: Vintage, 1997.

de Mause, L. *The Evolution of Childhood*. New York, NY: Psychohistory Press, 1974.

Delamar, Gloria T. *Mother Goose: From Nursery to Literature*. Jefferson, NC: McFarland, 1987.

Delamont, S. *Sex Roles and the School* (2nd ed.). London: Routledge, 1990.

Douglas, Ann. *The Feminization of American Culture*. New York, NY: Knopf, 1977.

Drake, St. Clair, and Horace Cayton. 1945. *Black Metropolis: A Study of Negro Life in a Northern City* (rev. ed.). Chicago, IL: University of Chicago Press, 1993.

Dreze, Jean, and Amartya Sen. *India: Development and Participation*. New Delhi and Oxford: Oxford University Press, 2002.

Duncan, N. *Sexual Bullying: Gender Conflict and Pupil Culture in Secondary Schools*. New York, NY: Routledge, 1999.

Dundas, Marjorie, ed. *Riddling Tales from Around the World*. Jackson, MS: University Press of Mississippi, 2002.

Durham, Meenakshi Gigi, and Douglas M. Kellner. *Media and Cultural Studies*. Malden, MA; Oxford, UK; Carlton, Victoria, Australia: Blackwell Publishing, 2006.

Eagly, A. H. *Sex Differences in Social Behavior: A Social Role Interpretation*. Hillsdale, MI: Lawrence Erlbaum Associates, 1987.

Edwards, D. Miall. *The Philosophy of Religion* (Indian edition). Kolkata: Progressive Publishers, 1975.

Elder, Glen H. "Appearance and Education in Marriage Mobility." *American Sociological Review* 34(4) (August 1969), 519–33.

Eliot, Lise. *Pink Brain, Blue Brain: How Small Differences Grow into Troublesome Gaps*. Boston, MA: Houghton Mifflin Harcourt, 2009.

Engineer, A. *The Rights of Women in Islam*. New Delhi: Sterling Publishers, 2004.

England, Paula, and George Farkas. *Households, Employment and Gender*. New York, NY: Aldine, 1986.

Erikson, E. H. *Childhood and Society*. New York, NY: W. W. Norton & Company, 1993.

Erikson, E. H. *Identity: Youth and Crisis* (No. 7). New York, NY: W. W. Norton & Company, 1994.

Ferree, M., and E. Hall. "Rethinking Stratification from a Feminist Perspective: Gender, Race, and Class in Mainstream Textbooks." *American Sociological Review* 61(6) (1996), 935.

Fine, Cordelia. *Delusions of Gender: How Our Minds, Society and Neurosexism Create Difference*. New York, NY: W. W. Norton & Company, 2010.

Fischer, Ernst. *The Necessity of Art*. Middlesex: Penguin Books, 1981.

Foucault, Michel. *The History of Sexuality*, Vol. 1. New York, NY: Vintage, 1980.

Franklin, S., ed. *The Sociology of Gender*. Cheltenham: Edward Elgar Publishing, 1996.

Friedman, Stewart D., and Jeffrey H. Greenhaus. *Work and Family: Allies or Enemies?* New York, NY: Oxford University Press, 2000.

Fu, Vincent Kang. "Racial Intermarriage Pairings." *Demography* 38 (2001), 147–59.

Fukuyama, Francis. *The End of Order*. London: Social Market Foundation, 1997.

Galambos, N. L., S. A. Berenbaum, and S. M. McHale. "*Gender development in Adolescence*." In *Handbook of Adolescent Psychology: Individual Bases of Adolescent Development* (3rd ed.), edited by R. M. Lerner and L. Steinberg, Vol. 1. Hoboken, NJ: John Wiley & Sons.

Geertz, Clifford. *Local Knowledge: Further Essays in Interpretive Anthropology*. New York, NY: Basic Books, 1983.

Ghadially, Rehana, ed. *Women in Indian Society*. New Delhi: SAGE Publications, 1988.

Giddens, A. *Sociology*, Cambridge: Polity Press, 1993.

Gill, N. Rosalind. *Gender and Media*. Cambridge: Polity Press, 2006.

Gillin, John Lewis, and John Philip Gillin. *Cultural Sociology*. New York, NY: The Macmillan Company, 1948.

Gleitman, H., A. J. Fridlund, and D. Reisberg. *Basic Psychology*. New York, NY: W. W. Norton & Company, 2000.

Glock, Charles, Ringer Benjamin, and Babbie Earl. *To Comfort and to Challenge*. Berkeley: University of California Press, 1967.

Goode, William J. "Family and Mobility." In *Class, Status and Power: Social Stratification in Comparative Perspective*, 2nd edition, edited by Reinhard Bendix and Seymour Martin Lipset. New York: Free Press, 1951.

———. *World Revolution and Family Patterns*, 2nd edition. New York, NY: Free Press, 1970.

Gottman, John. *The Seven Principles for Making Marriage Work*. New York, NY: Three Rivers Press, 1999.

Greenfield, P. M. *Mind and Media: The Effects of Television, Video Games, and Computers*. Cambridge, MA: Harvard University Press, 1984.

Hacking, Ian. The Social *Construction of What?* Cambridge, MA: Harvard University Press, 1999.

Haddad, Y. Y., and J. L. Esposito. *Islam, Gender and Social Change*. New York, NY: Oxford University Press, 1998.

Hallet, Martin, and Barbara Karasek, eds. *Folk and Fairy Tales* (2nd ed.). Peterborough: Broadview Press, 1996.

Handel, G. *Childhood Socialization*. New York, NY: Aldine de Gruyter, 1988.

Harris, J. R. "Where Is the Child's Environment? A Group Socialization Theory of Development." *Psychological Review* 102 (1995), 458–89.

Harrison, V. "Modern Women, Traditional Abrahamic Religions and Interpreting Sacred Texts." *Feminist Theology* 15 (2007), 145–59.

Hasan, M. "Feminism as Islamophobia: A Review of Misogyny Charges Against Islam." *Intellectual Discourse* 20 (2012), 55–78.

Havighurst, R. *Developmental Tasks and Education*. New York, NY: Plenum Press, 1952.

Henry, J. *Culture Against Man*. New York, NY: Vintage, 1963.

Hetherington, E. M., and R. D. Parke. *Child Psychology: A Contemporary Viewpoint* (5th ed.). New York, NY: McGraw-Hill College, 1999.

Heywood, Andrew. *Key Concepts in Politics*. Chennai: Palgrave, 2005.

Hill, Michael R. "American Sociological Association." In *Blackwell Encyclopedia of Sociology*, Vol. 1, edited by George Ritzer. Malden, MA: Blackwell Publishing, 2007.

Hvistendahl, Mara. *Unnatural Selection: Choosing Boys over Girls, and the Consequences of a World Full of Men*. New York, NY: Public Affairs, 2011.

International Gay and Lesbian Human Rights Commission [IGLHRC], 2005, Institutional Memoir of the 2005 Institute for Trans and Intersex Activist Training, 8, http://www.iglhrc.org/files/iglhrc/LAC/ITIAT-Aug06-E.pdf

Jackson, Rosemary. *Fantasy: The Literature of Subversion*. London: Methuen, 1981.

Jayaram, N. *On Civil Society*. New Delhi: SAGE Publications, 2005.

Kalia, Narendra Nath. "Women and Sexism: Language of Indian School Textbooks." In *Women in Indian Society*, edited by Rehana Ghadially. New Delhi: SAGE Publications, 1988.

Kane, Emily W. *Rethinking Gender and Sexuality in Childhood*. London: Bloomsbury, 2013.

———. *The Gender Trap: Parents and the Pitfalls of Raising Boys and Girls*. New York, NY: New York University Press, 2012.

Kant, Immanuel. *Observations on the Feelings of the Beautiful and Sublime*. Translated by John J. Goldthwait. Pacific Grove, California: University of California Press, 1960.

Kaplan, E. A. *Women and Film: Both Sides of the Camera*. New York, NY: Methuen, 1983.

Kaplan, P. A. *Child's Odyssey*. Saint Paul, MN: West Publishing Company, 1991.

Klein S. *Handbook for Achieving Sex Equity Through Education*. Baltimore, MD: The Johns Hopkins University Press, 1985.

Leaper, C., and R. S. Bigler. "Gender." In *Social Development: Relationships in Infancy, Childhood, and Adolescence*, edited by M. K. Underwood, and L. H. Rosen. New York, NY: Guildford Press, 2011.

Lee Bartky, Sandra. *Femininity and Domination: Studies in the Phenomenology of Oppression*. New York, NY: Routledge, 1990.

Lempers, J. D., and D. S. Clark-Lempers. "A Functional Comparison of Same-sex and Opposite Sex Friendships During Adolescence." *Journal of Adolescent Research* 8 (1993), 89–108.

Liddle, Joanna, and Roma Joshi. *Daughters of Independence – Gender, Caste and Class in India*. London: Zed Books Ltd., 1986.

Liu, F. "School Culture and Gender." In *The SAGE Handbook of Gender and Education*, edited by C. Skelton, B. Francis, and L. Smulyan. Thousand Oaks, CA: SAGE Publications, 2006.

Lorber, Judith. *Paradoxes of Gender*. New Haven, CT: Yale University Press, 1994.

Lucal, B., and A. Blackstone, eds. *The Sociology of Gender: Syllabi and Other Instructional Materials*, 5th edition. Washington, D.C.: American Sociological Association, 2002.

Luckmann, Thomas. *The Invisible Religion.* New York, NY: Macmillan, 1967.

Ma, X. *Gender Differences in Learning Outcomes.* Louisville, KT: University of Kentucky, 2007.

Mac an Ghaill, Mairtin. *The Making of Men: Masculinities, Sexualities and Schooling.* Buckingham: Open University Press, 1994.

Maccoby, E. E. "Gender and Relationships: A Developmental Account." *American Psychologist* 45 (1990), 513–20.

MacIver, R. M., and Charles H. Page. *Society.* London: Macmillan, 1965.

Macrae, C. N., C. Stangor, and M. Hewstone. *Stereotypes and Stereotyping.* New York, NY: The Guilford Press, 1996.

Majumdar, G. *Folk Tales of Bengal.* New Delhi: Sterling Publishers, 1911.

Majumdar, Rinita. *A Short Introduction to Feminist Theory.* Kolkata: Anustup, 2001.

Marsden, P. V. "Core Discussion Networks of Americans." *American Sociological Review* 52 (1987), 122–31.

Martin, Daniel D., and Janelle L. Wilson. "Role Theory." In *Encyclopedia of Social Theory*, edited by George Ritzer, Vol. 2, 651–55. Thousand Oaks, London, New Delhi: SAGE Publications, 2005.

Masuzawa, Tomoko. *The Invention of World Religions.* Chicago: The University of Chicago Press, 2005.

McRobbie, Angela. *The* Aftermath of Feminism: Gender, Culture and Social Change. London: SAGE Publications, 2008.

Mead, G. H. *Mind, Self and Society: From the Standpoint of a Social Behaviorist.* Chicago, IL: University of Chicago Press, 1934/1962.

Mead, George Herbert. *The Philosophy of the Present.* La Salle, IL: Open Court Publishing, 1959.

Merry, Sally Engle. *Gender Violence: A Cultural Perspective.* Chichester: Wiley-Blackwell, 2009.

Merton, Robert K. "Intermarriage and the Social Structure: Fact and Theory." *Psychiatry* 4 (1941), 361–74.

Milgram, S. *Obedience to Authority: An Experimental View.* New York, NY: Harper & Row, 1974.

Miller, Allan S., and Rodney Stark. *Gender and Religiousness: Can Socialization Explanations be Saved?* Chicago, IL: The University of Chicago, 2002.

Millet, Kate. *Sexual Politics.* New York, NY: Doubleday, 1970.

Misra, Gitanjali, and Radhika Chandiramani, eds. *Sexuality, Gender and Rights.* New Delhi: SAGE Publications, 2005.

Moses, J. Oneness. *Great Principles Shared by All Religions.* New York, NY: Random House, 2002.

Muncie, J., Margaret Wetherell, Mary Langan, Rudi Dallos, and Allan Cochrane. *Understanding the Family.* London: SAGE Publications, 1999.

Muus, R. E. *Theories of Adolescence.* New York, NY: McGraw-Hill, 1996.

Murdock, George Peter. *Social Structure.* New York: The Macmillan Company, 1949.

Northcutt, H. C. "Who Stays Home? Working Parents and Sick Children." *International Journal of Women's Studies* 6 (1983).

Nye, Malory. *Religion: The Basics.* New York, NY: Routledge, 2003.

O' Neill, Maggie, ed. *Adorno, Culture and Feminism*. Thousand Oaks, CA: SAGE Publications, 1999.

O'Neil, J. N. "Patterns of Gender Role Conflict and Strain." *Personnel and Guidance Journal* 60 (1981), 203–10.

Paechter, C. "Using Poststructuralist Ideas in Gender Theory and Research." In *Investigating Gender: Contemporary Perspectives in Education*, edited by B. Francis and C. Skelton. Buckingham: Open University Press, 2001.

Pagels, Elaine. *Adam, Eve and the Serpent*. New York, NY: Random House, 1988.

Papalia, D. E., S. W. Olds, and R. D. Feldman. *Human Development* (7th ed.). New York, NY: McGraw-Hill, 1998.

Parenti, M. *Make-Believe Media: The Politics of Entertainment*. New York, NY: St. Martin's Press, 1992.

Parpart, Jane L., M. Patricia Connelly, and V. Eudine Barriteau, eds. *Theoretical Perspectives on Gender and Development*. Canada: International Development Research Center, 2000.

Perry, David G., and Rachel E. Pauletty. "Gender and Adolescent Development." *Journal of Research on Adolescence* 21(1) (2011), 61–74.

Phillips, Anne. *Gender and Culture*. Cambridge, MA: Polity Press, 2010.

Piaget, Jean. *The Moral Judgement of the Child*. London: Kegan Paul, 1932.

Pilcher, Jane, and Imelda Whelehan. *50 Key Concepts in Gender Studies*. London: SAGE Publications, 2004.

Pleck, J. H. *The Myth of Masculinity*. Cambridge, MA: MIT Press, 1981.

Punwani, Jyoti. "Portrayal of Women on Television." In *Women in Indian Society*, edited by Rehana Ghadially. New Delhi: SAGE Publications, 1988.

Ouzgane, Lahoucine. "Women and Islam." *Postmodern Culture 3.3* (1993), Project MUSE. Retrieved 15 November 2012 from http://muse.jhu.edu/

Qian, Zhenchao. "Breaking Racial Barriers: Variations in Interracial Marriage between 1980 and 1990." *Demography* 34 (1997), 263–76.

Rage, Sharmila, ed. *Sociology of Gender*. New Delhi: SAGE Publications, 2003.

Rahman, F. *Major Themes of the Qur'an* (2nd ed.). Chicago, IL: University of Chicago Press, 2009.

Rao, V. V. P., and V. N. Rao. *Marriage, Family and Women in India*. Columbia: South Asian Books, 1982.

Radford Reuther, Rosemary. *Sexism and God-Talk: Towards a Feminist Theology*. Boston, MA: Beacon Press, 1983.

Rexroat, Cinthia, and Constance L. Shehan. "The Family Cycle and Spouses' Time in Housework." *Journal of Marriage and the Family* 49 (1987), 737–50.

Richardson, Laurel. *The Dynamics of Sex and Gender: A Sociological Perspective*. New York, NY: Harper & Row, 1988.

Ritzer, George. *Sociological Theory*, 3rd edition. Singapore: McGraw Hill, 1992.

Robyn Ryle. *Questioning Gender: A Sociological Perspective*. Los Angeles, CA: SAGE Publications, 2012.

Rose, A. J., G. G. Glick, and R. L. Smith. "Popularity and Gender: The Culture of Boys and Girls." In *Popularity in the Peer System*, edited by A. H. N. Cillessen, D. Schwartz, and L. Mayeux. New York, NY: Guilford Press, 2011.

Rosenfeld, Michael J. "A Critique of Exchange Theory in Mate Selection." *American Journal of Sociology* 110(5) (March, 2005), 1284–1325.

Roy, Kumkum. *The Power of Gender and the Gender of Power: Explorations in Early Indian History.* Oxford: Oxford University Press, 2010.

Roy, Manisha. "Concept of Femininity and Liberation." In *Women in Indian Society,* edited by Rehana Ghadially. New Delhi: SAGE Publications, 1988.

Russell, David L. *Literature for Children: A Short Introduction* (6th ed.). Boston, MA: Pearson, 2009.

Santrock, J. *Child Development,* 6th ed. Madison: Brown & Benchmark, 1994.

Schalet, Amy. *Not Under My Roof: Parents, Teens and the Culture of Sex.* Chicago, IL: University of Chicago Press, 2011.

Schipper, Mineke. *Never Marry a Woman with Big Feet.* New Haven, CT and London: Yale University Press, 2003.

Sen, Girish Chandra (Maulavi Bhai). *The Holy Koran* (Bengali Translation). Kolkata: Haraf Prakashani, 2011.

Sengupta, Sankar. *A Survey of Folklore Study of Bengal.* Calcutta: Indian Publications, 1970.

Shields, Stephanie A. "Functionalism, Darwinism and the Psychology of Women: A Study in Social Myth." *American Psychologist* 30 (1975), 739–54.

Siegler, Robert. *How Children Develop, Exploring Child Develop Student Media Tool Kit + Scientific American Reader to Accompany How Children Develop.* New York, NY: Worth Publishers, 2006.

Sinha, Santi. *Tushu.* Kolkata: Loksanskriti O Adibasi Sanskirti Kendra, 1998.

Smart, Barry. *Michel Foucault.* London: Routledge, 1985.

Srivastava, S. L. *Folk Culture and Oral Tradition.* New Delhi: Abhinav Publications, 1974.

Stark, Rodney. *Doing Sociology.* Belmont, CA: Wadsworth, 1992.

Statham, June. *Daughters and Sons: Experiences of Non-sexist Childraising.* Oxford: Blackwell, 1986.

Steinberg, Laurence. *Adolescence* (5th ed.). New York, NY: McGraw-Hill College, 1999.

———. *Adolescence.* New York, NY: McGraw-Hill, 2010.

Stromquist, N. P. "The Gender Socialization Process in Schools: A Cross-national Comparison." Paper commissioned for the EFA Global Monitoring Report 2008, *Education for All by 2015: Will We Make It?* New York, NY: UNESCO, 2007.

Swami Nirmalananda. *Baromaser Teroparban.* Kolkata: Pronob Math, 1978.

Tavris, C. *The Mismeasure of Woman.* New York, NY: Simon & Schuster, 1992.

Tagore, Abanindranath. *Banglar Brato.* Kolkata: Visva-Bharati, 1944.

Tanveer, Saiad Nasrin. "Musalman, Bangali O Nari: Samakalin Paschimbanga." In *Naribiswa,* edited by Pulak Chanda. Kolkata: Gangchil, 2008.

The Brothers Grimm. *The Complete Fairy Tales.* Hertfordshire: Wordsworth Editions, 1997.

Thompson, E. H. "Beneath the Status Characteristics: Gender Variations in Religiousness." *Journal for the Scientific Study of Religion* 30 (1991), 381–94.

Thorne, B. *Gender Play: Girls and Boys in School.* New Brunswick, NJ: Rutgers University Press, 1993.

Thornham, Sue. *Women, Feminism and Media.* Edinburgh: Edinburgh University Press, 2007.

Touchman, G. "Women's Depiction by the Mass Media." In *Feminist Frontiers: Rethinking Sex, Gender and Society*, edited by L. Richardson and V. Taylor. London: Addison-Wesley Publishing Co, 1983.

Tuckman, Bruce W., and M. Monetti David. *Educational Psychology*. Belmont, CA: Wadsworth, 2010.

Turner, Bryan S. *Religion and Social Theory*, 2nd ed. London: SAGE Publications, 1991.

Unger, R. K. *Female and Male*. New York, NY: Harper & Row, 1979.

Vetterling-Braggin, Mary, ed. *Sexist Language: A Modern Philosophical Analysis*. New Jersey: Totowa, Littlefield, Adams, 1981.

Wadud, A. *Qur'an and Woman: Rereading the Sacred Text from a Woman's Perspective*. New York, NY: Oxford University Press, 1999.

Walby, Sylvia. *Theorizing Patriarchy*. Oxford: Blackwell Publishing, 1990.

Walter, Tony, and Grace Davie. "The Religiosity of Women in the Modern West." *British Journal of Sociology* 49(4) (1998), 640–69.

Watson, John Broadus. *Behaviorism*. New York, NY: W.W. Norton & Company, 1925.

Webster's New World Dictionary. Webster New World, 1998.

Wharton, A. S. *The Sociology of Gender: An Introduction to Theory and Research*. Malden, MA: Blackwell Publishing, 2005.

Williams, T. M., ed. *The Impact of Television: A Natural Experiment in Three Communities*. Orlando, FL: Academic Press, 1986.

Williamson, Nancy. *Sons or Daughters: A Cross-Cultural Survey of Parental Preferences*, Beverly Hills, CA: SAGE Publications, 1976.

Witkin, W. Robert. *Adorno and Popular Culture*. Thousand Oaks, CA: SAGE Publications, 2001.

Witt, Susan D. "The Influence of Peers on Children's Socialization to Gender Roles." *Early Child Development and Care* 162(1) (2000), 1–7.

Wolf, S. Rowan. *The Dialectic of Social Inequality*, PhD thesis, 2008.

Young, R. A. "Vocational Choice and Values in Adolescent Women." *Sex Roles* 7/8 (1984), 485–92.

Youniss, J., and J. Smollar. *Adolescents' Relations with Mothers, Fathers, and Friends*. Chicago, IL: University of Chicago Press, 1985.

Yuksel, Wolfrang. *Women in Proverbs*. Oxford: Oxford University Press, 1993.

ZIPES, Jack. *When Dreams Came True: Classical Fairy Tales and Their Tradition*. London: Routledge, 1999.

———. *Fairy Tales and the Art of Subversion*. New York, NY: Wildman Press, 1983.

Index

About the Author

Sujit Kumar Chattopadhyay is former Chairman, West Bengal Regional School Service Commission (Western Region), Bankura. Prior to this, he was Associate Professor and Head of the Department of Political Science, Bankura Zilla Saradamani Mahila Mahavidyapith, West Bengal. He has done PhD on 'Gender Inequality, Popular Culture and Resistance: A Case Study of the District of Bankura', under the guidance of Professor Harihar Bhattacharyya from the University of Burdwan, West Bengal, in 2006. His published works include the books *Revisiting Vivekananda: From Revival to Renaissance* (2015), *Gender Inequality, Popular Culture and Resistance in Bankura District* (2016), *Fighting Gender Inequality: A Tribute to Nirbhaya* (2015), *Samajchitre Loksahitya* (2017), *Loksahitye Narir Sthan* (2017) and the edited volume *Politics of Discrimination and Problem of Democratic Governance: Issues, Experiences and Challenges* (2009). He is also the author of an anthology of poems in Bengali and some texts on gender and folklore. He has many published papers to his credit.